ECONOGUIDE® BUYING AND SELLING A HOME

D0747366

Help Us Keep This Guide Up to Date

Every effort has been made by the author and editors to make this guide as accurate and useful as possible. However, many things can change after a guide is published—new products and information becomes available, regulations change, techniques evolve, etc.

We would love to hear from you concerning your experiences with this guide and how you feel it could be improved and kept up to date. While we may not be able to respond to all comments and suggestions, we'll take them to heart, and we'll also make certain to share them with the author. Please send your comments and suggestions to the following address:

> The Globe Pequot Press
> Reader Response/Editorial Department
> P.O. Box 480
> Guilford, CT 06437

Or you may e-mail us at:

> editorial@globe-pequot.com

Thanks for your input, and happy travels!

ECONOGUIDE® SERIES

ECONOGUIDE® BUYING AND SELLING A HOME

COREY SANDLER

The
Globe
Pequot
Press

GUILFORD, CONNECTICUT

To Janice, again.
Home is where the heart is.

Copyright © 2003 by Word Association, Inc.

All rights reserved. No part of this book may be reproduced or transmitted in any form by any means, electronic or mechanical, including photocopying and recording, or by any information storage and retrieval system, except as may be expressly permitted by the 1976 Copyright Act or by the publisher. Requests for permission should be made in writing to The Globe Pequot Press, P.O. Box 480, Guilford, Connecticut 06437.

Econoguide is a registered trademark of Word Association, Inc.

Text design: Lesley Weissman-Cook

ISBN 0-7627-2493-5

Manufactured in the United States of America
First Edition/First Printing

CONTENTS

Acknowledgments   ix
Introduction   x

PART I: BUYING A HOUSE

1   So You Want to Buy a House?   1
The Pluses and Minuses of Buying a Home   2
A Quick Course in Tax Issues   3
Differentiating Between Needs and Wants   4

2   How to Buy a House: The First Steps   9
What Is a Buyer's Market?   10
What Is a Seller's Market?   10
Should You Hire an Agent?   11
When Should You Buy?   12
Finding a House by the Numbers   12
Buy First or Sell First?   13

3   How to Look at a Home   16
Used Homes versus New Homes   16
Your Home-Buying Checklist   18
Check Out the Neighborhood   18
Appraising a Home by Yourself   19

4   How to Make an Offer on a House   25
Opening Negotiations   26
The Elements and Contingencies of an Offer   27
The Seller's Response   34
Buying from a FSBO   35

PART II: AGENTS

5   Real Estate Agents   37
Choosing a Real Estate Agent to Sell Your House   37
Choosing a Real Estate Agent to Help You Buy a House   42

PART III: MORTGAGES

6   Choosing the Right Mortgage   47
Why Mortgages Are a Bargain   47
Which Mortgage?   48
Popular Mortgage Types   54
Borrowing More Than the Home Is Worth   59
Matching the Mortgage to Your Plans   60

7 Understanding Adjustable Rate Mortgages 63
The Components of an ARM 64

8 FHA, VA, and State Mortgage Programs 68
FHA-Insured Home Loans 69
VA-Guaranteed Loans 70
Rural Housing Loan Program 71
First-Time and Low-Income Buyer Programs 71

9 Types of Lenders 75
Who's Got the Money? 75
Where Does the Money Come From? 76
Seller Financing 78

10 Refinancing a Loan 81
Analyzing a Refinancing Option 82

11 Applying for a Mortgage 85
From Application to Closing 86
How Large a Loan Can You Obtain? 88
The Advantages of Preapproval 91
Your Credit Score 92
Should You Seek a Cosigner for a Loan? 95
Full Disclosure to the Borrower 96

12 Down Payments and Prepaid Points 98
The Theory of Down Payments 98
The Theory of Points 102
Zero-Cost Mortgages 103
How to Choose 105

13 Biweekly Payments, Equity Loans, and Reverse Mortgages 106
Biweekly or Extra-Payment Mortgages 106
Home Equity Loans and Second Mortgages 108
Reverse Mortgages 110

PART IV: LAND

14 Buying Land 113
Choosing a Piece of Land 113
Restrictions on Land Use 115
Contingencies on a Land Offer 116
Financing the Purchase of Land 116
Construction Costs 116

PART V: NEW HOMES

15 Buying a Brand-New Home   118
Tract or Production Homes   118
Factory-Built Housing   120
Buying a House from a Catalog   121
Taking Possession of a New Home   124

PART VI: CONDOS, CO-OPS, AND TIME-SHARES

16 Condominiums and Co-Ops   126
Buying a Condominium   126
Buying into a Cooperative   127
Town Houses and Duplex Developments   128

17 Vacation Homes and Time-Shares   129
You've Got to Know the Territory   129
Time-Shares and Fractional Ownership   130

PART VII: GOING TO CLOSING

18 Closing the Deal   132
Understanding Closing Fees   133
Negotiating Closing Costs   137
Title Insurance   139
Taking Title   140

PART VIII: INSURING YOUR HOME

19 Home Insurance and Home Warranties   143
The Lender's Requirements   143
Standard Home Insurance Coverage   144
How an Insurance Company Evaluates Your Application   147
Saving Money on Homeowners Insurance   149
Renters Insurance   149
Condo and Co-op Insurance   150
Flood Insurance   150
Home Warranties   151

PART IX: SELLING YOUR HOUSE

20 How to Get the Most for Your Home at Resale   153
How Much Is a House Worth?   154
The Dangers of Overpricing   155
Preparing a House for Sale   155

Should You Remodel? 157
Things You Can Do to Speed the Sale 158
Guaranteed Sales 158
Homes for Sale by the Owner (FSBOs) 159
Taxes on Sale of a Home 160

PART X: MOVING

21 Preparing for a Move   163

PART XI: REAL ESTATE IN CYBERSPACE

22 Enter the Web   166
How an On-line Mortgage Application Works 167
Real Estate Portals 168
Home Builders and Plans 168
Mortgage Portals 171
Government and Government-Sponsored Agencies 176
Moving Services 176

Appendix A: Home-Buying Comparison List 178
Appendix B: Residential Offer to Purchase 181
Appendix C: Property Condition Disclosure Statement 197
Appendix D: A Comparison List of Mortgage Candidates 204
Appendix E: Mortgage Types at a Glance 207
Appendix F: Uniform Residential Loan Application 212
Appendix G: Land-Buying Comparison List 218
Appendix H: Good Faith Estimate 221
Index 222
About the Author 228

All brands, product names, or other works mentioned in this book are trade-marks, registered trademarks, or copyrighted names of their respective owners or developers and are used in this book strictly for editorial purposes; no commercial claim to their use is made by the author or the publisher. Realtor® is a registered trademark of the National Association of Realtors.

ACKNOWLEDGMENTS

As always, dozens of hard-working and creative people helped move my words from the keyboard to the book you hold in your hands.

Among the many to thank are Mary Luders Norris of The Globe Pequot Press; we look forward to many years of partnership. Thanks, too, to editorial and production staff at Globe Pequot, including Liz Taylor, Justine Rathbun, Lesley Weissman-Cook, and Casey Shain.

Gene Brissie has been a believer for a decade, and the feeling is mutual.

And as always, thanks to Janice Keefe for running the office and putting up with me, a pair of major assignments.

INTRODUCTION

OVER THE YEARS I've bought three homes and one piece of property, as well as built a new house from scratch and expanded it twice. I've made offers on five homes . . . and backed out of accepted deals twice. Along the way, as best I can recall, I've received nine mortgages, three construction loans, and two home-equity loans.

My wife and I made a small profit on our first home, plowed it into a new house outside of New York City built "on spec" by a contractor, and watched its value soar by about $100,000 in a few years. In our spare time we bought a piece of land on a resort island and built a vacation home. When we sold the New York house to move to Boston due to a new job, we bought a spectacular house on a lake at the peak of a seller's market; when it came time to sell, we fell into the trough of a cyclical real estate slump and lost most of our previous profit.

We moved to our vacation home and expanded it once with more family space and bedrooms, and then a second time to add an office suite, a guest wing, and a new heating system. Along the way we've put perhaps $500,000 into a home that is now worth nearly $1 million. In the past decade we've refinanced the mortgage three times, using an adjustable loan when rates were high, locking in at a lower fixed rate after a few years, and then grabbing a new fixed-rate loan when rates dropped again. Now we're looking to convert the huge equity in the home into a tax-free profit we can use to buy a new home in a market not yet at its peak.

I tell you these details not to brag; the performance of our real estate investments has been good but could have been better. There are more than a few things I would have done differently. Instead, I've outlined some of my history to show just how complex the landscape is for many of today's homeowners. Consider this: My parents and my wife's parents each owned a total of just one home and stayed with the same mortgage from inception to the day it was fully paid off thirty years later.

LOOKING BACKWARD AND FORWARD

As the lawyers for mutual funds instruct their clients to say: Past history is no guarantee of future performance. But in general, owning a home is one of the most stable and productive investments you can make.

In 2001, in the face of a slowing economy and the shockwaves of the September 11 terrorist attacks, sales of new and existing single-family homes dipped but soon recovered. Overall sales in 2001 were up 2.7 percent over the year before, according to the National Association of Realtors (NAR). According to NAR, the average appreciation in value for homes varied from 5 to 8 percent, depending on region. This came at the same time as the stock market took a tumble and inflation rose just 2.7 percent. Mortgages originated in 2001 were at a historic high of about $2 trillion; the previous record had been $1.5 trillion, reached in 1998.

Coldwell Banker Real Estate Corporation's 2002 annual Home Price Comparison Index (HPCI) showed the average home value rose 7 percent over the previous year. Nationally, the HPCI revealed the cumulative average sales price of the study's subject home in the United States is $291,097, up from $269,241 in 2001. The study also determined that the most expensive market in the nation is Palo Alto, California ($1,263,250), and the most affordable market is Yankton, South Dakota ($101,062). Of the 317 U.S. markets assessed, 206 markets (about 65 percent) showed increases from 2001, and 114 of those (about 36 percent of the total) were up more than 10 percent. The company projected total annual sales of 5.75 million homes in 2002, the third-highest sales pace since record keeping began in 1968. Helping to propel the relatively strong real estate market was the decline in mortgage interest rates to their lowest levels in several decades, allowing more people to enter as first-time buyers and permitting those already there to pay more for housing.

Not all news is rosy: Surveys show that there continue to be racial strata in homeownership. According to various surveys, while approximately 73 percent of whites own homes, only 47 percent of African Americans do. The figures for Hispanics and Asian-Americans were 46 and 53 percent respectively. Across the nation, about one-third of American households live in rented quarters. The largest groups of renters are in New York, Los Angeles, Chicago, and Houston.

ABOUT THIS BOOK

My goal in the Econoguide series is to help readers get the most for their time and money. This book is not an academic treatise on real estate theory. It's also not a guide for the professional investor or an accountant. Instead, what you'll find here is news you can use: plain-language explanations of the process of buying and selling a home. I'll tell you what you need to know to make intelligent and fiscally smart decisions in deciding whether to buy a house, choosing a location, finding the best deal, and making an offer. Do you need a real estate agent? And if you hire one, is she really representing your interests, or is she on the seller's side?

Choosing the proper mortgage, and getting approved, is one of the most important financial decisions you will make. We'll explore the many different types of available loans and help you pick the right one for you. We'll also explore insurance and tax considerations, and how to be a savvy consumer at closing.

And then comes the time to sell your home. We'll help you decide on a strategy and whether to use a real estate agent. Then you can take the money you receive from the sale of your house and go back to chapter 1 to start the cycle all over again and find a new place to live.

We hope you find this book to be of value; please let us know how we can improve the book in future editions. (Please enclose a stamped envelope if you'd like a reply; no phone calls, please.)

Corey Sandler
Econoguide Books
P.O. Box 2779
Nantucket, MA 02584

To send electronic mail, use the following address: info@econoguide.com. You can also consult our Web page at: www.econoguide.com.

We hope you'll also consider the other books in the Econoguide series. You can find them at bookstores or ask your bookseller to order them. All are written by Corey Sandler.

Econoguide Walt Disney World®, Universal Orlando®
Econoguide Disneyland Resort®, Universal Studios Hollywood®
Econoguide Las Vegas
Econoguide Cruises
Econoguide How to Buy or Lease a Car

PART I
BUYING A HOUSE

CHAPTER ONE

SO YOU WANT TO BUY A HOUSE?

SOMEWHERE DEEP WITHIN modern man's and woman's DNA is a primal urge to own a home. The ideal used to be a little bungalow with a white picket fence and a flower garden; today it might be a split-level condo on the beach with a hot tub. Either way, the dream of home ownership is very much ingrained in our being.

Most of us don't like living in rented quarters and following someone else's rules—where, as Paul Simon wrote, one man's ceiling is another man's floor. And there is the nagging realization that all of those rent payments are an expense and not an investment; there's no holding on to them. But before we get deep into the whens, hows, and how muches of buying a house, it is very important to consider the whys and wherefores. Let's start with a few reasons *not* to buy a house:

■ Don't buy if you are not reasonably sure you will stay in one place for a few years.

■ Hold off if you are uncertain about your ability to commit to making a long-term contract to pay for a mortgage, insurance, property taxes, and repairs.

■ Wait if you're not ready to do the research to find the right house in the right town and neighborhood, paid for with the right financing.

Buying a house requires a significant investment in upfront costs and effort; the impact of the cost diminishes with time. If all you can see is a short-term view of your future, you'll almost certainly be better off renting an apartment or a house. You may be able to rent a nicer place to live at a lower cost per month than you pay for a starter house.

But if you think you can envision a reasonable level of stability in your personal and financial status for the next few years, you should consider buying property. Over time you'll build equity in the property and hope to also benefit from an increase in its value. And while rents tend to rise over time, the monthly payments on a fixed-rate mortgage do not. On average, a couple will move five to seven times. This includes a starter home, a job transfer or two, an upgrade, and a retirement home.

THE PLUSES AND MINUSES OF BUYING A HOME

There are some significant advantages to buying and owning a home, but it's not all gravy. Let's look at the pluses and minuses of buying a home:

+ **It's yours.** You can paint the kitchen green and the bedroom fuchsia, hang a chandelier over the bathtub, and do just about anything you want with your property—within the bounds of your local building and zoning codes. Way out in the country, the involvement of local government in what you do with your home is minimal; in a city, and especially in certain historic districts or planned communities, there may be rules and regulations that govern every detail of the exterior, from the color of your siding to the design of your mailbox. But it's your mailbox.

+ **Some of your monthly payment comes back to you in equity.** Unlike a rental bill, some of the monthly mortgage payment you make is applied against the outstanding principal—the proportion grows with each year you maintain the mortgage. Assuming that the property keeps its value or appreciates, those dollars will be yours at resale.

+ **You can profit from an increase in value.** If you sell the house for more than you paid for it, you can keep the profit or invest it in another home. While you own the house you can also tap into the equity in the home (its value above the amount of the outstanding balance) for other purposes.

+ **Your profit can be tax-free and interest costs tax-deductible.** This one-two gift from the government is the legacy of post–World War II plans to boost home ownership. For a married couple the first $500,000 of profit is tax-free. Any taxpayer can write off interest costs on a mortgage of up to $1 million. For most people, owning a home is the best tax break they can take advantage of.

+ **You can take advantage of *leverage.*** Done properly, the profit you make on the sale of a house comes from the use of other people's money. Consider the difference between making a $50,000 profit on a down payment of $200,000 of your own savings versus the same $50,000 profit on a $25,000 investment.

− **You could end up losing money on the house.** If property values decline or don't rise enough to cover the up-front cost of the mortgage and other factors, you could end up losing some or all of your down payment when it comes time to sell. In the worst situation you could end up owing money to the lender.

− **Unexpected repair and maintenance costs could clean out your savings.** There's no landlord to call when the heating system fails or the plumbing backs up. The bills land right on your desk.

− **You could suffer an opportunity loss on your down payment.** It costs you money to have your savings invested in the down payment for your home. If the house appreciates at a slower rate than you would have obtained by investing the cash elsewhere, you've lost income on those dollars.

— **You're no longer footloose and fancy-free.** It's not easy to pick up and move to another job or another place to stay when you have a substantial financial obligation like a home mortgage. Unless you're willing to unload the house at fire-sale prices (or are forced to do so), the process of selling a home usually takes several months or more to complete.

A QUICK COURSE IN TAX ISSUES

It is national, political, and economic policy to encourage home ownership. When you take out a mortgage, prepaid interest (points) can be deducted from taxes. While you own a house, most of the interest portion of your mortgage is tax-deductible. Even the costs of moving your possessions to a new home are deductible if they are in connection with a new job more than 50 miles farther from your old home.

The biggest break of all is this: **Profits on the sale of a house** are tax-free, up to $500,000 for a married couple or $250,000 for a single person. For tax purposes, the profit is calculated on the difference between the original purchase price of the home *plus* any major structural improvements—the **tax basis.** Keep copies of all major expenses for the home, and consult a tax advisor to properly calculate the tax basis for your home when it comes time to sell.

Points paid to the lender to obtain a mortgage are generally tax-deductible, reducing their cost to you as the borrower. The purpose of the points must be to prepay interest; they cannot be for origination fees or closing costs. (If you compare two mortgages that have the same total closing costs but find that one applies some of the money collected to an origination fee while the other uses points to prepay interest, choose the one that offers you the most tax benefit.) If the points are financed as part of the loan, the deduction for them must be spread out over the full term of the mortgage. On a thirty-year loan you'll have the benefit of about 3.3 percent of the points as a write-off each year—a rather insignificant amount. You can instead deduct the full cost of the points in the tax year in which you pay them under the following conditions:

■ The points must go for prepaid interest and must be in line with typical charges in your area.

■ You must pay the points from your own funds and not from the proceeds of the loan.

■ The loan must be for the purchase or refinance of your principal residence, or for the renovation of that residence.

Finally, the points are included in the determination of the maximum interest deduction on a residence. This limitation applies to the most expensive homes and accompanying mortgages.

Politicians, builders, and real estate agents have for decades pointed to the benefits of writing off the cost of interest paid on a home mortgage. That is still the case, although changing economic times have put a cap on the government's largesse. For your principal residence, only the interest on the first $1 million of the mortgage is deductible. The mortgage must be used for the purchase, refi-nance, or renovation of the home. If you refinance the home to take out equity for a purpose other than the purchase or renovation of the home, you can only deduct interest on the first $100,000 of debt. Consult with your tax advisor for the latest wrinkle, including special exemptions for funds raised by a refinancing of your home in order to pay for college expenses.

If you take out a mortgage that allows negative amortization, you may lose some of the benefit of the interest expense since in most cases it is converted into additional principal on the loan. Similarly, if you take out a loan for more than the value of the property, a portion of the interest cost may not be deductible since it would be considered a personal loan rather than a real estate loan.

All of this applies only to mortgages dated after October 13, 1987. On any loan in effect prior to that date, the full amount of interest is tax-deductible.

DIFFERENTIATING BETWEEN NEEDS AND WANTS

If you didn't quit after the analysis above, you're ready to start the process of buying a house. Get out your notebook and start jotting down your answers to the questions that follow.

Location. The old saw about real estate value is still apt: The top three attrib-utes of a great property are location, location, and location. A mansion next to a sewage plant is, to most buyers, a lot less desirable than a simple cottage with a million-dollar view. You can buy or build just about any type of home just about anywhere. So, start by choosing the proper location:

■ Do you need to be within commuting distance of your job? How far in miles and time are you willing to travel?
■ Is there mass transit nearby?
■ Do you want to be near family or friends, recreation, shopping, or a particu-lar school?
■ What are your quality-of-life desires? Do you want to live way out in the coun-try or in the heart of a city? Do you want to be near a major university and cul-tural centers, or do you want to be miles away from civilization? Do you want to be close enough to go skiing, boating, or golfing without an overnight trip?
■ What types of location will *disqualify* a particular home from consideration? Too close to factories, highways, airports, shopping malls? Too far from the fire station or the hospital?

Let's say you decide you are willing to commute as much as an hour. Get a good map and draw an X on your place of work. Use a marker to highlight major highways and commuter rail lines in all directions, and estimate the point at which they lie about one hour away from the X. Connect the points to create a rough circle; your primary hunting ground will lie within the circle.

Size and Design. Once you get beyond location, it's time to consider whether you really need a mansion with a formal garden and lily pond out back, or whether a comfy cottage with a rocking chair on the porch will do you fine. A random shuffle through home design books will show you four-bedroom contemporaries spreading over 3,583 square feet and a four-bedroom bungalow packed into a third of the space. The larger model might cost three times as much to build or buy.

Keep in mind that it can make perfect sense to buy a home with the intention of making major alterations immediately. You may be able to add a garage or a new wing of bedrooms, change the heating system, or relocate and pave the driveway. Be sure to consider the cost of any changes in your decision-making process.

- How many bedrooms and bathrooms do you need, now and in the foreseeable future? Do you plan to have more children? Do you expect to regain a room as a child flies from the nest?
- What other special needs or wants do you have: an office, a sprawling country kitchen, a screened porch, a hobby room?
- Do you need a garage? For how many vehicles?
- Is a basement essential? Is an accessible attic or storage space required?
- Are you looking for a particular architectural style: contemporary, ranch, Cape, bungalow, or Victorian?
- Do you require a large piece of property for privacy, or does the thought of lawn care and landscaping make you want to retreat to your apartment?
- What types of design will *disqualify* a particular home from consideration?

Special Features. Some home buyers start their wish lists with amenities the rest of us would all but ignore: Their home must have an oversized whirlpool tub or a fireplace or an artist's atelier in a Victorian-style cupola. Do you require skylights inside or a swimming pool outside?

- What special features are essential to your dream home?
- Can the features be added to an existing home?
- Do you have any special requirements for subsystems of the house: heating, cooling, telecommunications?
- What features will *disqualify* a house: a swimming pool, the location of particular rooms, type of utilities (gas versus electric, for example)?

Age and Condition. Do you want a brand-new home, untouched and untried? Or do you seek a home with old-fashioned construction and well-earned character? Buying a previously owned house is somewhat like buying a used car—the careful buyer makes sure he or she is buying a well-kept-up investment and not buying someone else's headache. The advantage of buying a used car is that the first owner is the one who has to deal with the depreciation—a rough rule of thumb is that a new car loses 40 to 50 percent of its value the minute you drive it off the lot. On the other hand, most previously owned homes have appreciated in value since they were first bought. The trick here is not to buy a home that has appreciated out of step with the rest of the market (or is priced as if it has).

- Do you want to look at new homes built "on spec" by a builder?
- Do you want to look at subdivisions where the builder is willing to customize a design on a lot you purchase there?
- Will you only consider a used home built within the past ten years with modern construction techniques, subsystems, and appliances?

- Are you willing to consider an older home in good condition, but with old-style amenities and features?
- Are you looking for an antique or historical home?
- Must everything in the home be in like-new condition, or are you willing to buy a home that needs updating and repair?
- Would you consider a "handyman's special" or a "fixer-upper," real estate agents' euphemisms for a real dump that needs a lot of work?

Price. The cost of a house, of course, is determined by all of the aforementioned variables. I live on a resort island where a handyman's special near the beach might sell for a million dollars. In some places older homes are more highly valued than new construction, while elsewhere the existing stock of homes is not valued very highly. In some parts of the country construction costs for new homes are around $100 per square foot, while elsewhere builders work for half that amount. In general, a new home will cost 10 to 25 percent more than a comparable previously occupied home, although it may come with more modern heating and cooling systems and appliances and the latest amenities. And it can be customized to your exact needs and wants.

About your price target: Although we all tend to think in terms of the purchase price of the home, the truth is that for most people a much more important figure is the monthly payment to finance that purchase. Once you determine how much you are willing (and able) to spend each month, you can determine how large a loan you can obtain. The size of the loan will fluctuate with rising and falling interest rates. (In chapter 11 I'll show you how to estimate the maximum monthly payment a conventional lender will allow you to undertake.)

- What is your price target? (This is not necessarily the maximum amount of money you will spend; in fact, you should keep the maximum amount a family secret, not sharing it with your real estate agent.)
- What types of mortgage have you considered that might permit you to spend a bit more for your house?
- Have you explored all of your options for a down payment that would reduce the monthly payment?

▇ YOUR WANTED LIST

If you're lucky, the end result of your self-examination will be a straightforward but detailed declarative sentence: "We want a four-bedroom new or nearly new two-story with a two-car garage, a full basement, and a fireplace or wood-burning stove, in the suburbs but not too far from shopping and services, and within a one-hour commute to downtown Boston." The more specific your list, the better you'll be able to wade through the coming overload of the Multiple Listing Service (MLS) book or local Web site. But don't expect to find a home that fits your bill exactly, and don't be surprised if you end up making an offer on a property very different from the one you first envisioned. It's the process that matters. If your dream house changes along the way, it will be after you have examined your needs and wants.

YOUR UNWANTED LIST

It's also important to know your own deal killers; call it an unwanted list. If there is no way, no how, that you're going to buy a concrete-block home with aluminum siding and no basement, put that on your list and share it with your real estate agent. On many issues there is no right and wrong; some people just love Capes and despise ranches, while others absolutely will not accept a two-story home. Here are some turnoffs; your list may be very different.

- Slab foundation or crawlspace
- Basement laundry or playroom
- A small lot, or one with neighboring dwellings on or near the side property line
- Less than your specified number of bedrooms or bathrooms
- Vinyl or aluminum siding, stucco, or false brick construction
- A well or septic tank instead of town water and sewer
- A master bedroom without a bathroom, or one that's too small, or on the wrong floor of the house
- More than a particular number of miles or commuting time from your job or other location
- A location on a major road with heavy traffic, on a remote and dark country road, or in a high-crime or declining neighborhood

By the way, if your agent insists on bringing you to homes that are on your unwanted list, he or she may be trying to keep another client happy by delivering some traffic to his door. In the process, the agent is wasting your time. You might want to reconsider your arrangement.

COMING TOGETHER

Finally, there is the little matter of the opinions of your wife or husband or children. I don't know of any modern families where one person makes important, life-changing decisions like the purchase of a new home without reaching some level of consensus with significant others. If there are any such autocracies, I can't imagine they produce happy families. I'm a big believer in the problem-solving capabilities of a yellow legal pad. (My father drew up a plus/minus chart before asking my mother to marry him.)

Here's one way to work toward a consensus: Have a family discussion about realistic expectations for a new home. Your child may want a ten-bedroom mansion with a roller coaster in the backyard, but that is not likely to happen. Agree together on a list of at least twenty attributes: country, city, modern, antique, big backyard, fireplace, basement workshop, sewing room, and so on. Continue the discussion to try to develop as much of a consensus before you vote. Talk about the advantages of country versus city, old brick versus new wood, and home designs.

Ask everyone to choose from that list their top ten attributes for a new home, ranking them in order and giving the most important a 1 and the least important a 10. Combine the lists into a single chart, adding the points together, and then divide the score for each attribute by the number of people voting. Anything that rates a 1 or 2 is an essential; if you're lucky, your family will be close enough to rank a few in that range. If the numbers are all in the middle—fours through sevens—you need to back up a few steps and try to come to a consensus on a few important issues and conduct the vote again. If you want to be very formal about it, you can remove the top two and bottom two attributes and conduct a second round of voting on the remaining six items to come up with secondary attributes.

But in most families, it's not the voting that matters: it's the time spent discussing needs, wants, and dreams—realistic or not. My teenaged daughter wanted a roller coaster in the backyard; I would have preferred the Alps out back and the ocean out front. My college-sophomore son wanted one room for his video game collection, a second for his books, and a third to store his unsorted laundry. Once those requests were unseconded, we moved on to a meaningful discussion.

CHAPTER TWO

HOW TO BUY A HOUSE: THE FIRST STEPS

BUYING A HOUSE is not quite the same as going down to the corner store to buy a book on the subject. You can examine a book before you make a purchase to evaluate its quality. You can compare it to others that are conveniently shelved nearby, and its price is clearly marked on the label. And, though the advice within may be more valuable than gold, buying a book is an inexpensive, casual transaction that will not have a permanent effect on your finances.

Compare that to buying a home. Can you tell the quality and potential headaches that lie hidden within the walls, beneath the floors, and inside the systems of a house? How easy do you imagine it is to compare one house to another when they are miles apart, years different in age, and built in completely different styles? And though the seller will put a price on the property, how do you know if it's a good deal, and how do you plan to handle the give-and-take of a negotiation?

In the previous chapter I've laid out some strategies to help you make some basic decisions about whether you are ready to buy a house and about the location, design, and price range. Now it's time to examine the process involved in getting ready to shop for a home. Here are the first steps:

1. Assess the market. Is this a seller's market, when prices are high and you'll be competing against other buyers? Or is it a buyer's market, when there are many more houses than customers?

2. Decide whether you'll hire an agent. A good real estate agent can be a lot of help in finding a home and making a successful offer, but you'll need to choose carefully and understand the economic and legal loyalties of the agent. You can also shop on your own.

3. Set your schedule. Is there a season when you'll get the best deal on a home? Should you make an offer on a new home before you've sold your old one?

WHAT IS A BUYER'S MARKET?

The short answer is: when there are more sellers than buyers. In general, it's a great situation to find yourself in, although you should find out why the market is so favorable to the buyer and unfavorable to the seller. Why should you care? Because someday you may want or need to sell the home. Here are some conditions that create a buyer's market and some comments about them:

■ A large number of homes for sale in a particular area. By itself, this may not be a bad thing. The inventory of homes may be the result of over-optimistic plans by builders or merely the consequences of regular cycles in the market.

■ Massive local layoffs. A major employer may be in financial difficulty or may have shut down, resulting in the loss of executive and lower-level jobs. Is this an isolated case, or is the local economy on the skids (which may result in further layoffs and a period of decline in sales of homes and real estate value)?

■ A reduction in the influx of new residents. Is there an environmental, economic, or other problem with the area that will continue to depress home values for some time to come?

■ Seasonal declines. Relatively fewer homes sell in the dead of winter, for example. However, that might be a great time to shop because sellers may be desperate to unload properties.

■ A national economic slowdown. This may be the best situation since it is a fair bet that the domestic economy will eventually recover from a recession or even a depression. People who bought homes in the recession of the early 1980s benefited greatly from the hot market of the next decades.

WHAT IS A SELLER'S MARKET?

Again, the short answer is simple: A seller's market is defined by many buyers pursuing a relatively small number of homes. This is great news for the seller since it means that prices will be high and homes should sell quickly. For the buyer it's a mixed blessing. On the down side, the cost of a house will be higher, there will be more competition for mortgage funding, and you will likely have to react quickly when you find a home that meets your needs. On the plus side, you'll know you're buying into a market where homes are very desirable, at least for the moment. Here are some conditions that contribute to a seller's market:

■ A relatively small number of homes for sale.

■ Low interest rates that spur many first-time buyers or encourage current homeowners to trade up.

■ A boost in local employment. A new factory or other major business can bring large numbers of executives and lower-level workers into the home market.

■ Seasonal boosts. In most parts of the country, more homes are sold between May and September than during the rest of the year. It's better shopping weather, and most families try to avoid uprooting children during the school year.

■ A national economic upturn. Although an improvement in the economy generally benefits everyone, it is also true that sooner or later the housing and other markets will reach the top of a cycle and start heading down. If you buy at the peak, it may be a number of years before prices come back up to that level again. (And as my father used to warn: They don't ring a bell at the top.)

■ HOW TO BUY IN A SELLER'S MARKET

How do you snap up a great house at a great price in a seller's market? Well, you may or may not be able to get a great price, but there are some things you can do to improve your chances of making a successful bid at a time when there is a real estate feeding frenzy. Here are a few:

■ If you are working with a real estate agent, make sure he or she is motivated to help you move quickly and understands your needs and wants, as well as your unwanted list.

■ Do your own research, and keep it current. Check Web sites for area real estate agents—some may post listings on their own site before they get them into the MLS. Make regular visits through the area of most interest to you. Ask friends or business acquaintances if they know of any homes about to go on the market. If you hear of one before it is listed, consider contacting the seller and discussing a direct offer on your own or with the aid of your agent.

■ Get prequalified for a mortgage. Your offer will be much more attractive to a seller if you can show that you are ready to move forward with financing.

■ Have a lawyer (if you plan to use one) and a home inspector lined up and ready to review the contract and the house itself on short notice. Again, you're seeking to make your offer with as few contingencies as possible.

■ Have funds available to write a substantial check for earnest money to accompany your offer. (Your real estate agent should advise you on local expectations for earnest money. If your offer is accepted, the check will usually be deposited in an escrow account and held until closing.)

SHOULD YOU HIRE AN AGENT?

You don't *need* an agent to buy a house. You might want one, though. A good agent can help you assess the market, select appropriate homes to consider, and help you obtain a mortgage.

Under the traditional arrangement, using a real estate agent won't cost you anything—at least directly. Agents are paid by the seller through a commission at closing. However, as I discuss in more detail in chapter 5, in most cases the agent who helps you buy a house is beholden to the seller. You'll have to look out for your own interests: don't reveal more information than you need to, and seek independent advice anytime you can.

Other options include hiring a buyer's agent, who works exclusively for you, or shopping on your own. The old-fashioned selling tools of a FOR SALE sign in the front yard and an occasional newspaper ad have been augmented in recent years by impressive Web sites and on-line multiple-listing services. You may also run into a FSBO: a home for sale by the owner. A well-informed consumer should be able to conduct a businesslike transaction without the involvement of a real estate agent on either side. However, if you buy directly from a FSBO, one or the other or both parties should engage a real estate attorney to manage the paperwork and closing process. In a straightforward deal, it may be possible to have one attorney handling the mechanics of the process for both parties, although in this case the lawyer is not looking out for either one's particular interests—just the paperwork. (I discuss FSBOs from the point of view of the seller in chapter 20.)

WHEN SHOULD YOU BUY?

Most families try to avoid uprooting their children in the middle of the school year, and for that reason the prime selling season in many neighborhoods runs from the late spring into mid-summer. If you're flexible with your own plans, a capable real estate agent ought to be able to help you choose the best time to shop. And if you're concerned about fitting your children into a school year, consider a short-term rental of a home or apartment in the school district where you're shopping.

Resorts have their own calendar. If you're buying a vacation home in ski country, the hot time for sales may be in the early fall before the first snowflakes fall. The best bargains may be found in the muddy spring and quiet summer. At a beach resort, sales may be hot during the heart of the summer season and fall off sharply in the fall and winter. The best deals may be available on a cold day in January, but optimism—and prices—may begin to creep up in the spring.

FINDING A HOUSE BY THE NUMBERS

Finding a house is a bit like finding a mate. It takes a bit of planning and a lot of luck. And, though you may find your soulmate, it is probably also true that there are almost certainly more than a few others out there who would have been quite acceptable. One difference, though, is that the search for a home can be conducted a bit more methodically. Here is one version of a step-by-step process to winnow out the wheat from the chaff. (In this example I'll assume you will be working with a real estate agent.)

1. Check out the market on your own first to get a sense of what's available and the price ranges. Ask friends and acquaintances for advice and drive through neighborhoods of interest to get some sense of the local atmosphere. Look for FOR SALE signs from real estate agencies and FSBO (for sale by owner) properties.

2. Do some research. Major real estate agencies place ads in free shopper publications or produce their own magazines to highlight their top listings. (Bear in mind that by the time a home is in print, it has most likely been listed for a few weeks and may have already been sold. If it's still available in a hot market, this might be a sign that it is overpriced or less desirable.)

3. Check the Internet. Many real estate agencies now post homes for sale on their own Web sites. In some cases listings appear on an agency's site before they are given to multiple-listings services. The advance notice may be a few days or just a few hours, but it might be enough for you to grab a hot property before the rest of the world catches on. (Internet Web sites are discussed in more detail in chapter 22.)

4. Study the MLS (Multiple Listing Service) book. Your agent should provide you with a current copy to read at home or at least allow you to examine a copy at the agency. In some areas the MLS is available on-line through a Web site. Ask for a lesson in interpreting the real estate shorthand. In some locations the MLS listings will include the actual address for a home, while in other places you'll need the agent's assistance to find the address. Look for neighborhoods and areas you have identified as places of interest as well as some that are a bit outside of the area. Ask your agent to investigate any properties you locate on your own.

5. Discuss what you have found with your agent. Make sure the agent knows what you are looking for; you don't want to work with an agent who wastes your time taking you to obviously inappropriate homes. (The agent may be trying to make the seller happy by bringing them visitors, even if they are not likely to buy.)

6. Schedule your tours. Learn as much as you can about places you will visit before heading out.

7. Some agents will direct you to visit open houses at some properties. Here the owner schedules a block of time during which time visitors can come by without an appointment. This may be a good way to make a quick and easy visit, although in a seller's market you could find yourself engaged in a bidding war that could result in a selling price above your target. If you see a home that is appealing, ask your agent if you can make an appointment before the open house for a private tour, and possibly a preemptive bid.

8. If you come across any FSBOs, consider whether you should visit on your own or with your agent. Some sellers refuse to deal with agents because they want to avoid paying a commission; others are willing to sign a one-time agreement with an agent who brings them a customer. If a FSBO will not deal with an agent, that does not prevent you from paying your agent to serve as an advisor on an offer to an unrepresented seller.

9. Go forth and shop. Take along a map or ask the agent to provide you with one so that you can understand where you're going and how the home might fit into your needs to be near work, shopping, or schools. Take lots of notes, and consider bringing a digital camera, video camera, or film camera to help you remember the places you have visited. (See appendix A for a comparison list to help you evaluate a home.)

BUY FIRST OR SELL FIRST?

Trading up from one house to another is a great way to make use of the equity you have built up in a home, but very few homeowners can afford to buy a second principal home while they still own the first. That brings up one of the thorniest problems for homebuyers: Should you buy a new home first or sell off your old one first? And how can you possibly manage to coordinate the two major events with the least disruption to your own plans as well as those of the buyer of your old house and the seller of the new one? There is no hard-and-fast rule here; each situation is different from another. The first and most important assumption here is that your personal finances are in good shape. If you are out of work, have a bad credit history, or have a high ratio of debt to income, you are going to have a hard enough time getting a new mortgage without having to consider obtaining a second mortgage on a new home before the first one is discharged.

If you want to work up a real headache, consider the complex chain of events involved in a purchase and sale transaction: The buyer of your old house may well be selling another home, while the seller of your new house is set to buy another home. Your deal is a link in a huge chain of events that has little to do with your specific plans.

■ BUY FIRST

If the real estate market is strong, meaning that houses are selling for good prices in a relatively short time after they are listed for sale, it may make sense to search for and make an offer on a new home before you sell your old dwelling. In this scenario you can devote your full attention to finding the best possible new home in the proper location, and you can make an offer for purchase that is not clouded by desperation. The risk, of course, is that your old house will not sell quickly enough to allow you to use the proceeds from the sale for a down payment on your new home and to clear your credit for the most advantageous mortgage. If that happens, there are some things you can do to get by in the short term:

■ You can make your purchase of the new home contingent on the sale of your old dwelling. The seller may not find this acceptable, especially in a hot real estate market. Put yourself in his shoes: Given a choice between a firm offer and one with contingencies, which one would you take? You can, though, sweeten the deal by offering a bit more money, or a larger nonrefundable deposit, along with the contingent offer.

■ You can use a home-equity line of credit on your old home as a "bridge" loan, together with some of your savings, to come up with a large down payment or even the full purchase price of the second home. Once you sell your first house, you can refinance the loan for the new house.

■ If you are being transferred by your employer, the company may offer a no-interest or low-interest bridge loan as part of its relocation package. The bridge loan becomes due once your old home sells.

■ You can move out of your old home and into the new home and become a short- or long-term landlord. The rental payments become income that should cover much or all of the first mortgage and reduce the ratio of debt to income that lenders check. Rental also brings some tax deductions. Consult your tax advisor to see whether it makes sense to continue renting out the home for an extended period or selling it to avoid having to pay capital gains taxes.

■ SELL FIRST

If you sell your house first, you can concentrate on obtaining the best possible price for your old home without having to accept a low-ball offer from a buyer who is smart enough to realize that you are facing a deadline on the closing for your new home. Here are some things you can do to give yourself a bit more breathing room:

■ Set the closing for the sale of your old home at 90 or 100 days instead of 30 or 60 days.

■ Ask the buyers to delay moving into the home after closing for a short period of time, renting it back to you for a month or two. (Their lawyer or insurance agent may warn of risk here.)

■ Plan on moving your possessions into temporary storage at a safe and secure warehouse, and find an apartment or house you can rent on a month-to-month basis as you look for a new home.

CHAPTER THREE

How to Look at a Home

OKAY, SO YOU DON'T NEED to be Bette Davis (as the evil adulteress in *Beyond the Forest*) to come to a famous quick appraisal of a home: "What a dump!" But that doesn't mean that a "handyman's special" can't be a great deal for the buyer willing to invest some time and money in fixing it up.

You don't need to be an architect or an engineer to appreciate quality in the construction and equipping of a home or to spot costly problems in need of repair. And you don't need to be a cop or a sociologist to spot a neighborhood that's bursting with wealth or on the decline. But very few of us, myself included, are capable of seeing and knowing all when it comes to looking at a home. That's why the best way to buy a home is to assemble a team of experts who know the real estate market, the neighborhood, and the complexities of construction.

If you use a real estate agent, you should ask for full details on the neighborhood and the town. When it comes time to make an offer on a home, I will recommend a bit later in this book that you make your offer contingent on receiving a satisfactory report from a qualified home inspector. But when it comes to winnowing out the wheat from the chaff as you tour available properties, you have to be your own first expert. You already know what's on your wanted and unwanted lists. Now become an impartial appraiser of each home you visit.

USED HOMES VERSUS NEW HOMES

When you buy a used car, you can benefit from the fact that its value has *depreciated*. In general, the older the car, the lower its value. This sort of calculus does not work, though, when it comes to most previously occupied homes. Assuming that the property has been maintained properly and the neighborhood has not gone into serious decline, nearly every home *appreciates* in value over the long term. And each time a home is sold, the current owner tries to lock in the purchase price as the basis for new appreciation when it comes to resale.

If the previous owner was the original buyer of the home, the actual amount of hard cash invested in the home may be much less than the market value: the original cost plus major renovations and improvements. For that reason an original owner may be more willing to accept a lower offer. You can also obtain a good price on an older house in need of renovation—the fabled handyman's special. You can add equity to the home through your own efforts and by careful expenditures with contractors.

■ WHY A NEW HOME COSTS MORE

The main reason why new homes cost more than older ones is that the developer or builder has laid out real dollars for current construction costs and real estate, as opposed to the paper profits considered when the owner of an older home sets a resale price. New homes are typically larger than existing homes, even when you compare a house with the same number of bedrooms and baths. Modern homeowners want larger bedrooms, bathrooms, and a place to install a 65-inch projection television. Where an older house may have had a small garage intended for a family sedan, newer homes typically have multiple-car spaces with room for monster SUVs. Modern homes may also use more robust construction techniques, improved insulation, and more efficient heating and cooling systems, and new construction may have to bear the costs of new roads, sewer, water, electricity, telephone, and other utility lines.

Each year, about 20 percent of home purchases are for new construction. The proportion of new homes varies from region to region, with a higher percentage of new construction in sunbelt states and lower in more densely populated big cities.

■ FIXING UP AN OLDER HOME

Some buyers are quite happy to make a silk purse from a sow's ear, buying a home in need of major repairs or renovations and then paying for construction or doing it themselves. Done properly, this is one way to quickly boost the value of a home. Some people move from home to home, building their net worth or equity with each move.

If you consider buying a handyman's special, be sure to seek the opinion of a home inspector or an engineer, and consider seeking tentative bids for major repair or maintenance before you make an offer. Don't accept the seller's or the broker's estimate of the cost of repairs—they are not experts on the subject, and both have a vested interest in downplaying the true cost.

Also be sure to consider the risk of spending too much money on upgrading an existing home, making it considerably more expensive than other homes in the neighborhood. Put yourself in the position of a shopper for a high-priced home: Do you want to buy the house of your dreams in a neighborhood of shanties?

YOUR HOME-BUYING CHECKLIST

Somewhere around the third or fourth house you've toured in one day, you're going to forget whether the one with the sunken living room had the cute little office over the garage, or if that was the fixer-upper with the subsiding septic tank. Although your real estate agent may be able to help you out with copies of listing sheets, I'd suggest you take matters into your own hands:

■ Take along a camera. Even better, make that a digital camera. Take a shot of the exterior of the home and a few interiors that distinguish it from others you visit.

■ Make notes about each house you visit.

■ Make a few copies of the Home-Buying Comparison List in appendix A at the end of this book and ask your real estate agent to help you fill it out as completely as possible.

CHECK OUT THE NEIGHBORHOOD

You've visited the house three sunny Sunday afternoons in a row. The house is lovely, the neighborhood is safe and serene, and you're prepared to make an offer. Are you really ready? What is the street like on Saturday night at midnight? Do the area teenagers use the park on the corner for parties? Does the guy across the street leave his high-intensity porch light—the one directly opposite the master bedroom of the house you want to buy—on all night? Does a neighbor rev up his motorcycle each morning at 6:00 A.M.? Does the street flood in a rainstorm? Is there a traffic jam each morning as commuters head for the interstate?

If you've got the time—and you should try to clear your schedule for this very important assignment—you should do a bit of lurking on the street where you'd like to live. Make a late-night cruise, an early-morning visit, and drop by for lunch. And while you're in the neighborhood, head over to the local police station and inquire about the local situation.

If you see or hear something that troubles you, rethink your interest in the home. If you're stopped on the street by the police or a neighborhood patrol, appreciate the fact that local eyes are wide open—and then try to find out if there is a particular reason for the security.

■ PRACTICE THE COMMUTE

Don't take someone else's word about traffic conditions and commuting time. Try to spend the time to make at least one practice commute from the home you are considering to your place of work. Ask the present owners or your real estate agent for advice on the best route to take. Leave at the time you would expect to depart if you lived there.

Traffic patterns differ from city to city; in many places, though, the heaviest traffic occurs during the morning commute, when there is a higher concentration of vehicles. The evening return is in some areas spread over a longer period. Is the commute mostly by superhighway or on local roads? Does traffic flow smoothly, or is it stop and start? Is the trip a pleasant one or a white-knuckle challenge? (Road designers in Massachusetts oriented the Mass Pike due east-west, meaning that the commute from one of my former homes in a suburb of Boston was directly into the sunrise each morning and into the sunset most nights.)

If you expect to take mass transportation to work, try the train or bus at the hour you would plan on commuting. Is the trip on time? Is there a parking space at the station and seats available from the station or stop you would use? Is the price of a monthly pass reasonable? Is the trip pleasant or a rolling torture? It's also worth practicing the drive to schools and shopping.

APPRAISING A HOME BY YOURSELF

Before you make an offer, do your own appraisal of the home. Here are the criteria:

Location. A fabulous home in the wrong place is a lot worse than a merely adequate one in the perfect location. Don't let infatuation with a particular home allow you to overlook problems with the neighborhood—declining values, crime, and pollution among them.

Comparables. In most cases, you don't want to own the most expensive house on the block unless there are clear signs that the neighborhood is in the process of upgrading and boosting values. Your real estate agent, if you have one, should be able to provide this information. If you're not represented, you can ask the seller to justify the price. If you're completely on your own, you can research recent home sales in many local newspapers.

Age and condition of the home. An old home in need of repairs is not necessarily something to avoid. You do, though, need to include expected expenses in your decision on an offering price. The cost of the home *plus* the cost of the expenses should be near the level of comparable homes in good repair.

The fact that a home is older does not necessarily detract from its value. Some older homes are well built and well maintained, with mature and well-tended landscaping. One area that needs to be closely examined in an older home is the quality and maintenance of home systems, including electrical, plumbing, heating, and air-conditioning.

As you appraise the home, you should think about which elements you expect to replace. For example, if the carpeting is old and worn, but you intend to replace it anyway, its condition doesn't matter to you—although you should keep your intentions to yourself. You may be able to justify your lower bid by pointing to deficiencies in some of the components of the house.

Walls and ceilings. Walls should be upright and unwarped, as well as free of major cracks and holes. The paint should be clean and fresh. Wallpaper should be properly attached, with matching seams. Look for mold or insect damage along the floor and ceiling joints.

The ceiling should not sag, and seams between plasterboard panels should be invisible. The paint should be clean and fresh here as well. Look for water stains that might indicate roof leaks or problems with plumbing overhead.

Floors. First of all, are they level, solid, and free of water stains that might indicate leaks and underlying damage to the floor and the structure of the home? Next, consider whether existing carpeting and tile is clean and in good condition. This is much more important if you expect to keep the flooring.

Keep in mind that you may use particular rooms differently from the homeowner. You should consider asking the homeowner to move pieces of furniture to permit you to examine the flooring.

Doors. Make sure all doors open and close easily. If they stick or don't close properly, this may be an indication that the house has settled unevenly or was not properly built in the first place. Do the same with all sliding glass doors, which are particularly subject to going out of plumb.

Examine the quality of the doors themselves. Solid wood doors do a much better job of stopping the transmission of noise than hollow-core doors. Check the functioning of locking mechanisms on interior and exterior doors.

Windows. All windows should be in place and fully operable. Look for signs of water leakage and rot. Screens should be clean and untorn.

Modern window systems are double- or triple-paned and do not require separate storm windows. On an older home, storm windows should be used. Windows should properly lock. At street level, look for additional security devices such as separate locks in the window channel.

Find out if drapes and window shades are included in the sale of the home. If so, check that they are properly attached to the wall or ceiling and that the mechanism to open and close them works properly. The material should be clean and in good repair.

Kitchen. You'll be spending a lot of time in the kitchen; make certain it is large enough and properly equipped for your purposes. Older homes generally have small kitchens and separate dining rooms; more modern homes often have larger "country" kitchens that include room for a table used for most meals.

The cabinets should be of good quality, and hinges and latches should function properly. Check for proper lighting and ventilation. The stove should have a range hood with an exhaust fan. The hood should have a vent to the outside to help clear cooking odors and smoke, or a good-quality filter for a "closed" system without a vent.

Determine which appliances are included in the sale of the home. Examine the stove, oven, microwave, dishwasher, garbage disposal, and other devices for obvious signs of disrepair and try them out; the homeowner's disclosure notice should declare any known problems. If the refrigerator is part of the deal, check its function. One quick test is to check the consistency of ice cream in the freezer (ask for permission from the owner before opening food). Also examine the sink for leaks and problems with the faucet. Be sure to check in the cabinet below the sink for water damage.

Bathrooms. Check for any signs of water damage around and under the sinks, toilet, tub, and shower stall. Look, too, for mold and mildew. Make sure the toilets function properly, with the mechanism turning off after use. The showers should have adequate water pressure, and shower doors or curtains should be in good condition.

Bathrooms need adequate ventilation. Test fans for proper draw. In some homes the bathroom has an independent heating system (one nicety is a heated towel rack), which should be tested.

Turn on the shower, flush the toilets, and walk through the house, listening for the plumbing sounds; some systems let you know the state of use of the plumbing anywhere in the house, whether or not this is something you want to hear.

Bedrooms. You'll be spending a lot of time in your private quarters; spend a while in the bedroom to gauge its comfort. Is it large enough for your furniture, including the bed, dressers, and television? If a television is part of your bedroom suite, is there a cable television outlet in the room? Is it in a quiet place, or right next to the kitchen or directly over the garage or the heating system?

Are there sufficient windows to allow ventilation? Check the orientation of the room. A bedroom with a southern exposure will be warmer than one on the north side of the house, while windows to the east face into the sunrise—which may or may not be what you want.

Closets. It is almost impossible to have too much storage space in a home. Check out the closets throughout the common areas of the house as well as in the bedrooms. In certain designs of houses, including saltboxes and Capes, there can be storage spaces under the eaves; other nooks include the space under stairways and in attic spaces.

Basements. There are cellars that are wet, creepy, and dark, useful only for access to the furnace and the house's pipes and wires. And then there are basements that are extensions of the house—places where you can store furniture and sporting equipment, keep a chest freezer, and use as a playroom for the kids.

Not every piece of land will allow construction of a full basement. If the water table is too close to the surface or there are other geological conditions, the builder may put in a half-height foundation called a crawlspace or, in some climates, place the home on a concrete slab. If there is a basement, check to see that it has a concrete floor and look for signs of leaks or other water damage. Look for signs of insect or pest infestation. If the house has a crawlspace, the home inspector you hire should make a visit to check for water damage and infestation.

If you intend to use the basement, it should have adequate lighting and electrical outlets. Casement windows should be designed to open when needed for ventilation. Proper design for a basement in most climates includes screened vents to allow moisture to exit in the summer; the vents should have closures to cut off the inflow of cold weather in the winter.

A nicety for basements is a utility washtub to clean up outdoor tools and wash the dog. Installation of a tub or a bathroom can be difficult in some basements that are below the outflow of the sewer pipes.

Attics. An older house may have a full-height attic that can be used for storage or even converted to use as an extra bedroom or office; the biggest challenge is to remove the excess heat that naturally accumulates there. More modern houses typically have half-height attics. Check the type of access; a full stairway or a telescoping pull-down stairway is much preferable to an opening that requires use of a ladder. The attic should include screened ventilation panels to exhaust heat and humidity.

Electrical, telephone, and cable-television wiring. It is almost a certainty that a home built more than five years ago will have an inadequate wiring design for modern homeowners with multiple television sets, a few personal computers, and other appliances. Telephone companies used to run just a single phone line to homes; today it is not uncommon for there to be a phone for the adults, one or more for the kids, and a line or two for computer modems or fax machines. Similarly, an older design with one electric outlet on each wall is likely to be inadequate for a home entertainment system with a television set, VCR, DVD player, video game console, and stereo system. Cable television lines that used to go to the rec room now are expected to extend to several bedrooms, the kitchen, and the den.

The home inspector should be able to examine the circuit breakers (or in a much older house, the fuse box) to determine the capacity of the electrical wiring and check for its state of repair. Although it is possible to expand the capabilities of the house's electrical wiring, this is not an inexpensive job. Inadequate telephone and television wiring can often be upgraded much more simply and less expensively by using state-of-the-art wireless networks that broadcast from a central point in the house.

Heating, cooling, and hot water systems. Have you ever had a house or apartment with *too much* hot water for showers and baths and an efficient and quiet heating and air-conditioning system that delivers precisely the temperature you want in every room of the house? Me neither. Do your own inspection of the major utility systems of the home—knowing that you will also be hiring a qualified home inspector to do the same before closing. Turn on the heating and the cooling and listen. Some systems are nearly silent, while others have squeaks and moans that would please the Addams Family but probably not yours. If you have any doubts about the safety, maintenance, or capability of the systems, you can ask to send in an inspector *before* you make an offer. If the homeowner refuses, I'd move on to another house.

In general, a modern heating or air-conditioning system will be much more efficient than an older one and may be in better repair. Be on the lookout for systems that are inappropriate for the local climate or energy prices. For example, although electric baseboard heating is very good at providing individualized heating from room to room, in many parts of the country the cost of electricity makes it very expensive to operate. Electric heat pumps are much more efficient for heating and cooling in most climates, although they may not be appropriate in places that get very cold in the winter. Your home inspector may be able to advise you about the possibility of converting an existing oil system to gas, or the other way around. You may also be able to have a local utility or heating contractor inspect the system before you make a final offer or go to closing.

If you are concerned about filtering out dust and allergens, a system that uses ducts to move hot or cool air through the house can work with an electrostatic or physical filter. Such systems can also be fitted with humidifiers for the winter and dehumidifiers for the summer.

An important feature in large homes is the division of rooms into heating zones. For example, separate thermostats could control the family room and kitchen where heat is needed during the day, and bedrooms could be made cooler during the day and warmer at bedtime.

The more bathrooms in the house—and the more teenagers—the more hot water you'll need for showers and baths, as well as for dishwashers and clothes washers. The three main types of hot water heaters are:

- **Storage.** Water in the tank is heated by an electrical coil or a burner fueled by natural gas, propane, or oil. Although modern tanks are well insulated, the water within will need to be regularly heated to keep it at the desired temperature even if water is not being drawn out of the tank.
- **Demand.** An electric element or a burner raises the temperature as cold water passes through a small tank only when it is needed. On the plus side, you won't run out of hot water; on the negative side, the flow rate is relatively slow—usually only enough to support one shower or washer at a time.
- **Indirect or tankless coil.** This design makes use of your home's heating system to also produce hot water. An indirect hot water tank channels the hot water produced by the heating system through a coil in a storage tank. In the winter hot water is produced at very low cost because the furnace is running much of the day in any case. In the summer the system is less efficient, although modern oil or gas furnaces with zone controls can be optimized to quickly heat just the hot water tank when needed. A tankless coil sends a cold water line through the boiler itself, requiring the furnace to run in order to make hot water.

A typical size for a hot water tank is about forty gallons, which may be insufficient for modern families. A typical shower or bath uses ten to twenty gallons, a dishwasher twelve to fourteen gallons, and a clothes washer ten to thirty-two gallons. If your family is likely to have three showers going at the same time in the morning while the dishwasher cleans up last night's dinner, you may need a larger tank. Again, a home inspector or engineer can help you assess the systems in the house you are considering.

Utility bills. Ask to see copies of the past year's bills for electricity, water, and sewer. (In many areas, the current bill will include a graph or chart showing the past year's usage.) The amount of the bill should give you an indication of how efficient the house's systems are. Keep in mind that the current owner may have a different mix of family members than you and otherwise use energy at a greater or lesser rate than you would. On the water bill, look for unexplained sharp increases in usage—this could be an indication of a leak somewhere on the homeowner's side of the water meter.

Odors, mold, and stains. Real estate agents will generally advise someone putting their home up for sale to have the rugs cleaned and the walls painted. On the day of an open house or a visit by a hot prospect, the agent might suggest baking bread or cooking a turkey to fill the place with mouthwatering, homey smells. That's good advice for the seller, but it might also mask odors and stains that could be a real problem for the next owner. Request a return visit when the homeowner is away, and spend the time to take a good sniff. Odors can be caused by mildew, pets, or pest infestation. Look for mold or mildew in the corners of ceilings, especially in bathrooms and kitchens.

If you or the home inspector find problems, obtain a price from a professional cleaning service and figure its cost in your bid for the home.

Exterior and roof. The home inspector will check the roof and exterior walls more closely. Before you make a bid, though, you should look for any obvious problems such as cracks in the foundation and missing shingles in the roof. Look for water stains and damage, especially under the eaves of the roof. Also examine the driveway and sidewalk for cracks and damage.

In most parts of the country, a properly functioning set of gutters and downspouts is essential to direct rainwater away from the house. You can quickly test the gutters by directing a water hose onto the roof. If water spills over the edges of the gutters, the downspouts are probably clogged.

Security. In addition to your survey of the neighborhood itself, check the home to see how well protected it is against intrusion. Are there heavy-duty locks on all doors? Are windows lockable? Is there exterior lighting?

A professionally installed and monitored burglar alarm is a definite plus. Keep in mind, though, that you may be obligated to pay a monthly charge to an alarm company. Check, too, that the home includes an adequate system of smoke detectors. Experts recommend a combination of hard-wired detectors that can sound an alarm throughout the house with a few battery-operated backup units.

Depending on the home, other valuable security features include carbon monoxide detectors near the heating system and water-level monitors in the basement or crawlspace.

CHAPTER FOUR

How to Make an Offer on a House

HOW MUCH IS A HOUSE WORTH? Is it:

■ The **asking price** set by the seller? In most cases, this is intended as a starting point for negotiations.

■ The **assessed value** determined by city or town taxing authorities? Depending on local practice, the assessed value may be close to the expected selling price for the home, or it may be only a fraction of that amount.

■ The **offering price** put forth by a would-be buyer? Opening offers are often considerably lower than the asking price. The final offering price, if accepted by the seller, becomes the selling price.

■ The **appraised value** an estimate of the likely selling price made by a real estate professional?

■ The **market value,** an informed estimate of the likely selling price of a particular home in its current condition over a reasonable period of time? The market value can fluctuate based on seasons, changes in local conditions, and the general economic climate. In most real estate environments, the market price is based on a selling period of thirty to ninety days. And, of course, an identical home in two different locations can have greatly different expected selling prices.

■ The **selling price,** the actual amount paid by the buyer to the seller in a real estate transaction?

These are all "prices" for a house. But for our purposes in this book about buying and selling a home, the most important are the *market value* and the ultimate figure, the *selling price.* In the end, a house is worth whatever the highest-bidding buyer is willing to pay.

OPENING NEGOTIATIONS

The first thing to understand about making an offer to purchase a home is this: Nearly every element of the deal is subject to negotiation. Only in the most severe of seller's markets should you consider agreeing to every element of the asking price and conditions, and even then, only if the conditions are acceptable even if they're not the way you would prefer them. You can ask for:

- A lower price
- Payment by the seller of some or all of the costs of closing
- Assistance by the seller in financing all or part of the mortgage
- A quicker (or slower) time to closing and occupancy
- Inclusion or exclusion of any piece of furniture, decoration, or appliance
- Repairs and fix-ups to the home
- Enhancements or changes to the home or property

There is no guarantee that any of your requests will be accepted, but there is little harm in asking—in a polite, businesslike manner—for a better deal. Your chances of success are greater in a buyer's market.

There are many theories on how to negotiate, and not all of them are compatible with each other or with every buyer's personality. Speaking for myself, I don't enjoy confrontation, but I am quite comfortable with stating and holding on to a position that is based on research and reason. In other words, I like to spend the time to become at least as knowledgeable as the person on the other side of the table.

Never tell your own agent anything that you don't want communicated to the seller. If you have engaged an exclusive buyer's agent, you should feel a bit more relaxed about your personal information and bargaining position, but it nevertheless makes no sense to be a completely open book to anyone but your banker and your spouse. To repeat: Don't disclose the price at which you will walk away, and make each offer as if it is the only one you intend to slide across the table.

It is fair to assume that the seller's asking price is higher than what they will accept. In a seller's market, though, the price may be firm, and in some instances multiple buyers may end up in a bidding war that results in offers above the asking price. If the seller is anxious to unload the property, the offering price may be below fair market value, and there may be resistance at going below its level.

The first question should be: What is this property worth? You need to know whether the offering price is realistic—within a few percent of fair market value one way or another—or whether the seller is out of line with the market. Your real estate agent may be of assistance in letting you know what sort of offers are considered appropriate in the local market. Remember, though, that unless you have an exclusive buyer's agent, you may not get a straight answer unless you phrase the question very specifically: "On comparable homes, what percentage of asking prices are sellers receiving in recent sales?"

If you learn that houses are selling for 93 percent of their listing price, *and if you believe the house is priced above fair market value,* you might make an offer that discounts the seller's price by 10 or 12 percent. You can expect that the seller's agent has done the same math for the client. But let's say that you find a house that is priced below the market, and you want to snap it up before someone else discovers its attractions. In that situation you might want to make a preemptive offer: accept the seller's offering price with minimal or no contingencies.

Some buyers try to steal a house by making lowball offers well below the asking price. They are prepared to be rejected by many sellers until sooner or later someone bites, or at least nibbles back with a counteroffer that comes way down. If that is your strategy, there is no reason to take a rude rejection personally. You do, though, run the risk of becoming branded in the local real estate market as a bottom-fisher. Agents who are aware of your tactics will be sure to tell their clients what they know about your past history.

Whatever you offer, I'd recommend you have a rationale. If you're in a buyer's market and want to play a polite form of real estate hardball, you can "load" your offer: With the assistance of your real estate agent, you can add to your offer a listing of comparable sales in the neighborhood and any repairs or maintenance issues you have with the home.

■ BOLSTERING YOUR BID

The letter accompanying your offer can also do a bit of salesmanship: For example, indicate that you have been prequalified for the loan and do not need to wait for the sale of a previous residence, and that you will not place any contingencies on the purchase other than a home inspector's report. Some agents recommend that you also throw a high and inside pitch: state that your offer is the only one you intend to make, and that you will not consider a counteroffer. If the seller accepts your pitch, you may be getting a great deal on a house. If the seller rejects the offer and comes back with a counteroffer despite your declaration, you have the option to go into negotiations or walk away.

■ MAKING A BID ON NEW CONSTRUCTION

If a real estate agent brings you to a developer or home builder, the agent expects to receive a commission from the seller if you purchase a home. Although that money does not come directly out of your pocket, you may end up paying what amounts to a 3 to 6 percent commission in the purchase price. If you walk in without an agent, you may be able to bargain down the price a bit because the builder or developer does not have to pay the commission. Then again, your agent may be able to help you negotiate a reduction in the price.

THE ELEMENTS AND CONTINGENCIES OF AN OFFER

Make all offers in writing, including the purchase price, anything you want the seller to perform, and any contingencies. Putting it down in words protects you (and the seller) from any misunderstandings and helps the seller's agent or lawyer draw up the documents for closing.

If you're working with an agent, you can use a preprinted purchase contract from the brokerage. (In some areas the form is called an offer or binder.) Be sure to review all of its elements; if you make an offer and it is accepted, you and the seller have entered into a contract with only limited escape clauses. (See appendix B for an example of a Residential Offer to Purchase contract.)

■ TIME LIMIT FOR ACCEPTANCE

An offer to purchase is generally written with a relatively short time limit for acceptance, often as short as twenty-four or forty-eight hours. As the would-be buyer, you don't want to leave your offer on the table for a long time for several reasons:

■ A short time period demands the immediate attention of the seller, moving along the negotiation.

■ You don't want to make it too easy for the seller to be able to use your offer as an incentive to make other buyers raise their offers.

■ You don't want to be out of the market for other homes for an extended period while you wait for a response from the seller.

Plan to keep in close contact with your real estate agent during the period the offer is open. In most situations you can withdraw your offer at any time before it has been accepted in the manner spelled out in the purchase agreement.

■ EARNEST MONEY

In most situations there is no requirement that the buyer include a deposit along with the offer to purchase a home. The contract alone, signed by the would-be buyer and accepted by the seller, is legally binding. However, it has become customary to include a check as an indication of the seriousness of your bid; that's why the deposit is often called **earnest money.** Although there really is no difference, a buyer presented with two identical offers—the same amount for the purchase of the property and the same contingencies—would probably accept the bid with a $5,000 deposit rather than the one with a $100 earnest money check.

The earnest money check is generally not deposited until and unless the seller accepts the offer. If the offer is rejected, the agent will return the check to you. In most deals, though, a trusted intermediary holds on to the earnest money until the conditions of the purchase agreement are satisfied. Depending on local custom and the language of the purchase contract, the check may be made out to the real estate brokerage, an attorney, or an escrow agent, identified on the check as "trustee," "fiduciary agent," "escrow agent," or other such restrictive title. The check should not be made out to the seller. In some states the earnest money is deposited in an escrow account. If the amount of the deposit is substantial, you should make sure the offer to purchase has language requiring it be held in an interest-bearing escrow account and that earned interest be credited to you at closing.

The purchase contract should also spell out the conditions under which the earnest money will be returned to you, including a reasonable time limit for its return. Under some contracts the deposit is not identified as returnable earnest money but rather as an **option** to purchase property—essentially, a payment for the right to buy the property within a specified period of time. Be sure you understand the language associated with the payment; an option is generally not returnable for any reason.

■ INSPECTION AND APPRAISAL CONTINGENCIES

The lender is not likely to grant a mortgage if its inspector finds the home is not in good condition or may decline a loan or require a larger down payment if its appraiser decides the property is selling for significantly above its fair market value. Either way, the financing contingency should allow you to cancel the offer.

In addition to inspections for infestation by pests and termites, in some areas it may be required that homes pass a check of the septic system if one is used. Other inspections may check for the presence of pollutants, urea formaldehyde insulation, aluminum electrical wiring, radon gases, and water quality. Many states require tests or disclosure of the presence of lead paint; FHA mortgages in all states for homes built before 1978 require the same.

Most offers also include the right to have a qualified home inspector check the property on the buyer's behalf. A typical contingency allows the buyer to cancel the offer if the inspector's report is not satisfactory in any way. If you do receive a less-than-acceptable report from the home inspector, the contingency should permit you to cancel the purchase offer or to reopen negotiations to allow the seller to make repairs or reduce the price to permit the buyer to bring the home to a satisfactory condition.

■ CONDITION OF THE HOME AND MAJOR SYSTEMS

The contract should include a guarantee by the seller that the home at closing will be in a condition no worse than it was at the time the purchase offer was received. Most contracts require the seller to remove all furniture and objects not included in the sale and to clean up dirt and debris throughout.

Unless an appliance is sold as is, it is expected to work properly at the time of the closing. In most cases, mortgage lenders will require that a furnace or heating system be in proper condition. Some sellers will provide a warranty on appliances and major systems of the house. The warranty functions like a service contract for repairs to certain devices. Buyers can also purchase a warranty on their own.

■ SELLER'S DISCLOSURE FORM

In most states the seller must disclose any known problems with the home. The intent is to protect the buyer against fraud—buying a home that requires major repairs in order to be made livable, for example. The form also ends up giving some protection to the seller, who might otherwise be open to a lawsuit about undisclosed problems. Of course, the form depends on the honesty of the seller. If you purchase a home and later find that serious roof leaks were hidden by a new paint job or that the furnace was held together with baling wire, you may still have a legal case against the seller. (See appendix C for an example of a Seller's Disclosure Form.)

■ HOME INSPECTIONS

Are you really ready to commit yourself to buying a $400,000 used home on the basis of your own, amateur walk-around examination of the property? Even if you know what to look for—for example, termite infestation, inadequate or below-code plumbing and electrical systems, a properly maintained heating and cooling equipment, and the structural soundness of the foundation, frame, and roof—have you inspected every corner, crawlspace, and utility closet in the home before you made your offer to the seller? Do you know if the existing structure and systems will support expansions and additions you plan as a buyer? The smart solution is to hire a professional home inspector, someone who will look out solely for your interests—not the seller's, the real estate agent's, or a home-repair or maintenance company's. It is not unreasonable to make the purchase of your home contingent upon receiving an acceptable report from a qualified inspector.

The inspector should be brought in after the offer to purchase is accepted by the seller, prior to executing the final purchase and sales agreement. Make certain that your attorney or real estate agent includes a clause in the contract making the purchase obligation contingent upon the findings of a professional home inspection. The clause should specify the terms to which both the buyer and seller are obligated.

The cost of a home inspection will vary by region and according to the size and complexity of the house. Typically an inspection will range in cost from about $200 to $400. Some inspectors have a basic rate that is adjusted upwards for older homes, very large homes, and those with unusual construction techniques. You can also expect to be charged a premium for rush jobs and for inspections conducted on weekends or holidays.

Only a handful of states require that home inspectors be licensed. Don't confuse "certification" or membership in an industry group with licensure. If your state does not issue licenses, however, spend the time to check out the qualifications of the inspector. Look for engineering or homebuilding experience and training, and assure yourself that there are no conflicts of interest between the inspector and the seller, agent, or home-repair companies: You don't want to deal with an inspector who has a business relationship with someone trying to sell you a home or with someone who wants to make repairs to it. The largest trade group is the American Association of Home Inspectors, which requires members to agree to their code of ethics.

If possible, I'd recommend that you ask that the seller not be present for the inspection. At the same time, you should ask to accompany the inspector on his rounds. To begin with, you'll be able to learn a great deal about the home and be able to ask questions about findings before you receive the written report of the inspection.

In general, you should consider having the following tests performed on the house as part of the inspection: termite and other insect and pest infestation, lead paint, and radon gas. In some states the seller is required to disclose whether lead paint or urea formaldehyde insulation was used in the home. Some lenders may require such tests in order to issue a mortgage. If the home uses a well or septic tank, separate tests of those systems are worthwhile.

In some cases a home seller may want to arrange for an inspection before putting the house on the market. The report of the inspector can be used to repair any major defects and be promoted in the listing as a qualification for the house. However, the seller could be opening the door to a lawsuit if all of the information in the report is not disclosed to a buyer, or if the inspection is found to have been less than professional or compromised by a conflict of interest.

Very few homes will receive a perfect report from the inspector. Some problems may be very minor, while others may require significant expenses for repair. According to industry groups, a typical home inspection recommends repairs costing 2 to 8 percent of the value of the structure. The most common items found to require repair include:

- Wood rot in decks and porches and other parts of the house in contact with soil or moisture
- Problems with roofs and roof venting systems, gutters, and downspouts
- Poor ventilation of the home
- Deteriorating chimneys
- Damage to tub and shower walls and bathroom floors
- Furnaces, hot water heaters, and air conditioners in need of cleaning or service
- Outdated electrical systems inadequate for modern demands, including computers, multiple televisions, and other devices

Home Inspector Resources

PROFESSIONAL ORGANIZATIONS

▶ American Society of Home Inspectors, (800) 743–2744; www.ashi.org.

▶ National Institute of Building Inspectors, (888) 281–6424; www.nibi.com.

DIRECTORIES

▶ Home Hero, (800) 964–0307; www.home inspectorlocator.com.

▶ Home Inspector eFinder, www.homeinspectorefinder. com.

▶ Home Inspections-USA, www.homeinspections-usa. com.

▶ Independent Home Inspectors of North America, www.independent inspectors.org.

If you receive a report from a home inspector that indicates significant problems with the house, you should consult with your real estate agent about your options. If your offer to purchase allows, you can withdraw your offer or ask for a reduction in the selling price to cover the cost of repairs. If you agree to allow the homeowner to make repairs, the purchase should be made contingent on a second home inspection to certify that the repairs were properly made.

Making Use of a Home Inspector's Report

If the home inspector you hire finds no significant problems with the house, you can proceed with an offer based entirely on the fair market value of the home. On the other hand, if you find serious problems, you have four options:

1. Walk away from someone else's headache. If you have already made an offer, invoke the contingency clause you included that says the bid is based on receiving a good report from a qualified home inspector. Your deposit should be returned from the real estate agency's escrow account.

2. Ask that the seller make and pay for certain repairs before closing.

3. Reduce your offer based on the anticipated expenses for repairs deemed necessary by the home inspector.

4. Accept the house as is, knowing that you'll have to spend money to bring it up to move-in condition.

In some circumstances, the lender's appraiser may find problems with the home that would cause a reduction in the amount of money available for a mortgage. For example, the appraiser might find the roof needs reshingling, reducing the value of the home by $10,000. As the would-be buyer, you have the same set of options: walk away, insist on a repair, reduce your offer, or pay for the repairs yourself.

■ FINANCING CONTINGENCY

It's not enough to make a successful offer for a piece of real estate; you've got to pay the bill when it comes time to close the deal. If you make a straight offer for purchase and it is accepted, you are legally obligated to come up with the amount due on the date specified. If you've got the cash and plan to show up at closing with a suitcase full of bills or a certified check, that shouldn't be a problem. But if you plan on taking out a mortgage, there is usually more than a little bit of uncertainty: Will the lending institution grant the loan, and if so, will it be at an interest rate and terms that you find acceptable? For that reason most offers to purchase include a financing contingency that says the deal will only go forward if a loan of a particular type and terms is received.

A typical contingency will indicate that the loan will go to closing if a loan is received by a particular date at or below a maximum interest rate and requiring no more than a specified down payment and discount points. If the buyer is unable to obtain financing, the deal can be canceled, and in most cases the contract requires the return of the entire earnest money deposit. The seller and real estate agents will judge the contingency to see that the would-be buyer is basing the offer on realistic expectations. (This is also an area where your own agent can help—or hurt—your chances of getting the home. Never tell your agent any details of your financial situation you don't want passed along to the seller.)

In a seller's market, you may find that some sellers will resist granting a very broad financing contingency. They will prefer to deal with someone who seems more certain of coming up with the needed funds or who expects a loan that is clearly in line with current offerings. As a buyer, you can greatly enhance your offer by getting preapproved for a loan, removing the need for a financing contingency clause. You can also include a financial statement with your offer, giving some indication of your ability to obtain a mortgage in a timely manner.

■ SALE OF A PREVIOUS HOME

It is not uncommon for a buyer to make a purchase offer contingent upon the sale of their current residence. In almost any deal, such a contingency greatly weakens the value of your offer if other buyers don't make similar demands. Just how much of a roadblock such a contingency represents generally depends greatly upon the local real estate market. In a booming seller's market, when homes are selling very quickly and at or near asking price, the seller may expect that your home will move as quickly as theirs did. In a very quiet buyer's market, the seller may be very unhappy with how long it took to dispose of their own home at the price they wanted and may not be willing to sweat out the buyer's sale of a previous home.

Your real estate agent may be of assistance in finding a way to help you purchase a new home while your old one is still on the market. Solutions include home-equity loans and short-term bridge loans.

■ SETTING A CLOSING DATE

Consider for a moment all of the various, complex issues that must be resolved before a real estate closing can be accomplished:

■ An attorney and title insurance company must research the title and certify that it is without defect or outstanding liens.

■ The home must pass government or lender-required inspections, including septic system, pest, and radon test.

■ The homeowner needs to receive and approve the report of a qualified home inspector or engineer.

■ The lending institution has to approve the mortgage.

■ In many states, attorneys need to prepare and review papers on behalf of the seller, buyer, and the lending institution.

■ The change in ownership needs to be recorded at various government offices.

■ The seller needs to arrange for a moving company and pack up the contents of the house prior to the closing date.

■ The buyer is usually granted a last-minute inspection of the home before closing to assure that it is in the promised condition and that any appliances, window treatments, and other furnishings are in place as agreed.

■ In most cases, the buyer needs to arrange for the coincidental sale of a previous home or termination of an existing lease.

It's enough to give a professional planner a headache. As a mere amateur, this is a case where a capable real estate agent may be able to keep the train on the tracks.

In most markets, the purchase agreement allows forty-five to sixty days for the completion of all of the aforementioned tasks. In most cases, the closing date can be set for a slightly longer period, although in many cases the lending institution will only lock in its rates and term for a limited period of time. And if you insist on a longer-than-typical period, your offer may be less attractive than one from another would-be buyer.

Once a purchase agreement has been accepted, you may be able to extend the closing date with the permission of the seller. In some cases, you may have to compensate the seller for any losses incurred because of the delay. If you are unable to meet the closing time, and no extension is granted, you may lose some or all of the earnest money if the purchased agreement includes such a provision.

In most agreements, possession of the house is conveyed at the time of clos-

Discrimination against Buyers

Discrimination against potential buyers on the basis of race, religion, or ethnic background is offensive, unethical . . . and most of the time, illegal. Put another way, an individual seller can still choose to sell or not sell to someone for any reason in most cases. The federal Fair Housing Law, part of the Civil Rights Act of 1968 and later revisions, says that real estate brokers, agents, mortgage lenders, and other professionals involved in the sale of homes cannot refuse to sell or rent to someone on the basis of race, religion, sex, ethnicity, or disability. They cannot set different conditions for one group of persons than another. They are also barred from attempts at convincing homeowners to sell their property because of an influx of a minority group, a practice called "blockbusting." Lending institutions are banned from "redlining" a neighborhood—refusing to lend—on the basis of a protected class. However, individuals can pretty much act independently, unless they fall under certain exceptions. The Fair Housing Law applies if:

- The seller owns more than three single-family homes.
- The seller has sold more than one house where he is not the resident.
- A broker or other real estate professional is involved.

And no matter the circumstances, discriminatory advertising is illegal.

At this writing, one loophole in the law is that sellers can refuse to sell to someone on the basis of sexual orientation.

If you suspect that a seller is engaging in discriminatory practices, contact your state attorney general for advice on filing a complaint. Other sources of help include the U.S. Department of Justice (202–514–4713 or www.usdoj. gov/crt/housing/faq.htm) or the HUD Housing Discrimination Hotline (800–669–9777 or www.hud.gov/complaints/housediscrim.cfm).

ing. It is possible to come to an agreement that allows the buyer to move into the home before closing or that permits the former owner to stay on in the house for a period after closing. However, you should involve an attorney in drafting a short-term lease to protect one side or another from liability claims and to stay on the right side of state and federal capital gains tax regulations.

THE SELLER'S RESPONSE

The seller can accept your offer, reject it outright, or make a counteroffer as a response. The "counter" can be made as an edit to your original proposal by changes to the figures and language or in the form of a new purchase offer contract proffered by the seller. In either case, the counteroffer is signed by the seller and becomes effective if you sign it as the buyer.

If you receive a counteroffer, the ball is back in your court. You have the same options: accept, reject, or respond. Your real estate agent may be able to assist you in deciding whether to raise your offer, improve its terms, or to move on to another property. (Remember that most agents are paid entirely from the proceeds of a sale, and it is always in their interest to get you to buy something rather than walk away.)

Some sellers are perfectly happy to engage in several rounds—or more—of offer and counteroffer, while others will dig in their heels at their original price or after a drop to what they consider to be their lowest acceptable price. (In some instances, your agent may be able to inform you of past unsuccessful negotiations that will give you an idea of the seller's true expectations.)

Some sellers may reject your proposal but encourage you to raise your offer or improve the terms. This is often a bad situation for the buyer: You have no assurance that the seller will accept an increased bid, and you may be an unwilling or unknowing participant in an attempt by the seller to get another would-be buyer to boost his offer.

You or your real estate agent should respond to any verbal representation by the seller by requesting a written counteroffer. In theory, a seller should have only one active counteroffer. If two or more counters are in the marketplace, both could be accepted, leading to legal complications. (In some instances, a seller may notify multiple bidders of a counteroffer, promising to sell to the first buyer to deliver an acceptance and earnest money.)

If you walk away from a property, be sure to ask your real estate agent to monitor its status even as you look at other houses. It is quite possible that the seller will realize that the offer he rejected from you might be the best one he can expect at the moment. The seller could come back and ask you to resubmit your offer with a promise to accept it.

BUYING FROM A FSBO

In some areas, it is not unusual to see homes for sale by owner (known in the real estate trade as FSBOs, pronounced "fiz-bohs"). For whatever reason—usually economic—a homeowner chooses to offer a home for sale without involvement of a real estate agent.

A common error by FSBO sellers is to think that by selling the house by themselves they will receive a higher price than they would by listing with an agent. The most likely outcome is that they will end up receiving about the same price either way. What they may save is the 6 percent they would pay to brokers, or perhaps just half of that commission if the purchaser is represented by a buyer's agent.

Owners attempting to sell a home by themselves often set their expectations on the listing price of neighborhood homes, as opposed to the actual selling price, which is usually lower. As a would-be buyer of a FSBO home, you should also try to determine if the home had previously been offered by a real estate agent. It may be the case that the sellers were asking an unreasonable amount of money for their home, or that there are problems with the house such that agents will not handle it.

If you are shopping for a home and are considering a home for sale by the owner, it might be worthwhile to ask a real estate agent to approach the seller on your behalf. The seller may have to agree to pay a commission to the agent if you buy the house, or less commonly, you may have to pay your own agent. But in either case, you will have the protection of a real estate professional in your corner.

If an agent is involved, the commission should be half of the standard amount since only one side of the transaction will be represented. It may also be appropriate to ask for a commission of just a percentage or two since the agent has had no involvement in the marketing of the home.

PART II

AGENTS

CHAPTER FIVE

REAL ESTATE AGENTS

WHOM DO YOU WORK FOR? The short answer is: You work for the person or company that pays your salary. Now answer this question: Whom does your real estate agent work for? Although the agent may be helping you as a buyer, in almost every instance the commission check comes from the seller. As a seller, that's fine. You want someone to look out for your interests first. As a buyer, this may not be good news. Later in this section I'll discuss some ways that a buyer can find an agent who will be exclusively on his side in the house-hunting and purchasing game.

CHOOSING A REAL ESTATE AGENT TO SELL YOUR HOUSE

Think of choosing a real estate agent as *hiring* a salesperson for your house. You should research the market and interview candidates as if your bottom line depended on it. Your perfect candidate should know the neighborhood, understand real estate law and practice, be a crackerjack salesperson, and—depending on the local market conditions—be willing to bargain with you on the commission charged.

Although it is possible to discover an unproven rookie on the verge of an all-star season, it may not make sense for you to take on that sort of a challenge. The fact is that the right candidate is often the agent who is in the midst of a sustained winning streak. You want an agent who sells a high percentage of listings he accepts. A strong performer sells at least 75 percent.

Ask friends and business acquaintances for recommendations. Many local newspapers publish real estate transactions, including the names of the agents. You can check with the local real estate board or state real estate commission for any formal complaints filed against particular agents. Then schedule a round of interviews. Here are some questions to ask:

■ How many comparable homes in this area have you sold in the past year? Can you provide me with the names and phone numbers of some of your customers?

■ Tell me your view of the current market in this area. How will these conditions affect the sale of my home?

■ What homes currently on the market or soon to be for sale will be competitive with mine?

■ What suggestions do you have to make my home easier to sell?

■ How often will you communicate with me while the home is listed with you?

■ What percentage of your listings are sold before the listing expires?

■ What percentage of the asking price do your clients typically receive?

■ How much commission do you charge? If I am willing to work with you to make this home as marketable as possible, are you willing to accept a lower commission?

■ BROKER VERSUS AGENT VERSUS REALTOR

There are real estate agents, and there are Realtors. A Realtor is a member of the National Association of Realtors, a real estate trade association. Members have to pass a certification test and abide by that group's code of ethics. That said, the difference between a real estate agent and a Realtor can be great or none at all. It's much more important that you find someone who will bring the right combination of skills and resources for your assignment—with or without a registered trademark after their name. Whatever they call themselves, the person who is helping you sell your home or showing you a new one is a commissioned salesperson. In most cases, she doesn't earn a penny unless you sell your home or buy a new one with her aid.

The three most common titles are broker, agent, or Realtor. A broker is usually the owner or a principal of a licensed real estate brokerage. A licensed broker working for another broker might take the title of broker associate or associate broker. In most cases, though, when you sign a listing agreement your contract is with the brokerage and not with a particular agent.

An agent is a trained salesperson who works for a licensed broker. Some are on salary, while most are essentially independent contractors paid entirely with the proceeds of commissions. How much of the commission they hold on to depends on their success and their deal with the broker. The hottest salespeople can often keep nearly all of a commission—they are valuable to the brokerage in attracting customers and other agents, and the owner doesn't want to risk losing the number-one agent to a competitor.

At one time nearly every brokerage was locally owned and operated, trading on the connections established by the broker and staff. Today the trend is toward franchise affiliation with a national company. Among major franchises are Century 21, Coldwell Banker, ERA, Prudential, and RE/MAX. The advantage to the brokerage of buying a franchise is a tie-in to the national advertising and marketing of the parent company. The brokerage gets to include the well-known logo of the franchisor on its yard signs and local advertising, and it may even get to wear garish yellow, red, or green blazers.

As a buyer, you may find the Web sites of the franchisors a valuable place to do some research from hundreds or thousands of miles away, well before you sign an agreement with an agent to represent you in your search for a home. However, there is no certainty that a franchised brokerage will give you any better service than an independent one. You should still interview potential brokerages and check with friends, family, and business associates for recommendations and wave-offs.

Three of the largest—Century 21, Coldwell Banker, and ERA—are all owned by the same company, Cendant Corporation. Century 21 Real Estate Corporation (www.century21.com) claims to be the franchisor of the world's largest residential real estate sales organization, with more than 6,600 independently owned and operated franchised broker offices in more than thirty countries and territories worldwide. Coldwell Banker Real Estate Corporation (www.coldwell banker.com) has more than 3,000 independently owned and operated residential and commercial real estate offices that employ more than 75,000 sales associates around the world. ERA Franchise Systems, Inc. (www.ERA.com) includes more than 2,500 independently owned and operated brokerage offices with more than 28,000 brokers and sales associates throughout the United States and twenty-six other countries and territories.

The other two largest networks of brokerages are RE/MAX and Prudential. RE/MAX (www.remax.com) works with more than 73,000 sales associates in more than 4,200 offices worldwide. The Prudential Real Estate Network (www. prudential.com/realestate), part of the massive Prudential insurance and financial services company, has 1,540 quality real estate offices, and approximately 43,000 sales professionals located in fifty states and five Canadian provinces.

■ ONE BROKER OR TWO?

If you are selling a house and looking for a new one in the same area, you'll have to decide whether to deal with one real estate agent or two. Working with just one agent may be easier for you, especially if you are convinced that the agent is working hard and well on your behalf. (And there is no reason for the agent not to give you extra effort since he stands to make a commission on both transactions.) But you should make your decision based on separate appraisals of the agent's abilities and connections. Some agents would seem to be better suited to market your existing home and tap into their network of brokers to bring in qualified buyers. Other agents are very good at knowing the market of available homes and helping buyers in making a reasonable and successful bid. Only occasionally do the two sets of skills and connections coincide in the same person. If you do end up giving both the sale of your home and the purchase of a new home to one agent, this should be a good opportunity to negotiate a reduced commission on the sale of your old home.

■ TYPES OF LISTINGS FOR SALE

Most real estate agents want you just for themselves. They'll promise to spend money on advertising, work the telephones with other agents, and offer advice on pricing and marketing your home. In return, they don't want another agent or agency to swoop in and sell your house and collect the commission. For that reason, you'll likely be asked to sign some form of an exclusive listing that binds you to the agency.

The standard agreement between a seller and a real estate broker assigns the **exclusive right to sell.** During the term of the contract the listing agent receives a commission however the home is sold—by the listing agent, by another brokerage, or by the seller directly.

Under an **exclusive agency** agreement, only one agency represents you as the seller, and it will be paid a commission if it participates in any way in the sale of the house. If you find a buyer on your own and do not involve the broker, you do not have to pay a commission. This sort of agreement can include a blanket exclusion for any clients that you find, or for one or more named would-be buyers you dealt with before signing the agreement with an agency.

The least-binding arrangement is an **open** or **nonexclusive** agreement. This commits the seller to pay a specified commission percent to any agent who brings in a buyer whose offer you accept and go through to closing with. Since the seller is essentially handling the marketing end of the transaction, the typical commission paid is half of the standard rate—just the portion that would ordinarily go to the agent representing the buyer. This sort of listing is often used by homeowners who are also attempting to sell their property by themselves, and in some markets where no multiple listing service is available.

If you sign an open or nonexclusive agreement with a broker, make sure it has a reasonably short expiration date. If not, you will be unable to sign an exclusive agreement with another agent if you change your mind about how you want to market your home.

■ THE LISTING CONTRACT

The contract you sign with a brokerage includes legal boilerplate about your obligations to the listing agency and, generally, some much less specific details of what the brokerage will do for you. The more particulars you can get into the contract—advertising, open houses, and other marketing plans—the better. One essential detail is the **expiration date** for the contract, or the **contract term.** A brokerage will want to lock you in for as long as possible, justifying this exclusivity by pointing to the amount of time and money it intends to spend on your behalf. From the seller's point of view, it generally makes sense to seek as short a term as is reasonable. You can always extend the agreement, but a short term allows you to keep the pressure on the agent with the implied or explicit threat that you will sign with another brokerage if the house is not sold before the expiration date.

Typical terms range from three months to six months. Research the average time to sale for comparable homes in your market. If homes are usually selling in just a few weeks, keep the term short. If houses are taking four or five months to sell, a brokerage may not want to take on a listing, or may not put much effort behind it, if the term is only three months.

The contract usually includes some language that allows you to cancel the agreement for nonperformance by the broker. This is usually a pretty difficult case to prove unless the contract includes specifics about the number and type of ads, open houses, and other efforts. In any case, read the contract carefully to assure yourself that there are no financial penalties to you if you cancel the agreement or if you allow it to lapse at the end of the term. (Some agreements allow the broker to demand repayment for specific services such as advertising space.) Some contracts include a **protection period** that extends after the expiration period that requires payment of commission if the house ends up being sold to a buyer brought to the table by the original listing agent.

■ COMMISSIONS

In most cases, agents receive their income through a commission on sales. If there are two agents or brokerages involved—one for the seller and one for the buyer—the commission is usually split evenly between them.

The commission paid to a broker is not set by law; it is a negotiable amount. On the average, the commission is usually between 5 and 7 percent, and it is usually paid at closing from the proceeds of the sale. In a seller's market—when houses are selling especially quickly—it is not unreasonable to ask a broker to reduce the commission because the investment of time and money will be minimal. In a buyer's market—when brokers have to fight very hard for every sale—you can expect to find agents holding a firm line on the commission rate. Beyond that, there are all sorts of situations where you may want to try to adjust the commission rate. Among them:

■ A house has languished on the market for a long time and is not attracting many shoppers. The seller can advise brokers of a cash bonus or an increase in the commission as one way to make the house stand out a bit from others on the market—at least to brokers.

■ A house has languished on the market for a long time and has finally received an offer that is below the seller's expectations but close enough to consider. The seller can contact the selling broker and ask for a reduction in the agreed-upon commission in order to finally sell the home. This sort of approach might work well near the end of the exclusivity agreement. A smart broker realizes it is better to make less profit than no profit.

■ DISCOUNT BROKERS

One recent wrinkle in real estate sales has been the arrival of discount brokers. These companies promise to make use of modern marketing tools—the multiple listing service, the Internet, and print advertising—to sell homes. They market heavily to brokers serving buyers. Those brokers can expect to receive their usual commission of 2.5 to 3 percent (half of the typical full commission).

If you consider a discount broker, be sure you understand exactly what you are giving up and what you are receiving. In a hot market, it may be quite acceptable to promote your home primarily through an MLS. In a slow market, more may be required—either by you as the seller, or by a real estate agent who has a financial stake in seeing that the house is sold quickly and at a good price.

Reasons to Ask for Reduced Commission

▶ If you find a buyer who has not dealt with your listing agent.

▶ If the house sells immediately, before the broker has placed advertising or otherwise spent time and money on marketing.

▶ If the house does not sell for an extended period of time and the offer on the table is not quite acceptable to you, but could be made so by a reduction in commission cost.

▶ If the listing broker also delivers the buyer, in which case the company stands to collect both halves of the commission.

▶ If you agree up front to take on some of the work involved in marketing the house, including advertising and open houses. Some discount brokers will make exactly this pitch, offering to share some of the tasks in return for a reduced commission.

A typical discount broker agreement calls for the payment of a fee—perhaps $300 to $600—for the listing of the home in an MLS and on Internet sites. Once a home is sold, the owner is obligated to pay just the buyer's agent a commission, which should reduce the payment by half.

Watch out for some discount brokers that charge fees for services such as showing the home or making phone calls to buyer's brokers or directly to clients. Although there is nothing wrong with paying someone for work performed, these fees could end up negating the advantage of using a discount broker. Be sure there is a cap on fees and that the charges themselves are reasonable.

In general, I would advise considering the use of a discount broker only in a hot seller's market. At the same time, if the market is so hot that all a real estate agent has to do is let the world know a house is for sale, you should also consider asking a traditional agent to reduce the commission on the listing.

CHOOSING A REAL ESTATE AGENT TO HELP YOU BUY A HOUSE

Although I have advised that you "hire" a real estate agent to help you sell your home, that's not quite the case when you are selecting an agent to help you buy a home or property. That's because a real estate agent or a Realtor is a salesperson who is paid—by the seller—with a percentage of the selling price of the home or land.

As such, your agent may try very hard to make you happy and do a good job in finding properties that meet your desires, but when it comes to closing the deal, her interests align with the seller and not the buyer. The higher the selling price—and by extension, the more she helps the seller take cash out of your hands—the more money she makes.

Most agents are legally bound to help the seller get the most money and the best terms in the sale of the house, even if they have brought the buyer to the party. Assume that anything and everything you tell your agent will be made known to the seller. The agent may be required by law to disclose everything she knows about your financial circumstances and bargaining position to the seller. Here's what that means:

- If you make an offer of $275,000 but tell your agent that the maximum amount of money you have available to spend is $300,000, your agent may well communicate that information to the selling agent or the seller. You're better off telling your agent that $275,000 is as high as you will go, even if you are prepared to go a bit higher.
- The fact that you are desperate to buy a house because you are approaching the closing on the sale of your previous home may be important to you, but it is not the sort of inside edge you want to convey to the seller by way of your agent.
- Although you are certain of your ability to come up with a down payment and meet monthly mortgage bills, there may be details of your personal financial situation that don't reflect well on you. This is something you don't want communicated to a seller, or to anyone other than a bank or lending institution with a real need to know.

■ HOW AN AGENT WILL HELP YOU FIND A HOUSE TO BUY

You've asked an agent from a Century 21 brokerage to show you around town on the basis of its incessant advertising about how broad and deep its knowledge of the real estate market is and its hundreds of thousands of listings. Where does the agent take you on your expedition? To a home with a great big FOR SALE sign from Prudential Real Estate? It makes sense when you consider the fact that no real estate brokerage or national franchisor has a complete monopoly on all houses for sale. (That's a good thing, since in theory it prevents monopolistic practices like price-fixing and manipulation of commissions and fees. It is worth noting, though, that the real estate market is dominated by several huge groups of franchised brokers, including one set—Century 21, Coldwell Banker, and ERA—that are all owned by the same company, Cendant Corporation.)

You could, of course, only look at homes that are listed by the agent you have engaged to help you in your search. He'd be happy to do so, especially since he stands the chance to collect a full commission from the seller and sometimes a bonus from the broker who owns the agency. However, in nearly every marketplace, area brokerages cooperate in a multiple listing service. Any member of the association is able to show and sell homes (and land) listed in the MLS book, and increasingly, in an on-line regional MLS Web site.

Inherent in the idea of an MLS is the fact that real estate agents share the commission on a sale. Although there are some differences from area to area, in general real estate agents charge a commission of 5 to 8 percent on the sale of a home. A typical arrangement calls for an even split of the commission between the seller's broker and the broker representing the buyer. The brokers will in turn pay the agent a proportion of the commission received.

■ EXCLUSIVITY AGREEMENTS FOR BUYERS

If you are shown a house by an agent, the seller of the home is generally obligated to pay a commission if a sale results. For that reason, some agents start out their relationship with a buyer with a day of drive-by showings that cover much of the available market. Unless that sort of a grand tour makes sense to you, I'd resist such an untargeted tour.

True Story

My soon-to-be wife and I were shopping for our first home in upstate New York. We signed an agreement promising to work only with one agency, and we had already visited a number of homes with our assigned agent, including a few on which we were considering making an offer. But it was quickly apparent to us that we had hired a turkey. The agent knew less about the area than we did. She was a terrifying driver, an awful navigator, and, to make things ridiculous, she kept complaining to us about the cost of gasoline. After a few weekends of shopping, we had enjoyed about as much of her company as we could stand.

We made a phone call to the owner of the company and requested that we be assigned a new agent. He agreed—in fact, he took over our account personally, and very soon afterward we made a successful offer on a house. Whatever arrangements the owner made with the original agent were happily none of our concern.

If you are convinced you are not receiving proper service, ask to be released—in writing—from the exclusive buyer's agreement. If the broker refuses, contact the local real estate association or Board of Realtors and enlist its help. It is not in the interest of a brokerage or the real estate community for you to be busy spreading the news of your dissatisfaction. You can ratchet up the pressure a bit by suggesting you will conduct a campaign in the local newspaper and civic groups.

The practice is not common in all areas, but some real estate agents will ask clients to sign an exclusive buyer's agreement that commits you to working only with a particular agency. Similarly, some buyer's agents will ask you to sign a contract, sometimes calling for payment of a retainer or fee for their services. I would recommend against paying a significant up-front fee or retainer. If you do sign an agreement, don't allow a brokerage to tie you up for the whole planet, or more precisely, an area well outside of its expertise. Limit an agreement to include homes within a particular county, MLS region, or township.

The fact that you have an exclusive agreement with a brokerage doesn't mean that you can't also look on your own. If you find a FSBO or even a house listed by another brokerage but not one shown to you by your agent, you are generally free to make any arrangements on your own, including making an offer without being represented by an agent. The only reason to do so on your own would be if you expect the seller to reduce the price by most or all of the commission she would otherwise pay to an agent representing the buyer.

In most cases, the agreement you sign obligates you to a real estate agency and not directly to a particular agent. That could be a good thing if you find that you are not getting along with the agent or doubt his capabilities. You are well within your rights to approach the manager or owner of an agency and politely request a change of agents. There is no incentive for an agency to refuse to attempt to accommodate its clients. You can just wait out the expiration of your agreement to walk away—that's one reason to keep the exclusive period short.

■ OPEN HOUSES

If you walk into an open house without the company of a real estate agent, you will almost certainly be greeted by the seller's agent and probably be asked to sign a registry book. The owner's agent would be very happy to sell you the house directly—unless the seller makes other arrangements, the agent stands to collect both halves of the real estate commission. In any case, if you do identify yourself at the open house, you can expect to be contacted by real estate agents who are looking for buyers to represent. You don't have to engage their services, but you should interview a few to see if any of them bring something to the table that would help you in your quest.

■ HIRING A BUYER'S AGENT

A buyer's agent is legally bound to put your interests ahead of the seller's, even if the seller is paying her commission. In most states you can find real estate agents who proclaim themselves as **exclusive buyer's agents**. They operate very much like a seller's agent, but they are obligated to represent only the buyer in the search for the best purchase price and terms. Unlike a seller's agent, a buyer's agent is supposed to help you uncover any defects with homes, property, and the components of the contract. Any information you provide is required to be held confidential; in fact, if you're a rock star or an Academy Award–winning actress, or otherwise want to maintain complete privacy, a buyer's agent can represent you anonymously—at least through the closing.

Some buyer's agents will charge a flat fee for their services, while others will make their income from buyer's agent's portion of the real estate commission. Even though that fee is paid by the seller, they are bound to the buyer. In some regions, the buyer's agent will ask for a retainer of several hundred dollars while she represents you; the fee is refunded if you purchase a home with the agent's assistance. If the buyer's agent does intend to split the commission with the seller's agent, you should expect a full explanation of the process to assure yourself that there is no conflict of interest.

As an exclusive buyer's agent, the brokerage does not accept listings of property for sale, eliminating any bias toward its own financial interest. And, a buyer's agent is usually willing to direct you to MLS and exclusive listings of any seller's agent. The agent may also show you homes for sale by the owner and new homes under construction; in such a case the agent may seek to negotiate an agreement with the seller for a commission or may come to you as the buyer to pay the fee.

To find a buyer's agent, look for membership in a national group that sets standards for buyer's agents. These include:

■ **The National Association of Exclusive Buyer Agents (NAEBA),** (800) 500–3569; www.naeba.org.

■ **The Real Estate Buyer's Agent Council,** (800) 648–6224; www.rebac.net.

■ **Buyer's Resource,** (800) 359–4092; www.buyersresource.com.

Be sure to carefully read the agreement the agent asks you to sign to make sure that your interests as the buyer are identified as paramount. In most cases, a buyer's agent will use a version of the purchase and sale agreement that includes some extra protections for the buyer.

In a handful of states you'll also find **transaction brokers,** who are essentially managers of the real estate process. Sometimes referred to as facilitators or statutory agents, they are supposed to be even-handed with both buyer and seller, keeping confidential any information that would benefit one or the other. They provide little or no marketing assistance to sellers and minimal house-finding services to shoppers. In return, though, they usually charge a flat fee or a reduced commission for managing the business side of the deal.

The worst case is a **dual agent,** who represents both the seller and the buyer within the same brokerage. Being a dual agent is legal if it is disclosed to the buyer. Try to avoid such a situation—there is no incentive (or legal stance) for an agent to look out for your interests here. Put another way, an agent with two masters serves neither one well.

If you engage an agent and she refers you to listings held by the brokerage she works for, she has become a dual agent. That's why you should pay attention to the listing broker for every house you visit. It may be as obvious as the big sign on the front lawn, or you may have to look closely at the MLS information. Discuss with the agent your concern about dual agency and ask what she can possibly say that would relieve you of your anxiety about a conflict of interest. There is, in fact, very little relief to be had.

Is there a meaningful difference between seller's and buyer's agents? Yes and no. It depends very much on your wants and needs and the particular skills of the agent. Here are the formal differences, as set by state laws and real estate codes.

Services	Seller's Agent	Buyer's Agent
Shows MLS and other listed properties	✔	✔
Shows FSBO properties, homes under construction, homes held by banks or lending institutions	Uncertain	✔
Helps link the buyer to sources of financing	✔	✔
Provides information on comparable sales and details of the property itself	✔	✔
Advises against purchase of a property with defects or problems with deed		✔
Prepares and maintains necessary documents for offer, escrow, and closing	✔	✔
Helps the seller get the most for the property and the best terms	✔	
Protects the interests of the buyer alone		✔
Keeps confidential all of buyer's financial information related to the offer		✔

PART III

MORTGAGES

CHAPTER SIX

CHOOSING THE RIGHT MORTGAGE

MOST BOOKS LIKE THIS start out by saying: Buying a home is the single most expensive purchase in most people's lives. That is simply not true. The most expensive purchase in most people's lives is a home mortgage. Think about it: If you buy a $310,000 home with a typical 20 percent down payment, a thirty-year fixed-rate mortgage at 7 percent will cost about $350,000 in interest *plus* repayment of $250,000 in principal. That's $310,000 for the house and $350,000 for the mortgage.

WHY MORTGAGES ARE A BARGAIN

Almost no one buys a home for cash. Even if you could come up with a few hundred thousand dollars or more, in most cases this is not a good use of your money. Most financial advisors will tell you that you'll be better off *leveraging* a relatively small amount of money—typically 20 percent of the purchase cost—and making use of the bank's money. Assuming that the value of the house appreciates over time, you'll be making a nice return on a small investment. You can take the cash you have not spent on purchasing the home and invest it elsewhere.

To emphasize the point, domestic policy encourages home purchase and ownership by allowing tax write-off of interest costs and prepaid points. Using a mortgage also allows most buyers to purchase a better home, or one in a better location, than they could otherwise afford. Unless money is no object—in which case you don't need this book, or any other—you'll likely need to apply for a mortgage for your home.

▮ THE DIFFERENCE BETWEEN A MORTGAGE AND A CAR LOAN

When you borrow to purchase an automobile, you are taking out a *personal property* or *chattel* loan. Although the loan is secured by an interest in the car, that property is moveable. And most personal property *depreciates* over time, losing much of its value during the term of the loan. The owner can run away, the vehicle can be stolen, or it can be destroyed. Although the lender requires you to cover its interest with insurance, there is still a fair amount of risk of financial loss. For that reason, interest rates on an automobile loan are usually higher than those for real estate.

A mortgage, though, is a *real property* loan. The lender's money is again secured by an interest in the real estate and protected from loss by insurance the borrower is required to purchase. Most real property *appreciates* in value over time, and except in the most unusual of circumstances, the land itself will not disappear or become unusable. The lender typically offers a relatively low interest rate for a real property loan because the risk is comparatively less than for personal property. And the risk to the lender is even less if the buyer makes a substantial down payment on the property since the lender has first claim on the proceeds from the insurance or forced sale of the home because of default. If the lender has issued a mortgage for 80 percent of the purchase price (with a 20 percent down payment by the borrower), the lender is well cushioned against loss.

■ SHOPPING FOR A MORTGAGE

Sometimes it seems as if every other commercial on television or pop-up ad on your computer screen is sponsored by one or another bank or lending institution trying to convince you that its offices are more convenient, its coffee is fresher, and its loan officers are much friendlier than the others'. All of this may be true, but the essential fact is this: The only thing that is really important is getting the best possible mortgage loan. Keep your eye on the prize. Saving 1 percent on a thirty-year fixed-rate mortgage for $250,000 will reduce the cost about $2,000 per month, or $60,000 if you keep the loan to maturity. That will buy a lot of coffee.

Although mortgage lenders go on and on about how nice they are, and how they really, really care about the people they help to buy their dream homes, here's another truth: Very, very few mortgages end up being held by the original lenders. Most mortgages are sold to private or government-backed investors almost immediately. In many instances, a typical mortgage may be sold several times in its life.

In most cases, the owner of a mortgage obligation does not "service" the loan: send out monthly bills, accept payments, and otherwise deal with the borrower. Third-party mortgage service companies do the work for lenders, and they are interested only in collecting the money and keeping their own costs as low as possible. And they don't offer you a cup of coffee; their real customer is the current owner of the mortgage obligation and not the borrower.

WHICH MORTGAGE?

The good news is that there are dozens—maybe hundreds—of different mortgage plans available to the savvy consumer. The bad news is that when it comes to picking the best one for you, it's often a matter of comparing apples, oranges, and cabbages. The basic major differences between loans are:

■ **The term, or amortization period.** A thirty-year loan is set up to conclude in that number of years, either as the result of the completion of monthly payoff of interest and principal or after a balloon payment pays off the outstanding balance.
■ **The interest rate.** Rates can be fixed—unchangeable over the course of the term—or adjusted upward or downward monthly, annually, or after a specified number of years based on the performance of an independent economic index.
■ **The up-front costs.** Interest rates can be reduced by the payment of points or loan discount fees, which are additional profit for the lender.

See appendix D for a checklist you can use to compare the elements of various mortgages you are considering. Make as many copies as you need for serious loan candidates. Also see appendix E for a listing of mortgage types.

■ INTEREST RATES

Second only to the amount of the loan itself (the cost of the house minus any down payment plus any financed closing costs), the most important number in calculating the cost of a mortgage over a particular period of time is the interest rate. The interest rate on a mortgage tells you the charge on the outstanding balance of the loan. All other things being equal, a lower interest rate means a lower cost for a mortgage. If you are offered two loans for the same amount of money, for the same period of time (the term), and with identical up-front costs, choose the one with the lower interest rate.

However, things are rarely so simple. Nearly every mortgage includes a number of other costs, including loan origination fees, closing costs, and if the down payment is below a certain level, mortgage insurance. And many loans also link their particular interest rate to the payment of "points," which are prepaid interest. A rough rule of thumb: One point is equal to about one-eighth of a percentage point on the interest rate of a thirty-year fixed-rate mortgage. For example, a thirty-year mortgage that requires payment of two points has about the same cost as a zero-points mortgage that bears an interest rate one-quarter percent higher.

There is nothing wrong with paying points, but their cost needs to be included in any comparison of one mortgage to another. If you pay points, you are raising the effective yield on the mortgage for the lender. From the borrower's point of view, you are receiving less cash in the loan, although the face value remains unchanged. For example, if you pay two points on a $200,000 loan—$4,000 up front—the effect is that you will receive only $196,000 toward the home purchase, although your outstanding principal will begin at $200,000 and interest will be charged against that amount.

Federal regulations require lenders to calculate a restating of the interest rate: the **annual percentage rate,** which includes these costs as well as compounded interest (interest on accumulated interest due). An APR rate allows you to directly compare the true cost of a loan if a fixed-rate mortgage is held for its full term. It is of less value when comparing adjustable loans because their rising and falling rates may be based on different indexes and there may be differing caps on the adjustment and maximum level of the rate. The cleanest comparison of APRs puts loans of the same term against each other. If you compare a thirty-year loan to a fifteen-year loan, the APR on the shorter loan will be higher because any points included in the loan amount are amortized over fifteen years instead of thirty. You can find all manner of monthly payment and loan amortization tables at any of dozens of mortgage and financial-tool Web sites. A few examples: www.financialpowertools.com/amortization_calculator, www.eloan.com, and www.mortgage.com.

Here's a quick way to calculate the monthly payment on a fifteen- or thirty-year fixed mortgage. To figure the monthly cost of principal and interest, multiply the number of thousands in the loan by the cost per thousand. The cost per thousand is rounded off slightly, and therefore actual monthly payments may be slightly different. The interest rates shown here are in quarter-point increments. If the actual interest rate is quoted in eighths of a point, you can interpolate between figures for an approximation.

MORTGAGE PAYMENT TABLE

Interest rate	Thirty-year fixed interest loan	Fifteen-year fixed interest loan
(Payment per thousand dollars in loan)		
4.0 percent	$4.77	$7.40
4.25	$4.92	$7.52
4.5	$5.07	$7.65
4.75	$5.22	$7.78
5.0	$5.37	$7.91
5.25	$5.52	$8.04
5.5	$5.68	$8.19
5.75	$5.84	$8.30
6.0	$6.00	$8.44
6.25	$6.16	$8.57
6.5	$6.32	$8.71
6.75	$6.49	$8.85
7.0	$6.65	$8.99
7.25	$6.82	$9.13
7.5	$6.99	$9.27
7.75	$7.16	$9.41
8.0	$7.34	$9.56
8.25	$7.51	$9.70
8.5	$7.69	$9.85
8.75	$7.87	$9.99
9.0	$8.05	$10.14
9.25	$8.23	$10.29
9.5	$8.41	$10.44
9.75	$8.59	$10.59
10.0	$8.78	$10.75

For example, for a thirty-year loan of $240,000 at 5.5 percent, multiply the number of thousands (240) times $5.68 to yield a monthly payment for principal and interest of $1,363.20.

■ REGULATION Z

If you find the thicket of mortgage types, rates, discounts, charges, and terms to be painfully confusing, just imagine what it would be without the assistance of something called Regulation Z. More formally, the regulation is the implementation by the Federal Reserve System of the Federal Truth in Lending Act. The key element of the regulation is a uniform method to compute the cost of credit and a specified format for disclosure of the important rates, charges, and terms in a mortgage. The rule applies to any commercial lender; it generally does not apply in transactions entirely between individuals. The regulation requires lenders to:

■ Provide borrowers with clearly written information on essential credit terms of the agreement, including the cost of credit expressed as an annual percentage rate

■ Follow consistent and fair rules when it comes to advertising mortgage rates and terms

■ Provide a good-faith estimation of closing costs for residential mortgages before the contract is signed

■ Follow a prescribed process to respond to and deal with consumer complaints about errors

■ FIXED VERSUS ADJUSTABLE INTEREST RATES

Until a few decades ago, nearly all mortgages were long-term contracts based on an unchanging interest rate, with payments covering the cost of interest as well as a steady reduction of the principal of the loan. The beauty of the fixed-interest mortgage is the predictability and stability of the monthly payment for principal and interest; both the borrower and the lender know what to expect throughout the course of the agreement. That very stability, though, is also one of its disadvantages. Lenders know that interest rates—on money they borrow as well as money they lend—cycle up and down. For that reason, rates on a fixed-interest loan are typically set higher than the prevailing short-term interest rates with hopes that the lender will make a profit over the long term as market rates rise and fall. As a borrower you face the same uncertainty, knowing that the deal you sign today could carry a higher interest rate and monthly payment than one you could obtain in a few months or a few years. And though the monthly payment that covers principal and interest will remain the same over the entire course of the loan, payments over the first fifteen or twenty years of the loan are mostly directed at paying off the interest cost. (The amount of money directed to reduction of the principal doesn't reach 50 percent of the monthly payment until somewhere in the twenty-second year of a thirty-year loan.)

■ TIME IS THE MOST IMPORTANT QUESTION

You should expect any lender you deal with to help you compare one mortgage against another. The fact is that in most cases, the lender expects to make—on average—about the same profit on any of the programs offered. The better on-line mortgage Web sites also include calculators that allow you to analyze two or more programs at a time.

In order to make the most accurate comparison, there is one very important estimation you need to make: About how long do you expect to live in the house you are financing? It is also valuable to make an informed guess about the direction of interest rates, which tend to go up and down in cycles. If rates are at or near historic lows, as they were in 2002, it's a fair bet that they will trend upward over the coming decade. On the other hand, when rates are at painfully high levels, as they were in 1981 when average thirty-year fixed-rate loans demanded 18.45 percent interest, it's reasonable to expect the trend will be downward over time.

Here are two essential questions to ask yourself:

1. Do you expect to stay in your home for many years—seven to ten years or more? If so, your emphasis should be on getting the lowest available interest rate. If rates are low, take a fixed-rate mortgage. If rates are high, consider an adjustable rate mortgage and hope to ride it down to a better rate. Once it has declined, you can lock in a lower fixed rate or refinance.

Consider that saving 0.5 percent on a $200,000, thirty-year fixed mortgage rate will save about $69.10 per month for each of 360 months, or a total of $24,876 in interest costs. If it costs you $3,000 in prepaid points to get that lower rate, you will be ahead of the game in just three and a half years and saving money every month after then.

The biggest advantage of a long-term fixed-interest mortgage is predictability. You'll know right at the outset how much interest you will pay for principal and interest for every month of the loan. In the first half of the loan, most of your payment goes to pay off interest costs and therefore is tax-deductible. The disadvantage is that the initial rate is usually higher than the initial rate on an adjustable mortgage, although monthly payments on ARMs generally go up in the first few years and tend to decline slowly if interest rates go down for all loans.

2. Do you plan to sell the home (or refinance) after a relatively short time, say three to five years? In that case, your emphasis should be on obtaining a mortgage with low up-front and closing costs, coupled with a reasonable interest rate.

■ PREPAYMENT PENALTIES

Lenders make their profit off the interest payments that are made over the course of a loan. Lenders usually want—or need—payments for at least several years to cover their expenses and go into the black. However, homeowners in the past few decades have tended to hold on to their mortgages for shorter and shorter lengths of time. To begin with, the upward march of real estate value has lead many homeowners to trade up from one house to another. At the same time, sharp fluctuations in interest rates and the accompanying popularity of adjustable rate mortgages have also encouraged borrowers to refinance their loans when interest rates decline.

Most mortgages do not include a prepayment penalty, but some lenders will offer a slightly lower rate or a cash rebate to borrowers who agree to accept a penalty clause. (Prepayment penalties are not legal in some states, and in other areas there are limitations on the type of loans to which they can be attached.) If you are reasonably certain you will stay in a home for several years or more, it might be worthwhile to accept a prepayment penalty that expires before your expected departure or refinancing. On the other hand, if you think you might be transferred in your job or you want to be free to refinance for a better rate, you should probably stay away from a mortgage that includes the penalty.

Here is an example of a $200,000 five-year fixed thirty-year loan (fixed for the first sixty months and then adjustable every six months after then) offered with and without the prepayment penalty:

■ **No prepayment penalty:** 5.875 percent, no points, and $228 rebate at closing. The monthly payment for principal and interest is $1,183. After three years, you will have paid $42,360.

■ **With prepayment penalty:** 5.75 percent, no points, and $404 rebate at closing. The monthly payment for principal and interest is $1,167. After three years, you will have paid $41,608.

If you prepay more than 20 percent of the original loan amount in any twelve-month period during the first three years, you will incur a prepayment penalty equal to six months' interest on the amount prepaid that exceeds 20 percent of the original loan amount. No penalty will be charged if you sell the property after the first year. If you stay the three years without prepaying more than 20 percent of the loan, or hold off on reselling the property for a year after closing, you'll be about $750 ahead of the game. Beyond then you will be saving about an eighth of a point in interest, at least until the loan adjusts upward. However, if the penalty is incurred, you could end up paying thousands of dollars in penalties.

Be sure you understand whether a mortgage includes a prepayment penalty, and the terms under which it might be invoked.

■ PRIVATE MORTGAGE INSURANCE (PMI)

Every mortgage represents a bit of a gamble: The lender is expecting and hoping that the borrower will be willing and able to pay off the loan. One way in which lenders hope to reduce the chances that a borrower will default on a loan is to require a significant down payment. The theory is that if you have a large amount of your own money invested in the home, you're not going to walk away. Conversely, if you have little or no money sunk into the purchase, you may consider the mortgage to be more like a rental payment. For that reason, many mortgage lenders require a down payment of at least 20 percent. One way to get around the minimum down payment is to purchase private mortgage insurance (PMI) that protects the lender from default and allows resale of the mortgage to third-party investors like the Federal National Mortgage Association (FNMA) and the Federal Home Loan Mortgage Corporation (FHLMC).

PMI premiums can be paid as part of the monthly payment or in an annual bill. The charge is based on the amount and terms of the mortgage as well as the loan-to-value ratio. There is also a single-premium plan that pays for the coverage for several years or more, sometimes through the time when the borrower is expected to reach the 20 percent level. The advantage to this scheme is that it allows the borrower to include the cost of PMI in the amount borrowed, reducing closing costs and increasing the interest deduction. If you sell the home while the policy is still in effect, you should be able to obtain a refund for years not used.

If you do take out a loan that requires purchase of PMI, be sure to consult the mortgage lender to find out if you are permitted to cancel the insurance once you reach 20 percent equity. There is no reason to hold on to PMI any longer than you are required to; it protects the lender and not you.

POPULAR MORTGAGE TYPES

The main distinction between classes of mortgages is fixed versus adjustable. Within each class, mortgages may be based on various terms and include differing features such as the right of the borrower to prepay the loan ahead of its scheduled end and the ability to allow a subsequent buyer to "assume" the loan. In this section, we'll look at the most popular mortgage types.

■ THIRTY-YEAR FIXED-RATE MORTGAGE

The thirty-year fixed mortgage is, in most economic climates, the most popular home loan. This sort of loan is based on an interest rate that is fixed for the entire period of the loan. The monthly payment for interest and for reduction of the principal does not change.

A long-term fixed-rate loan generally works well for buyers who expect not to sell their home or refinance for at least five to ten years and who expect interest rates to increase during that period. It's also a conservative bet if you are uncertain about rate trends. A fixed-rate mortgage allows you to plan way ahead, knowing that changes to the financial environment will not change your monthly payment. If interest rates soar well above the level in your mortgage agreement, you'll be ahead of the game. If rates decline sharply, you can consider refinancing the loan at a lower rate.

The main drawback to a fixed-rate mortgage is the low amount of money applied to reducing the principal in the early years of the loan. If you sell the home or refinance in the first few years, your payments will have been almost exclusively applied to interest costs. Just as an example, on a $200,000 loan at 7 percent, at the end of two years you will have paid about $27,725 in interest and reduced the principal by just $4,210.

■ FIFTEEN-YEAR OR TWENTY-YEAR FIXED-RATE MORTGAGES

A fifteen- or twenty-year fixed-rate mortgage is different from a thirty-year fixed-rate mortgage only in the length of the term. Your monthly payments for principal and interest will not change over the life of the loan, but because you are committed to paying off the loan over a shorter period, the monthly payment will be higher than for a thirty-year loan. However, the loan will be paid off ten or fifteen years sooner.

A fifteen- or twenty-year fixed-rate loan might be appropriate for buyers who want to accelerate free-and-clear ownership of their home. For example, if you expect to retire in fewer than thirty years and want to avoid a mortgage in retirement. The advantage of such a loan is that it accelerates the time to paying off the amount borrowed. Because there are higher monthly payments—typically 15 to 30 percent higher than for a thirty-year mortgage—some borrowers may find they do not qualify for the shorter term.

Fifteen-Year versus Thirty-Year Fixed-Rate Loans

A shorter-term fixed-rate loan costs much less in interest cost than a longer-term deal, and you will end up with full ownership of your home much quicker. On the down side, your monthly payments will be higher, and the tax write-off of interest begins to decline much quicker. Because of the higher required monthly payment, some borrowers may find it harder to qualify for a shorter-term loan.

Here is a comparison of fifteen-, twenty- and thirty-year $200,000 fixed interest rate loans, each at 7 percent:

	Fifteen-year loan	Twenty-year loan	Thirty-year loan
Monthly payment*	$1,797.66	$1,550.60	$1,330.60
Total interest	$123,578.18	$172,142.89	$279,017.80
Total cost*	$323,578.18	$372,142.89	$479,017.80

(*Principal and interest)

The amount of money directed to reduction of the principal reaches 50 percent of the monthly payment early in the sixth year of a fifteen-year loan.

■ ONE-YEAR ADJUSTABLE RATE MORTGAGE (ARM)

A basic adjustable rate mortgage is based on a thirty-year amortization schedule in which the interest rate (and therefore the portion of the monthly payment that is the interest cost) is subject to change every twelve months, based on a margin above an independently calculated index typically based on U.S. Treasury bills or other dollar-based investments. The ARM agreement spells out the time frame for adjustments, the index on which the rate is based, and usually includes a "cap" that limits how much the interest rate can rise with each adjustment and a maximum level for the rate over the full course of the term. (Typical caps are 2 percent per year with a 6 percent ceiling. For example, if the initial rate is 4 percent, the interest rate can go up no more than 2 percent in any adjustment and cannot reach beyond 10 percent.)

In return for accepting an adjustable rate—especially one with as short an adjustment period as one year—the lender will usually offer a low introductory rate well below those offered for fixed-rate mortgages. Because the introductory rate is a "buy down" to make the rate more appealing, in most cases you can expect the rate to rise in the first adjustment and perhaps one or two subsequent adjustments regardless of the trend of interest rates. After then, the rate will track the index more directly. If interest rates continue to rise and you hold on to an ARM, you may end up paying much more for an adjustable mortgage compared to a fixed-rate loan over the course of a thirty-year term. If rates decline, you may pay less over the term.

An ARM may be appropriate if you can afford the monthly payment at any level up to the maximum cap (the lender can provide you the principal and interest charge at that level) and are willing to take a chance on the mid- and long-term trends for interest rates.

■ THREE-YEAR ADJUSTABLE RATE MORTGAGE (ARM)

A three-year ARM is identical to a one-year ARM, except that the interest rate (and the monthly payment) is subject to change every three years. A three-year ARM is considered less risky than a one-year adjustable mortgage because the interest cost is predictable for that period. Because many ARMs use a lower introductory rate for the initial period, in most cases you can expect them to increase by the amount of the cap after three years, which allows you to predict the interest and monthly payment for the first six years with a reasonable degree of certainty. This type of loan is very appropriate if you expect to stay in your new home for three to six years or so, and if you can afford to pay the maximum monthly payment that the cap would permit during that period.

■ FIVE-YEAR ADJUSTABLE RATE MORTGAGE (ARM)

A five-year ARM represents a compromise between shorter adjustment period adjustable rate loans and a fixed-rate mortgage. The interest rate (and thus the monthly payment) of the thirty-year loan is subject to change every five years. Because of the long period between the inception of the loan and the first adjustment, the interest rate on a five-year ARM will generally be higher than that quoted for the initial period of a one- or three-year ARM. A five-year ARM may be most appropriate for buyers who expect to stay in their home for five to ten years and can afford the maximum monthly payment that the cap would permit during that period.

■ 3/1 ADJUSTABLE RATE MORTGAGE (ARM)

The 3/1 ARM is a variant of the adjustable rate mortgage that sets a fixed rate for the initial period of three years and then allows adjustments to the interest rate (and thus the monthly payment) every year for the remaining twenty-seven years of the thirty-year term. Lenders will usually set the interest rate for this sort of loan lower than that for a three-year ARM since they can expect the rate to go up in three years in most instances and can adjust the rate annually after then in response to market conditions. This is a good choice if you expect to keep the mortgage for just three years; otherwise, a three-year ARM may be a better choice.

5/1 ADJUSTABLE RATE MORTGAGE (ARM)

The 5/1 ARM is a version of the adjustable rate mortgage that sets a fixed rate for the initial period of five years and then allows adjustments to the interest rate (and thus the monthly payment) every year for the remaining twenty-five years of the thirty-year term. If you expect to stay in your home for a shorter period, a 5/25 balloon mortgage (see page 58) may be a better choice.

7/1 ADJUSTABLE RATE MORTGAGE (ARM)

This version of the ARM sets a fixed rate for the initial period of seven years and then allows adjustments to the interest rate (and thus the monthly payment) every year for the remaining twenty-three years of the thirty-year term. This loan, which comes at a higher interest rate than for ARMs with a shorter initial period before adjustment, may make sense if you expect to stay in the mortgage for at least seven years. If you expect to stay for a shorter period, a 7/23 balloon mortgage (see page 59) may be a better choice.

10/1 ADJUSTABLE RATE MORTGAGE (ARM)

The 10/1 ARM is a version of the adjustable rate mortgage that sets a fixed rate for the initial period of ten years and then allows adjustments to the interest rate (and thus the monthly payment) every year for the remaining twenty years of the thirty-year term. This loan, which comes at a higher interest rate than for ARMs with a shorter initial period before adjustment, may make sense if you expect to stay in the mortgage for at least ten years.

GRADUATED PAYMENT MORTGAGE (GPM)

A graduated payment mortgage (GPM) is a specialized program for first-time buyers and others who expect their financial situations to improve over time. A version of an ARM that allows payments to be lower in the early years of the agreement, this sort of loan is usually offered by lenders participating in the Section 245 program administered by the Department of Housing and Urban Development. Lenders structure the loan around a fixed rate for fifteen or thirty years, and then reduce the monthly payment in the initial years well below the level that would be required to pay off the loan. For a number of years—typically five, but sometimes longer—the monthly payments rise once a year until they reach a maximum level sufficient to pay off the principal of the loan. During the early years of a GPM, the loan usually goes into negative amortization, meaning that unpaid interest costs will be added to the outstanding principal.

A typical GPM sets up monthly payments to rise 7.5 to 12.5 percent in each of the first five years. After then the payments are fixed and will not change. The advantage to the borrower is that she may be able to obtain a larger mortgage than she would otherwise be qualified for, and she can hope (if not plan) that her income will rise to match the increasing monthly payments. The disadvantages include the fact that this sort of structure usually ends up adding about 10 to 12 percent of the original loan amount to the principal in negative amortization. And, the base interest rate for a GPM is usually about 0.5 to 0.75 percent higher than a fixed-rate mortgage, resulting in a higher overall cost.

GPMs usually have no prepayment penalty, allowing the borrower to refinance to a lower-cost loan when conditions are right; however, borrowers may owe more than the original amount of the loan in the first ten years or so because of negative amortization. The pain will be less in times when real estate is appreciating rapidly, more so if home values increase slowly or are in an occasional downturn.

■ BALLOON MORTGAGES

A balloon loan is a form of mortgage in which monthly payments take care of most or all of the interest, but the principal is not fully amortized over the term. As a result, monthly payments are relatively low, but at the end of the term of the loan the remaining principal is due in full or must be refinanced. A typical balloon loan has payments based on a twenty-five- or thirty-year term but comes to maturity in five, seven, or ten years when a final balloon payment of the outstanding principal and any owed interest is due.

Although it may be a scary thought to face a huge bill in five, seven, or ten years—typical terms for a balloon mortgage—there are some circumstances where this type of loan may make very good sense:

■ You expect to resell the home by the end of the term of the loan. The best scenario here also calls for a reasonable growth in the value of the home itself; otherwise you will be "upside-down" on the loan, owing more to the bank than you will receive in proceeds from the sale.

■ You expect your family income to increase markedly in coming years, allowing you to refinance the mortgage on better terms.

■ You expect to receive a lump-sum amount of money within the term of the balloon mortgage. (For example, an inheritance, royalty, proceeds from the sale of another home or a business, or a retirement payment.) You can use the lump sum to pay off the loan or as a substantial down payment on a refinancing of the mortgage. (Make sure that the balloon mortgage contract allows prepayment without penalty.)

However, there is always the risk that at the time when the balloon payment comes due your financial or work situation may have changed to the point where you will be unable to obtain refinancing. In a worst case, you could be forced to sell the home to raise the money to pay the balloon, or even forced to default. One way to protect against such a risk is to include a **rollover option** in the balloon mortgage. This states that if the buyer does not come forth with the balloon payment at the specified time, the mortgage will automatically convert to a thirty-year adjustable loan. You'll probably end up with a rather hefty interest rate and may have to pay a fee for the conversion, but if you have no other choice, you will at least be able to keep your home and a mortgage.

5/25 Balloon Mortgage

Under this scheme, the monthly payment is calculated as if you will pay off the loan over thirty years, but the agreement requires the borrower to repay the outstanding balance in a lump sum after five years. You can do so by refinancing the loan or selling the home. The interest rate on a 5/25 balloon mortgage may be set lower than for a five-year or 5/1 adjustable. Unless there is a rollover provision, the lender is not obligated to keep the loan active beyond the five-year period. With a rollover, a new loan is issued based on interest rates in effect at the time. Generally the rates on balloon mortgages are 0.25 to 0.75 percent less than thirty-year fixed mortgages, but during the initial period (in this case, five years), payments are similar. A balloon mortgage is appropriate if you are certain you will not stay in the home beyond the initial term, and if you are reasonably sure you will have no difficulty in reselling the home at or above the purchase price or obtaining refinancing.

7/23 Balloon Mortgage
A 7/23 balloon mortgage is based on a thirty-year amortization schedule with a requirement that the outstanding balance be paid off after seven years.

▇ 5/25 OR 7/23 TWO-STEP MORTGAGE
A two-step mortgage is a variant of an ARM available in some markets: a thirty-year mortgage in which the initial five or seven years are fixed, and then the interest rate is adjusted once and set for the remaining twenty-five or twenty-three years of the loan. If you expect to stay in the home for less than five or seven years, a better bet might be a 5/25 balloon or 7/23 balloon loan if the interest rate is better and if you are reasonably sure you will have no difficulty in reselling the home at or above the purchase price or obtaining refinancing.

▇ SHORTER-TERM FIXED-RATE MORTGAGES
If you've got the available cash and expect your financial situation to remain stable for a long period of time, one other way to greatly reduce your interest costs and reduce the principal quickly is to accept a loan with a ten-, fifteen-, twenty-, or twenty-five-year term. The down side to such a loan: You will be locked into a higher monthly payment regardless of any changes in your financial situation, and you may not qualify for as much of a loan because of the higher payment.

BORROWING MORE THAN THE HOME IS WORTH

When it comes to finances, you can do just about anything—if you're willing to pay the price. Throughout this entire section on mortgages, I've talked about lenders insisting on keeping to a particular loan-to-value (LTV) ratio based on an appraisal, and about how lenders like to see a good-size down payment to increase the owner's personal investment in the property and bring the LTV ratio down. That is all true, but there are also ways in which you can take out a loan for more than the value of the home.

One such program, offered by many large lenders, permits borrowers to take out a mortgage for as much as 107 percent of the value of the home for the purposes of paying off existing debt or to amortize the closing costs (including points). The price for such a deal: a loan with a total interest rate several points higher than for a loan of 80 percent of the appraised value. In essence, with this sort of loan what you are doing is taking out a conventional mortgage for as large a LTV ratio as possible and then wrapping around a personal loan for the remainder. Because the personal loan does not use the property as collateral, it is based on a higher interest rate. The monthly payment blends the cost of both loans into a single amount.

You'll also find programs that offer second mortgages for as much as 125 percent of the value of your home. In this case, the lender is allowing you to tap into a combination of the equity you have paid against the first mortgage, the increase in value of the home since the original loan was written, and a personal loan for the remainder. As this book was written, a second mortgage for as much as 125 percent of the value of the home carried an interest rate as much as five points higher than a conventional first loan.

I would only recommend either type of loan as the solution to a short-term need, such as to pay off an existing mortgage or to finance home renovations or improvements. The goal would be to either pay off the expensive new loan quickly, or to refinance the entire property into a single conventional mortgage based on the increased value of the home.

MATCHING THE MORTGAGE TO YOUR PLANS

There are very few hard-and-fast rules about choosing one set of mortgage terms over another. However, in general, you are better off paying points to reduce the interest cost if you expect to continue ownership of the home for five to ten years. Similarly, an adjustable mortgage will usually cost less than a fixed-rate conventional loan over the same five- to ten-year period. However, if you expect to stay in the home for longer than that, and if interest rates are trending upward, in most cases the conventional mortgage will eventually prove to be a better deal.

Here are some examples of comparisons conducted using the calculators offered on the www.e-loan.com Web site:

$200,000 mortgage	Loan A One-Year ARM	Loan B Five-Year Fixed
Initial interest rate	3.0 percent	6.375 percent
Points	3.85	0 with $276 credit
First year monthly payment	$843	$1,248
First adjustment	Twelve months	Sixty months
Lifetime cap	9.0 percent	12.375 percent
Index type	One-year Treasury Bill	Six-month LIBOR index
Margin above index	2.75 percent	2.25 percent
Periodic adjustment	Twelve months	Six months
Total cost after five years (closing costs plus interest and principal payments)	**$83,954**	**$76,909**

In the above comparison, although Loan A, the one-year ARM, has a much lower monthly payment of $843 in the first month, by the end of the five-year period it can be expected to rise to about $1,533. Add in the cost of points and Loan B, the five-year fixed mortgage, will be a better deal by about $7,000.

Now, let's compare the same Loan B to another five-year fixed mortgage, this one requiring payment of points but delivering a lower interest rate:

$200,000 mortgage	Loan B Five-Year Fixed	Loan C Five-Year Fixed
Initial interest rate	6.375 percent	4.5 percent
Points	0 with $276 credit	3.781
First year monthly payment	$1,248	$1,013
First adjustment	Sixty months	Sixty months
Lifetime cap	12.375 percent	9.5 percent
Index type	Six-month LIBOR index	One-year Treasury Bill
Margin above index	2.25 percent	2.75 percent
Periodic adjustment	Six months	Twelve months
Total cost after five years (closing costs plus interest and principal payments)	**$76,909**	**$70,685**

In this instance, even with payment of points—a cost of $7,562 on a $200,000 loan—Loan C is a better deal over a five-year period. Paying the points up front will save about $6,224 during the course of the loan. And, Loan C also has a lower lifetime cap, which could save thousands of dollars if interest rates trend up sharply.

Finally, I asked the computer to compare the same Loan C to a conventional thirty-year fixed mortgage and extended the period to ten years:

$200,000 mortgage	Loan C Five-Year Fixed	Loan D Thirty-Year Fixed
Initial interest rate	4.5 percent	6.75 percent
Points	3.781	0 with $126 credit
First year monthly payment	$1,013	$1,297
First adjustment	Sixty months	None
Lifetime cap	9.5 percent	6.75 percent
Index type	One-year Treasury Bill	None
Margin above index	2.75 percent	None
Periodic adjustment	Twelve months	None
Total cost after ten years (closing costs plus interest and principal payments)	**$158,586**	**$157,859**

In this comparison, the cost of the two loans after ten years is very close, with Loan D possibly ahead by $728 if assumptions about the adjustable interest rates on Loan C prove to be correct. However, a more detailed analysis that includes the tax benefits of prepaying points and the write-off of interest expenses reverses the results, recommending the five-year fixed loan for the ten-year period. But if you plan to keep the home for much longer, perhaps twenty to thirty years, the fixed-interest mortgage will generally break even around the twentieth year and end up costing less after then.

CHAPTER SEVEN

UNDERSTANDING ADJUSTABLE RATE MORTGAGES

INTEREST RATES, like most everything else in economics, tend to move in a cycle. If you average out minor week-to-week swings, interest rates tend to travel in a relatively smooth bell curve. Sometimes the rate of change is more severe than at other times, but it is usually obvious when rates are headed up or down.

For most of modern times in the United States, home mortgages were based on a fixed interest rate. If the cost of money was 7 percent when you took out a thirty-year loan, your agreement with the bank or lending institution set out 360 equal monthly payments for interest and principal. But in the early 1970s, interest rates began to rise sharply in the face of political and economic issues, including an oil embargo and general inflation. Rates in mid-1973 were 7.7 percent. By late 1978 they crossed 10 percent and continued to rise through the 1980s, reaching a peak in September 1981 of 18.45 percent. By late 1998 they had dropped back below 7 percent, and after a few upward ticks, they were around 6 percent in the fall of 2002.

During the 1970s peak, many lenders began offering a mortgage based on a different structure that tracked the market rates for loans. Under an adjustable rate mortgage (ARM), the interest rate on the loan is adjusted on a regular basis as stated in the agreement. If rates have gone down, the interest charges would decline, and if they have gone up, the charges can rise. Things are a bit more complex than that, of course. ARMs use various ways to calculate the interest charges, and some are more volatile than others. And market pressures and federal regulations have also brought about "caps" that limit the amount a rate can rise in a particular period and that also set a ceiling on the maximum rate that can be charged.

Today an adjustable mortgage is perfect for someone who can't abide the status quo. If you think that today's interest rates are high and headed higher, an ARM is generally a good idea. If you get into an ARM at or near the top of the roller coaster ride, you can ride the rates down and convert to a fixed rate if your agreement permits or refinance. If you take out an ARM when rates are low, you are all but sure to ride the interest curve uphill.

Because an ARM reduces some of the lender's risk—getting stuck with outstanding loans that pay interest well below the market—lenders generally offer initial rates that are a percent or more lower than those on fixed interest mortgages. An ARM can be doubly attractive to borrowers: In addition to the fact that lower interest reduces the overall cost of a mortgage, the fact that the monthly payment usually starts out lower than an equivalent fixed-rate loan may allow borrowers to take out a larger mortgage. (An initially lower monthly payment may bring you within the lender's required ratios for total indebtedness to income and total housing costs to income.)

Most ARMs are offered with an introductory or "teaser" rate that is set artificially low to entice customers. Such a rate is already below where the ARM would be after the margin is applied to the index; even if interest rates go down between the closing and the first adjustment period, the rate on an ARM with a teaser rate will probably go up toward market rates. Note, though, that some lenders will not calculate their ratios based entirely on the teaser rate. Instead, they apply a formula that averages the teaser rate and subsequent expected rises.

THE COMPONENTS OF AN ARM

Here are some key elements of ARMs that you need to understand:

Adjustment period. The lender can construct a loan with just about any period of time between adjustments. Most common are six-month, one-year, three-year, and five-year periods. In general, a lender wants as short an adjustment period as possible, allowing the cost of the mortgage to closely track the cost of funds. ARMs with shorter adjustment periods are usually offered at lower introductory rates than those with longer periods. As a borrower, it is often to your advantage to have as lengthy a period between adjustments as possible. A longer adjustment period gives you greater stability and allows you to make long-term plans for your household budget.

Introductory or starting rate. Many lenders seek to entice borrowers by setting the initial interest rate on an ARM several points below rates on thirty-year fixed loans. The catch, of course, is that the starting rate is all but guaranteed to increase when the time comes for the first adjustment to the loan, even if interest rates have declined in that period. Still, a combination of a low starting rate and an interim cap make the cost of an ARM much lower than that of a fixed-rate loan in the short term, making this a good choice if you expect to live in the home for only a few years.

Interim or periodic cap. Nearly all ARMs include a limit on the amount the interest rate can increase with each scheduled adjustment. A typical interim cap would limit the increase to no more than 2 percent with each adjustment. Loans with shorter periods such as monthly or six-month adjustables might have a cap of 1 percent. Most ARMs also apply a cap to interest rate decreases. As such, an interim cap protects against huge boosts in times of rapidly rising interest rates but may also slow the reduction of rates when interest costs decline.

As an example, if the calculated interest rate of the index plus margin were to increase by 3 percent between adjustment periods but the interim cap limited boosts to no more than 2 percent, your interest rate would go up 2 percent at the time of adjustment. If the rate was to remain unchanged, at the next adjustment your interest rate would climb by another 1 percent to reach the calculated rate. In most cases, the cap applies only to upward moves. Some loans, though, apply the cap to reductions as well. In an ARM with a short period between adjustments—six months or one year—a cap on reductions may not have much effect. But if adjustments are several years apart, you might not be able to take full advantage of a drop of a few percent.

Payment cap. Some ARMs are tied to an index plus a margin but apply a cap to the amount of the monthly payment for principal and interest rather than to the interest rate. Such a plan can protect you against having to bust your budget to come up with the monthly payment. However, in order to apply a cap to the payment, the loan can go into negative amortization, meaning that the amount of the principal of the loan can increase. When interest rates decline, your payment will be applied to the additional accrued interest and, once that has been paid off, to the principal and ongoing interest charges.

Lifetime cap. Most ARMs set a cap on the maximum interest rate that can be applied to the loan by adjustments. For example, a loan might have a 2 percent interim cap and a 6 percent lifetime cap. If the loan started out at 5 percent, it could rise to no higher than 11 percent, and only in increments of 2 percent or less. If a loan reaches its lifetime cap, it will remain at that rate until the index and margin drop below that level. Some ARMs also include a cap for the minimum level for the rate.

Index. Adjustable mortgages "tie" their interest rate to an independent and publicly published index. For example, the rate might be tied to one-year, three-year, or five-year Treasury securities; average six-month certificates of deposit; the LIBOR (London Interbank Offered Rate); the 11th District Cost of Funds (COFI); or the prime rate. Although each of the indexes does a pretty good job of reflecting economic conditions, each varies slightly in how quickly it responds to changes in the market. Some move more quickly upward than down, while others use a moving average to smooth out short-term rises and falls. A lender is required to provide a historical report on the actions of the index. Look to see the behavior of the index in times of rapid rises in interest costs.

Here are some of the more common indexes:

■ **COFI Cost of Funds Index.** Based on the average interest rate paid on deposits at savings institutions, there are various indexes for each of the regional districts around the nation. The most commonly used bellwether is the 11th district of Arizona, California, and Nevada. COFI is more commonly used in western states and tends to rise and fall more slowly than Treasury securities.

■ **Treasury Bill Index.** The Federal Reserve Board publishes a weekly index of constant maturity interest rates on Treasury securities of various terms. The index tends to be pretty volatile, going up and down quickly as conditions change. The six-month T-bill index is the most volatile measure, while those tracking securities with maturity of one year and longer are slightly less mercurial.

■ **LIBOR.** This index is based on the rate charged among banks in London on short-term dollar-denominated deposits. LIBOR indexes are published for one-, three-, and six-month periods. LIBOR rates are usually close to those for one-year Treasury securities but are relatively stable.

■ **Prime Rate Index.** This measure tracks the rate banks charge their best customers for short-term loans. It is indirectly linked to federal monetary policy. The prime rate tends to be stable for long periods of time, moving up or down in relatively large increments when the Federal Reserve Board makes adjustments to rates among banks.

■ **Average Mortgage Rate.** This is a monthly index based on the average interest rates on mortgages issued by major lenders. Because it is looking backward, it tends to lag behind rapid changes in the market. And in any case, it is a relatively stable index.

Margin. The lender adds a "margin" to the index to come up with the interest rate charged on your loan, producing a profit over the cost of the money. If the index used in the mortgage is 4.75 percent and there is a margin of 2.5 percent, the "fully indexed rate" charged to borrowers is 7.25 percent. The index is used as a barometer; in most cases, the lender does not pay its rate for money. However, the margin will usually differ depending on the index used. For example, the prime rate is usually several points higher than a Treasury security index. The margin may also be set slightly higher for loans that are a high proportion of the property's value as opposed to one made to a borrower who has made a substantial down payment or holds a large amount of equity in the home.

Convertibility. Can you lock in an ARM at a fixed rate in the future? For example, if interest rates decline markedly, the borrower under an ARM might want to convert to the current fixed rate. Some ARMs charge a one-time fee for the conversion. The loan agreement usually sets specific times when the option to convert can be exercised.

Prepayment. Is there a fee or penalty for paying off the ARM ahead of its scheduled termination? Most loans do not penalize borrowers who sell their homes or refinance the mortgage early, but some lenders may add a charge if the payoff comes very early in the term of the loan.

Assumability. Are you able to transfer the mortgage to another borrower who meets the lender's qualifications? A borrower might want to assume your obligation if interest rates have increased and your ARM is at a level that is below the market. The borrower will also save on appraisal and closing costs. A purchaser might have to obtain a second, or wraparound, mortgage to pay the original owner for the home.

■ AN EXAMPLE OF AN ARM

Here is an example of an ARM with an introductory or teaser rate:

■ Introductory rate: 3 percent

■ Index: One-year Treasury Bill Index, which at the time of the loan was 1.8 percent

- Margin: 2.75 percent above the index
- Interim cap: 2 percent
- Lifetime cap: 6 percent

With that information, we know that the introductory rate of 3 percent is below where the rate would ordinarily be: the index of 1.8 percent plus a margin of 2.75 percent, or 4.55 percent. At the first adjustment, if rates were to remain unchanged, the interest rate would rise to 4.55 percent. If rates were to go up, the interest on the loan could go up to as much as 5 percent—the interim cap. The only way the interest rate could stay at 3 percent would be if the T-bill index value was to plummet to near zero, or 0.25 percent. That's a rather drastic level and not very likely.

▓ CONVERTIBLE LOANS

A good compromise for many buyers is to mix the advantage of the generally lower rates offered on adjustable mortgages with the opportunity to convert the loan to a fixed interest rate at a time or times specified in the agreement. This is a good solution for buyers at a time of relatively high interest rates who are expecting a decline. Be sure you understand the conversion option. Some mortgages include just a single conversion period several years into the term, while other agreements might permit conversion once a year on the anniversary of the closing. An agreement with a longer window of time for conversion is much more valuable than one with just a single period, allowing you to wait for a decline in rates. There may be a small fee for the conversion.

▓ BUY-DOWNS

In some cases, a builder or the seller of a home may seek to entice you to make a purchase by "buying down" the initial interest rate on an ARM. This amounts to making a prepaid interest payment to the lender. (Think of this as equivalent to the special deals regularly offered by new-car dealers. You'll see something like, "3 percent interest or $1,000 cash back." You'll need to do the math to see which works out to be a better deal for you.)

The buy-down comes at a cost, one way or another. If you accept the reduced interest rate, you'll likely be paying a bit more for the home. If you choose to seek your own financing, the seller should be willing to reduce the cost of the house by an amount equivalent to the cost of a buy-down.

Be sure you understand all of the terms of an ARM with a buy-down. In some instances, the first adjustment of the rate may have an expanded cap or no cap at all. For example, if prevailing interest rates are 7 percent and an ARM is offered with a special introductory rate of 2 percent, some deals might allow the rate to jump all the way to 7 percent at the end of the initial period. In that case, you might find a better deal with a mortgage that does not include the buy-down. If you do, ask the seller to give you the money that would have been spent to reduce the buy-down mortgage.

For one impartial appraisal of ARMs, consult the Federal Reserve Board's Web site at www.federalreserve.gov/pubs/brochures/arms/arms.pdf.

CHAPTER EIGHT

FHA, VA, AND STATE MORTGAGE PROGRAMS

TALK AS THEY DO about the glories of free enterprise and their desire to keep out of the way of business, politicians are nevertheless very eager to inject the federal and state government into the pursuit of the American dream of home ownership. From the end of the Great Depression, into the post–World War II baby boom, and through today, numerous government programs have helped millions of people obtain mortgages. The principal agencies involved are the FHA (the Federal Housing Administration, part of the Department of Housing and Urban Development) and the VA (the Veterans Administration).

The FHA protects the lender from loss on mortgages written under its program, promising to step in and pay off the loan in the event of default. The VA program is slightly different, guaranteeing a portion of the loan—essentially extending the down payment—so that in the event of a default the lender is sure to receive as much as 25 percent of the loan from the VA as well as the proceeds from resale of the property. (In certain circumstances, the VA pursues the borrower to recoup any losses it suffers.) Either way, the lender is all but fully protected against loss and therefore willing to offer funding at a lower interest rate.

In any case, as a borrower you do not deal directly with the VA or FHA. You'll make your application for a mortgage to a lending institution or bank, and if the numbers are right, your business will be offered to the VA, FHA, or the secondary market. Secondary lenders that help provide funds to lending institutions include a trio of organizations that are directly or indirectly derived from the federal government: Fannie Mae, Freddie Mac, and Ginnie Mae. (I'll discuss these secondary lenders in chapter 9.)

FHA-INSURED HOME LOANS

The Federal Housing Administration helps entice lending institutions to make mortgages available to almost any applicant by insuring the loans against default. The loans, both fixed rate and adjustable, usually require only a minimal down payment of 5 percent or less. FHA has both single-family (one- to four-unit homes) and multifamily (five or more units) mortgage lending programs. VA- and FHA-backed mortgages were very popular immediately after World War II, but their appeal declined as home prices rose and the amount of money available for these loans remained relatively low. Today, they are once again popular, after adjustments to the loan amounts were made.

The FHA doesn't set interest rates or decide whether the lender can collect points. Its mortgage insurance is aimed at allowing smaller down payments and loans to people who might be considered "marginal" by lenders not receiving insurance. Loans are available for as much as 97 percent of the value of the home (up to the maximum FHA lending limit). The buyer, though, must pay for mortgage insurance. FHA standards for loans call for housing expenses to be 29 percent or less of gross income, and total indebtedness of 41 percent or less of gross income.

The standard FHA mortgage insurance premium for a thirty-year conventional loan is in two parts: an annual mutual mortgage insurance (MMI) premium of 0.5 percent of the loan amount and an up-front mortgage insurance premium (MIP) of 1.5 percent. If the loan is paid off or refinanced within the first seven years, the unused portion of the up-front MIP is refunded. In addition, once the outstanding principal balance reaches 78 percent of the original purchase price, the MMI will automatically be canceled. On a fifteen-year conventional mortgage with a down payment greater than 10 percent of the purchase price, MMI is not required. The up-front MMI and most other closing costs can be included in the mortgage amount, and FHA-backed loans are assumable by qualified borrowers. FHA loans are available through many lending institutions, savings banks, and commercial banks.

Advantages of an FHA loan include the fact that the loan is assumable if the new buyer meets income and credit qualifications. The original mortgagee, though, may continue to be liable for the loan for a period after it is assumed. An FHA loan can also be prepaid without penalty at any time.

In order to receive an FHA-backed loan, the property also has to pass inspection. A seller may have to perform repairs and in some instances bring the home and property up to current building codes in order to receive certification. A buyer of a home using the FHA program knows that the home has passed at least that level of inspection.

The limitations of an FHA loan include the maximum loan amount, which is regularly adjusted but is still well below average market value in many parts of the country. In order to qualify for a loan with a down payment of as little as 3 percent, the buyer must plan to live in the home. FHA financing for a home purchased as an investment requires a down payment of at least 15 percent. There are also rules on the source of the down payment; among them is a ban on a second mortgage for that purpose on the property you're buying. You can, though, take out a second mortgage on other property you may own and use those funds as a down payment.

For information on FHA loans, consult www.hud.gov/buying/index.cfm.

■ FHA 203K REHAB PROGRAM

The FHA also administers a special program intended to help buyers purchase or refinance a principal residence or investment property that will be renovated. The mortgage can even be used to fund complete rebuilding of the existing property if the original foundation remains in place. The borrower must meet standard FHA credit qualifications.

VA-GUARANTEED LOANS

In a plan little changed since it helped boost the economy after the end of World War II, the Department of Veterans Affairs offers loan guarantees that protect a portion of a mortgage against foreclosure. Because of this, lenders are able to offer lower interest rates and other advantageous terms. The VA does not set a maximum amount for loans, but it does have a maximum guarantee amount of no more than $50,750 on loans of $144,000 and more. And there is a limit on the total amount of guarantee a veteran can receive.

VA loans are offered by authorized lending institutions and banks. In order to be eligible to receive a VA guarantee, you must have served on active duty in the military and received an honorable discharge. The number of days of required service varies. Veterans of World War II, the Korean conflict, and the Vietnam era must have had at least ninety days of service. Reservists and National Guard members who were involved in the Persian Gulf conflict of 1990 must have served ninety days. Veterans with service only in peacetime must have had at least 180 days of active service prior to 1980, or two years after then. There are also eligibility periods for recent members of the Selected Reserve, including the National Guard.

Before the VA will issue a mortgage, the property has to be appraised. A Certificate of Reasonable Value is issued and forms the basis for the amount of the loan. Most purchase and sale agreements allow the would-be buyer to back out of the deal if the property's selling price turns out to be out of line with the appraised price. The veteran must plan to occupy the home. If it is a multifamily structure, the applicant must occupy one of the units.

The basic funding fee for a VA guarantee is 2 percent of the loan amount. If a down payment of 10 percent is made, the fee is reduced to 1.25 percent. (Reservists pay slightly higher.) The fee to refinance an existing VA home loan with a new VA home loan to lower the existing interest rate is 0.5 percent.

Another wrinkle: Veterans who have taken out a VA loan in years past may be able to obtain another guarantee if they have any "remaining entitlement." In 2002 the maximum amount of a mortgage that the VA would cover was $36,000; older loans would have been up against a lower guarantee of as little as $10,000. Veterans can tap into the difference between the current maximum and the amount they used in a previous loan. The full entitlement can be restored in certain situations: If the previous property was sold and the loan paid in full, or if the VA loan was assumed by another veteran who agrees to substitute his entitlement for the same amount used in the original loan.

For information about VA loans, consult www.homeloans.va.gov or call (800) 827–1000.

RURAL HOUSING LOAN PROGRAM

The Rural Housing Service, part of the U.S. Department of Agriculture, offers loan guarantees for rural properties. Borrowers must meet income requirements and property must lie within areas designated as farming regions. For information consult www.rurdev.usda.gov/rhs or call (202) 720–4323.

FIRST-TIME AND LOW-INCOME BUYER PROGRAMS

For many would-be homebuyers, the biggest obstacle to buying a home is not the ability to pay the monthly mortgage payment—in many instances, a mortgage is pretty close to a rent payment—but instead a problem with coming up with a down payment. Most standard mortgages from banks and lending institutions require a substantial down payment of at least 20 percent—$40,000 on a $200,000 home—or the payment of an additional monthly or annual fee for private mortgage insurance (PMI), which can add hundreds or thousands of dollars per year to the cost of a loan.

For many first-time homeowners and others without sufficient resources, a good solution is offered by local and state agencies that use bonds to raise funds as assistance for a down payment in the form of subsidized loans or outright grants. Other programs subsidize the interest rates. In order to be eligible for a down payment program, you'll generally need to establish your ability to pay closing costs and the monthly mortgage payment as well as prove you have a good credit history. Most programs are aimed at low-income families, but the cutoff level takes into account the size of your family and other factors.

Other sources of money for a down payment include gifts—some newlyweds set up their bridal registry to collect money for a down payment. Or you may receive assistance from family. If the gift will come directly to the bank or lending institution from someone else, the lender may require evidence that the gift was indeed an irrevocable gift without any conditions or interest charges. One way to avoid the hassle of proving the legitimacy of a gift is to arrange to receive it a few months before applying for a loan and incorporating it into your assets.

You can also borrow from a 401K retirement account if your employer has one set up. The program allows you to withdraw funds, without penalty, for use as a down payment, but you will need to arrange to pay back the funds over a specific period of time. On the down side, you will lose the income growth you would have received if the money had stayed in your retirement account during the time it was used for the down payment.

■ STATE HOUSING AND FINANCE AUTHORITIES

Every state has some form of a housing finance authority that administers a wide range of programs, from providing information to would-be borrowers to underwriting programs that guarantee loans or assist borrowers in coming up with the down payment for a mortgage. Here are the contact numbers:

Alabama Housing Finance Authority, (205) 242–4310; www.ahfa.com

Alaska Housing Finance Corp., (907) 561–1900; www.ahfc.state.ak.us

Arizona Department of Commerce Office of Housing Development, (602) 280–1365; www.housingaz.com

Arkansas Development Finance Authority, (501) 682–5900; www.access arkansas.org/adfa

California Department of Housing & Community Development, (916) 322–1560; www.hcd.ca.gov

California Housing Finance Agency, (916) 322–3991; www.chfa.ca.gov

Colorado Housing and Finance Authority, (303) 297–2432 or (800) 877–2432; www.colohfa.org

Connecticut Housing Finance Authority, (203) 721–9501; www.chfa.org

Delaware State Housing Authority, Division of Housing and Community Development, (302) 739–4263; www2.state.de.us/dsha

DC Housing Finance Agency, (202) 535–1353; www.dchfa.org

Florida Housing Finance Agency, (904) 488–4197; www.floridahousing.org

Georgia Residential Finance Authority, (404) 679–4840

Hawaii Housing Authority, (808) 848–3277; www.hcdch.state.hi.us

Idaho Housing Agency, (208) 336–0161; www.ihfa.org

Illinois Housing Development Authority, (800) 942–8439 or (312) 836–5200; www.ihda.org

Indiana Housing Finance Authority, (317) 232–7777; www.in.gov/ihfa

Iowa Finance Authority, (515) 281–4058; www.ifahome.com

Kansas Office of Commerce and Housing, (913) 296–3481; http://kdoch.state.ks.us

Kentucky Housing Corporation, (800) 633–8896 or (502) 564–7630; www.kyhousing.org

Louisiana Housing Finance Agency, (504) 925–3675; www.lhfa.state.la.us

Maine State Housing Authority, (800) 452–4668 or (207) 626–4600; www.mainehousing.org

Maryland Department of Housing and Community Development, (301) 974–2176; www.dhcd.state.md.us

Massachusetts Housing Finance Agency, (617) 451–3480; www.mhfa.com

Michigan State Housing Development Authority, (800) 327–9158 or (517) 373–8370; www.michigan.gov/mshda

Minnesota Housing Finance Agency, (800) 652–9747 or (612) 296–9951; www.mhfa.state.mn.us

Mississippi Home Corporation, (601) 359–6700; www.mshomecorp.com

Missouri Housing Development Commission, (816) 756–3790; www.mhdc. com

Montana Board of Housing, Department of Commerce, (406) 444–3040; www.commerce.state.mt.us

Nebraska Investment Finance Authority, (402) 434–3900; www.nifa.org

Nevada Department of Business and Industry Housing Division, (702) 687–4258; http://nvhousing.state.nv.us/

New Hampshire Housing Finance Authority, (603) 472–8623; www.nhhfa. org

New Jersey Division of Housing and Community Resources, (800) 654–6873 or (609) 890–1300; www.state.nj.us/dca/dhcr

New Mexico Mortgage Finance Authority, (800) 444–6880 or (505) 843–6880; www.nmmfa.org

New York State Housing Finance Agency, (212) 688–4000; www.nyhomes. org

State of New York Division of Housing and Community Renewal, (718) 519–5700; www.dhcr.state.ny.us

North Carolina Housing Finance Agency, (919) 781–6115; www.nchfa.com

North Dakota Housing Finance Agency, (701) 224–3434; www.ndhfa.org

Ohio Housing Finance Agency, (614) 466–7970; www.odod.state.oh.us/ohfa

Oklahoma Housing Finance Agency, (800) 256–1489 or (405) 848–1144; www.ohfa.org

Oregon Housing and Community Services, (503) 378–4343; www.hcs.state. or.us

Pennsylvania Housing Finance Agency, (717) 780–3800; www.phfa.org

Puerto Rico Housing Finance Authority, www.gdb-pur.com

Rhode Island Housing and Mortgage Finance Corp., (401) 751–5566; www. rihousing.com

South Carolina State Housing Financing and Development Authority, (803) 734–8836; www.sha.state.sc.us

South Dakota Housing Development Authority, (605) 773–3181; www. sdhda.org

Tennessee Housing Development Agency, (615) 741–4979; www.state.tn. us/thda

Texas Department of Housing and Community Affairs, (512) 475–3800; www.tdhca.state.tx.us

Utah Housing Finance Agency, (801) 521–6950; www.utahhousingcorp.org

Vermont Housing Finance Agency, (800) 222–8342 or (802) 864–5743; www. vhfa.org

Vermont State Housing Authority, (802) 828–3295; www.vhfa.org

Virginia Housing Development Authority, (804) 782–1986; www.vhda.com

Washington State Housing Finance Commission, (206) 464–7139; www.wshfc.org

West Virginia Housing Development Fund, (304) 345–6475; www.wvhdf.com

Wisconsin Housing and Economic Development Authority, (800) 362–2767; www.wheda.com

Wyoming Community Development Authority, (307) 265–0603; www.wyomingcda.com

CHAPTER NINE

TYPES OF LENDERS

WE'VE COME A LONG, LONG WAY from the Bailey Bros. Building and Loan Association of *It's a Wonderful Life,* a place where the Bailey family becomes personally involved in both the collection of savings from their neighbors and the disbursement of mortgages. Today, very few savings and loan associations make home loans based on local deposits. Almost all mortgage loans use funds supplied by investors. In this chapter, we'll look at the most common sources of mortgages, and where these institutions and sellers get their money.

WHO'S GOT THE MONEY?

In 2001 American homeowners took out mortgages totaling some $2 trillion. That's trillion with a *T,* or roughly equivalent to the *entire* Gross Domestic Product of France plus Canada. With interest rates dropping to near-historic lows and the value of real estate staying strong, the amount of money laid out in new mortgages was expected to set a new record in 2002. Where does all this money come from? Fifty years ago, most of the money for mortgages came from the deposits in savings and loan institutions. Today, most of the funds come from investors who buy shares or own bonds in mortgage securities and from private placements by huge corporate and retirement fund groups.

The largest percentage of mortgages today are written by independent **mortgage companies.** Their loans can be entirely private, or they can participate in various government programs, including FHA-insured and VA-guaranteed loans. Applicants will have to meet standards set by secondary market lenders who buy up large groups of mortgages and trade them as market instruments. Among these are the quasi-governmental consortiums known as Fannie Mae and Freddie Mac. Borrowers will be assigned to a mortgage servicing company that will collect payments.

Savings and loans and savings banks still make mortgage loans, offering a local face to the process. You may even know the bank's officers, and they may know you. Most of the mortgages they offer are also resold in the secondary market to investors. Savings banks may be better suited to offer FHA and VA loans. Local banks are often a good source for short-term construction loans since they may already be familiar with area builders and also have relationships with inspectors and government agencies involved in approval of new construction.

Large **commercial banks** may offer loans for residences directly or through a mortgage company they own. Nearly all mortgages are resold on the secondary market.

If you're short on time or have a very unusual financial need or history, you might want to hire a **mortgage broker** to search out the best available loan for you. Some brokers charge a flat fee or may require payment of points as a fee—not as tax-deductible prepaid interest. In some instances, a real estate broker or agent may register with a state agency as a mortgage broker, ostensibly as a service to her clients. If you consider a mortgage broker, start by looking for the best deal on your own. There is no advantage to hiring someone to come up with a loan no better than one you have already located. Then assure yourself that the broker has no obligation to lenders—the broker should work only for you. Be sure to include the broker's fee in your comparison of relative costs of various mortgages.

In certain markets and market conditions, the owner of a home may "take back paper," loaning some or all of the purchase price to the buyer in **seller financing.**

WHERE DOES THE MONEY COME FROM?

Funds for a mortgage can come from just about anywhere. A savings bank can lend some of the holdings on deposit, which was the original concept behind savings and loan associations. A commercial bank can sell bonds or other financial instruments to investors. In seller financing, there typically is no actual cash involved. More commonly, though, funds come from secondary lenders, including a trio of organizations that are directly or indirectly derived from the federal government: Fannie Mae, Freddie Mac, and Ginnie Mae. You'll hear these organizations described with terms like government-sponsored enterprises.

Each of these associations raises money through the sale of bonds or other securities and then purchases mortgages from banks, lending institutions, and brokers. The originator of the loan gets to keep a percentage of the loan amount as profit and may also service the mortgage—collect monthly payments and supervise tax and insurance collections and disbursements—but the mortgage itself is held by the secondary lender.

Fannie Mae (the name is derived from the Federal National Mortgage Association) began in 1938 as an agency of the federal government, created to bring stability to the domestic housing market as the country recovered from the

Depression. In 1968 Fannie Mae became a privately owned and managed corporation under a charter granted by the U.S. Congress. Fannie Mae's loan limits vary from year to year. The association's charter ties the maximum it will loan to the Federal Housing Finance Board's (FHFB) October single-family home price survey. In 2002 the loan limit was set at $300,700, with higher limits for loans on multifamily properties and loans to families in certain localities.

Freddie Mac (the operating name for the Federal Home Loan Mortgage Corporation) is a government-sponsored corporation owned by stockholders. Its board of directors consists of eighteen members (thirteen are elected each year by stockholders, and the other five are appointed by the President of the United States). Freddie Mac buys residential mortgages and funds them in the capital markets using mortgage-backed securities or other debt instruments.

While Freddie Mac and Fannie Mae have similar charters and are both publicly traded corporations, the two companies often pursue different business strategies, competing for portfolios and helping to keep mortgage costs down.

The third major player in the secondary market is **Ginnie Mae** (the Government National Mortgage Association), which is a wholly owned government corporation within the U.S. Department of Housing and Urban Development (HUD). Unlike Freddie Mac and Fannie Mae, Ginnie Mae's guarantees on mortgages are backed by the full faith and credit of the U.S. government. Its purpose is to serve low-to moderate-income homebuyers. Some loans are funded as private placements to investors, including **REITs** (real estate investment trusts) that purchase baskets of loans and then trade as bondlike financial instruments.

■ CONFORMING AND NONCONFORMING LOANS

Mortgages that meet the standards of Fannie Mae or Freddie Mac, up to their current limits, are considered "conforming" loans. A loan for an amount above the limit is considered a "nonconforming" or jumbo loan. If a lender makes a loan from its own resources and does not resell it on the secondary market, it is referred to as a **portfolio loan.**

■ JUMBO MORTGAGES

In 2002 the maximum for a conforming loan from secondary market underwriters such as Fannie Mae or Freddie Mac for a single-family owner-occupied home was $300,700. What if you can afford a more expensive house and the mortgage to pay it off? The solution is a nonconforming, or jumbo, mortgage.

As with anything else in finance, you can usually get what you want ... for a price. Major lenders make jumbo loans and keep them in their own portfolio or sell them to private investors, since they cannot resell them on the secondary market. Jumbo loans usually apply an interest rate about one-quarter to one-half a point higher than for a conforming loan.

Since the loan will not go through Fannie Mae or Freddie Mac, the lender has greater flexibility in determining its criteria for a loan, including debt ratios. However, for conformity, many lenders use the same standards for all loans. Another wrinkle calls for the lender to issue a conforming mortgage for up to the maximum amount permitted and then another mortgage at a slightly higher rate for the remainder of the amount borrowed. You'll have a single monthly payment, with the varying costs of the two loans blended together in a wraparound.

Be sure you examine the total cost of the loan package, including points and closing costs that might be required for both mortgages. And be sure you understand the terms of the loan agreement. If you have any extra cash, you want to be able to pay off the higher-cost wraparound mortgage first.

SELLER FINANCING

When a buyer talks about seeking "creative financing," he or she is usually aiming to get some assistance from the seller, either in the form of a buy-down, a wraparound, or a mortgage outside of the traditional lending-institution channels. Although everyone loves to get a bargain, including a great deal on a mortgage, the fact is that most people looking for creative financing are doing so because they are otherwise unable to qualify for the full amount of a loan from a commercial lender.

In real estate parlance, when a seller agrees to finance all or part of the purchase of property, it is called "carrying back paper." Professionals also distinguish between "hard money," which is cash paid by a lending institution to a third party to enable the buyer to take possession of property, and "soft money," which is a paper transfer of the equity in a property from the seller to a buyer.

As a buyer, getting a loan from the seller may be a great way to buy a house. You may be able to get past previous credit problems, an uneven financial history, or buy more of a house than you would otherwise be qualified for. From the seller's point of view, things are sometimes not quite as clear-cut. Most sellers don't want to get into the business of making loans. Seller financing is more likely to be offered when the real estate market is soft—a buyer's market.

A privately issued mortgage is no less legally binding than one issued by a huge bank or lending institution. The loan is in most instances secured by an interest in property itself, and the buyer is ordinarily required to purchase homeowners insurance that protects the lender against loss. But some buyers may consider a mortgage issued by an individual to be less of an entanglement than one from a corporation, and an individual may not have the legal firepower to go after a buyer in default. If the owner of a piece of property does choose to offer financing directly to a buyer, it may be to help out a buyer who might not otherwise qualify for a mortgage from a lending institution or to gain a source of regular income. (If the seller offers financing at an interest rate below the market level, this amounts to a significant discount on the selling price of the home. If the rate is at market level, the seller may receive a higher rate of return from the mortgage than from other investments.)

Some owner-financed mortgages are intended as short-term assistance to the buyer until his personal finances or the market improves. The mortgage may be set up to require a balloon payment of the entire principal in several years. It is also common for the mortgage to include a due-on-sale provision that requires full repayment of the mortgage if the property is resold.

In most parts of the country it is pretty uncommon for a seller to take back paper for the entire purchase price of a home. To begin with, most sellers are looking to make use of the equity in their property to buy another home or for other purposes and are not interested in a thirty-year repayment schedule. Much more common is a second mortgage that extends the buyer's borrowing power to provide the funds for a down payment on a primary mortgage, or makes up the difference between the maximum amount a buyer can borrow from a lending institution and the cost of the property. The second mortgage can be a separate loan, or it can be blended into a wraparound that incorporates the seller's original mortgage or in another combination of loans.

The seller might make available a **carry-back second mortgage,** usually offered when a buyer can assume the existing mortgage on a property. The carry-back second mortgage covers the difference between the outstanding balance of the first mortgage and the selling price of the home. The carry-back is subordinate to the first mortgage, meaning that the issuer of the first mortgage gets paid first in the event of a resale or default. Many carry-back second mortgages are set up as short-term loans with a balloon payment.

Another alternative is a **wraparound mortgage.** In this arrangement the seller holds on to the original mortgage and continues to make payments on it. The buyer is given a new note that covers the full selling price, minus any down payment. The interest rate is usually "blended" between the assumable rate and the market rate for the secondary amount. This arrangement usually results in a lower interest cost for the buyer. In some arrangements a neutral third party is included to service the loan.

Sellers generally want to keep their loans to buyers as short-term as possible to limit their exposure to risk and to get their equity out of the home as quickly as possible. At the same time, though, many primary lenders have rules that limit the ability of an applicant to use second mortgages to buy a property, holding to their ratios for total indebtedness to income. Their interest, of course, is to try to assure that buyers are able to pay off their obligation. Lending institutions may require that second mortgages be written for a term of at least five years, which reduces the monthly payment.

It is also relatively common for sellers to make unwritten or hidden agreements with the buyer that affects the term of a second mortgage. For example, to satisfy the requirements of the primary lender, a seller might agree to a second mortgage with a five- or ten-year term but come to a separate agreement with the buyer that requires repayment in just two years. Such a hidden agreement may never be discovered by the primary lender, but if the buyer defaults on the mortgage, the whole deal might be exposed—and the buyer (and perhaps the seller) could face charges of fraud. Be sure to involve an attorney in checking the terms of an owner-financed mortgage.

■ LAND CONTRACTS

In some parts of the country a seller may offer a land contract, which amounts to an installment plan for the purchase of property. The title remains with the seller until the contract is fully paid, or at some other agreed-upon point. An attorney should closely review any such arrangement to make certain both parties are properly protected.

■ WHAT A BUYER CAN ASK OF THE SELLER

If the seller is willing to take back a note, here are some of the elements of the deal that a buyer can ask for:

■ A higher loan-to-value ratio, or more of a loan than your income would otherwise qualify you for. As a buyer, in most cases you are taking advantage of the seller's difficulty in unloading the property. There is little good reason for a seller to get involved in a risky loan or one that would pay less than could be earned on other investments. In effect, a seller who offers a lower-than-market-rate loan is reducing the net value received in the transaction.

■ Conversely, a buyer who might not otherwise qualify for a loan might offer an above-market-rate to the seller to induce a sale. This sort of deal might appeal to retired sellers who don't need the full amount of the proceeds immediately but would like to receive a steady stream of income based on an advantageous interest rate. (Be sure to consult an attorney about regulations on excessive interest rates—called usury—that apply in some states.)

■ The term of the loan can be agreed to for any length by the parties. Many sellers want a second mortgage to be as short as possible, as little as one to two years, with a balloon payment at maturity. Borrowers often want a longer period for the loan. In any case, primary lenders may disapprove of a second mortgage with a short term, figuring that this threatens the ability of the borrower to repay the larger first mortgage.

■ If the seller permits (or is especially desperate), the buyer may agree to an automatic rollover or refinancing of a second mortgage at the end of its term. This helps the buyer make long-term plans and slightly improves the chances that the loan will not go into default. Such a clause might state that the interest rate on the refinanced loan will be tied to a particular market index, much like the way an ARM works.

■ A buyer can ask for a *subordination* clause that locks a second mortgage into that position. Without such a clause, in most cases if the first mortgage is paid off or refinanced, any secondary mortgage moves up to hold first claim on the property in the event of default. If that happens, as the buyer you may have difficulty obtaining new financing. To the seller who hopes for the quick payoff of the paper she holds, though, a subordination may mean the second mortgage will be once again pushed to the back.

CHAPTER TEN

REFINANCING A LOAN

HOW OFTEN HAVE YOU BOUGHT a new computer, a television set, or a camera and then watched as prices tumbled a few weeks later? As bad as that may make you feel, it's probably only a few hundred dollars, and the pain is over quickly. Now consider taking out a mortgage and watching as interest rates drop to historic lows. Each time you write out a check for the monthly payment, you could be spending hundreds of dollars more than the guy up the block with a new mortgage—thousands a year for many years to come. Just because you have signed on the bottom line for a thirty-year mortgage, that doesn't mean you have to stay with that burden for three decades. Your options include:

- Selling the home and paying off the balance with some or all of the proceeds
- Paying off the outstanding balance with cash from another source
- Refinancing the mortgage at a more advantageous rate or term, or for other reasons

Nearly every home mortgage includes the right to repay the loan before the due date without penalty. There is no reason to accept a mortgage without that feature.

If you've taken out an ARM that permits you to "lock in" at a fixed rate, take advantage of that painless and free (or nearly free) option. If you have a conventional fixed-rate mortgage, you'll need to run the numbers to find the point at which it makes sense to take out a new, lower-cost loan. Remember that you'll generally have to pay a full set of closing costs, including application fee, appraisal, title insurance, attorney fees, and, depending on the loan, prepaid points.

Many homeowners, especially younger ones, can be expected to move a few times in their working careers or to choose to trade up to a larger or more luxurious house. And savvy consumers also track interest rates, looking for the proper moment to refinance an existing mortgage at a lower monthly cost. Just as an example, consider the effect of improving a loan's interest rate by two percentage points: Your current mortgage, a thirty-year, $100,000 loan at 9 percent, costs $804.62 per month for principal and interest costs. You are considering a thirty-year, $100,000 loan at 7 percent, which costs $665.30 per month for principal and interest costs. A two-point difference for the same loan will save about $139.32 per month, $1,671.84 per year, or about $50,000 over the course of thirty years.

In the abstract, any improvement in the interest rate will be to your benefit. However, you have to take into account the fact that if you refinance your loan, you will likely have to pay application, appraisal, insurance, attorney, and other fees and may also have to pay loan origination fees (points). You'll need to run the numbers on any refinancing decision, including all of the costs. And then you'll need to estimate how much longer you'll live in your home in order to see if a new mortgage makes sense.

Based on the example above, here are several options that were available in late 2002:

■ **Loan A:** A thirty-year, $100,000 loan with zero points and a $270 credit, at a 6.925 percent APR. Closing costs are approximately $1,300, and the monthly payment for principal and interest would be about $657.

■ **Loan B:** A thirty-year, $100,000 loan with 3.697 points, at a 6.429 percent APR. Closing costs are approximately $5,267, and the monthly payment for principal and interest would be about $600.

■ **Loan C:** A 30-year, $100,000 loan with a five-year fixed rate at 5.105 APR, and then an adjustable rate with a cap of 9.625 percent. The loan requires payment of 3.676 points, and total closing costs would be approximately $5,246. The monthly payment for principal and interest in the first five years would be about $514.

Use one of the many available loan comparison calculators on-line, or through the lending company or bank you are dealing with.

In the case of the aforementioned three mortgages, there are three different outcomes depending on the length of time you expect to own the home and (with less certainty) on the rise and fall of interest rates. If you were planning to sell your home after about five years, the best deal would be Loan C, which is based on a reduced interest rate for that period, even with the hefty points charged. However, if you hold on to the home for more than five years, you can expect the rate to rise above the original rate and possibly to a level above that of fixed rates. On the other hand, the more-expensive Loan B would be a better choice if you expect to stay in the home (and keep the same mortgage) for thirty years. An analysis shows a likely break-even after twenty years compared to the rising charges of Loan C.

To gauge your own refinancing situation, use one of the many loan-comparison calculators on-line or through the lending company or bank you are dealing with.

ANALYZING A REFINANCING OPTION

The old rule of thumb was that it made sense to refinance if interest rates have declined to at least two percentage points below what you're paying on your current loan. Today, though, the increased value of homes, some reductions in closing costs, and some new forms of mortgage loans has narrowed the spread. In most situations, if rates have declined significantly, it makes sense to replace an existing fixed-rate mortgage with a new, lower-cost fixed-rate loan. If you have an ARM, it is usually a good idea to change over to a fixed rate at that time.

As you begin to consider refinancing, there is one important question to answer at the start: How long do you expect to maintain ownership of the property? If you expect to sell (or refinance again) within a few years, it is pretty unlikely that your savings on the monthly payments in that period will make up for the cost of closing on a new loan. However, in a typical refinance, somewhere around three to five years out comes the break-even point, and after then you're ahead of the game.

Here's an example of an analysis where a drop of 1.25 percent on a mortgage, even with hefty up-front costs, still makes sense for a homeowner who expects to stay put for three years. I began with an existing thirty-year mortgage with an outstanding balance of $203,000 and a historically reasonable 7 percent interest rate. I compared that to a new fixed-rate mortgage for the same amount and term at 5.75 percent. To get that rate at the time I researched the comparison, you'd have to pay 2.395 points, plus closing costs of about $3,921.

The analysis shows that if you can come up with the $8,793 due at closing, you would reduce your monthly payment by about $278. You'd be in the hole for the first two years and seven months; after then you'd be ahead of the game. If you were to hold on to the mortgage for a total of fifteen years, you'd be way ahead, having paid about $41,247 *less* in interest. Here are the numbers:

	Current Mortgage	Refinance
Principal	$203,000	$203,000
Interest rate	7.0	5.75
Term	thirty years	thirty years
Prepaid points	n/a	2.395
Other closing costs	n/a	$3,921
Total due at closing	n/a	$8,793
Monthly payment	$1,463	$1,185
Monthly savings	n/a	$278
Break-even point	n/a	two years, seven months

Note that this simple analysis does not take into account the loss of income on the $8,793 due at closing. I'd add a few months to the bottom line, coming up with an estimate of three full years to break even.

You can do your own analysis at any of numerous refinancing sites on the Internet, or at your own desk with a spreadsheet or a pen and paper. Start by gathering the following information for your current mortgage and any proposed replacement:

■ **Principal.** For simplicity's sake, assume that the amount due under the new loan will be equal to the current balance on the current loan.

- **Interest rate.**
- **Points and closing costs for the new loan.** Determine the prepaid points and closing costs due under the new loan. Any expenses already paid for the current mortgage are not relevant to the comparison.
- **Monthly payment.** Again, for simplicity's sake, compare the monthly payment just for principal and interest, leaving out tax and insurance escrows since these costs should be unchanged in the new loan.

Here's the formula:

1. Subtract the **new monthly payment** from the **current monthly payment** to determine the **monthly savings.**

2. Divide the **total due at closing** by the **monthly savings.**

3. The result is the **number of months to break even.** Remember that this result does not take into account the loss of income on the closing costs or the tax write-off of points paid on the new mortgage.

It's worth noting that when you refinance a loan, you will be starting the amortization schedule from the top. In the first ten years or so of a mortgage, almost all of your monthly payment goes to paying interest costs. The principal is reduced by only a small amount with each monthly payment. If you've had your previous loan in place for a few years, you've begun to whittle away at the principal. You'll lose that progress with the new loan.

I'm also not dealing here with the idea of refinancing a loan and taking out cash in the process. For example, if the interest rate goes down, you could choose to keep the same monthly payment and receive a check for part of the built-up equity in the home. If you're interested in this sort of refinancing, which could be used to pay for renovation or expansion of the home or for other purposes, consult the lending institution and your financial advisor for suggestions as they apply to your particular situation.

■ TAX ISSUES OF REFINANCING

Be sure to consult with your tax advisor to make sure that your refinancing plan does not have an adverse effect on your tax liabilities. As this book went to press, the IRS rule regarding prepaid points paid on a refinancing is that the cost must be deducted over the life of the loan, not the year the new mortgage was issued. This lessens the benefit of the tax deduction for those points. However, if the purpose of the refinancing is to obtain cash for home improvements, some or all of the points may be deductible in the tax year they were paid. Again, consult your tax advisor.

CHAPTER ELEVEN

APPLYING FOR A MORTGAGE

BEFORE YOU PUT PEN TO PAPER on the application, be sure you understand the lender's policies. Is there an application or loan origination fee? What happens to that money if your request for a mortgage is not approved, or if you choose not to accept the loan? Can you lock in the interest rate at the time of the application?

Some old-style lending institutions hand applicants a packet of forms and send them home to plow through them. Higher-volume lenders may help you fill out the papers at their offices or over the phone. The burgeoning world of on-line lenders allows much or all of the application to be filled out over the Internet. (See appendix F for an example of a Uniform Residential Loan Application.) Whatever the process, you'll need a stack of papers of your own to answer the questions on the form. Here's a guide:

■ **Summarize your income.** You'll need copies of your most recent federal W2 and 1099 tax forms and state filings, as well as your most recent pay stub showing salary. If you are self-employed, you should have copies of your business taxes. Your accountant can help you prepare a profit and loss statement.

■ **Know your assets.** Bring copies of your current savings and checking statements, as well as documentation for other investments, including mutual funds, stocks, bonds, and real estate.

■ **Know your liabilities.** The lender will need to know your prospective housing expenses—the expected monthly payment, state and local property taxes, and insurance premiums—to calculate a housing cost ratio. You will also need to provide information on all outstanding loans, including credit cards, mortgages, automobile loans, and student loans.

■ **List your references.** You'll be asked for the names of past and current employers, businesses, and individuals who can vouch for some or all of the information on the form.

If you're applying for a loan on a particular property, you should bring a copy of the purchase contract for the house. It will include such essential data as the legal description of the property (in most areas, a description of the metes and bounds or a plat number that references listings in government recordings).

If you are relying on a gift for some or all of the down payment for the home, the lender will likely want to see an irrevocable gift letter that proves that you are not liable for repayment of the money. Similarly, if you have a private loan arrangement with a family member, friend, or the seller of the home you are buying, you will need to document the terms of that loan.

FROM APPLICATION TO CLOSING

If you're in a real hurry—and very lucky (and your credit and asset history is very well documented)—you can hope to go from application to closing in as little as a week. More commonly, the excruciating wait can take six to eight weeks. (Not every applicant wants closing to happen too quickly. Some applicants may be waiting for the closing on the sale of a previous home and arranging to move.)

Within three business days after you make an application, the lender must give you a Good Faith Estimate of your closing costs as well as a statement that shows your estimated monthly payment and the cost of your finance charges. After then, the lender has to go through all of its steps: qualifying you as a borrower, appraising the home, ordering necessary inspections and tests, and obtaining title insurance and attorney's review. In most cases, the lender also arranges to resell your loan to a secondary lender.

Keep in touch with the lending institution. Here's where those "we're so friendly" companies that advertise on television or the Internet can be put to the test. Find out if there are any snags in the process and if there is any assistance you can provide to the lender. A good real estate agent will get into the process as well, especially if you have applied for a mortgage from a local lender. It's in the agent's interests to have the loan proceed smoothly to closing.

■ RATE LOCKS

In most cases, it can take from four to twelve weeks for a mortgage to be approved and a closing scheduled. In times of economic volatility, interest rates can change daily. Most lenders offer applicants the choice between accepting whatever rate is available on the day of closing or "locking in" the rate at the time of application. Again, depending on market conditions, there may be a fee for the lock-in, or it may be included without additional charge as a benefit of a particular lending institution.

Typical lock-in periods are thirty to forty-five days. In times when rates are relatively stable or heading down, most lenders will offer a lock-in option as a free option. If rates are climbing, though, they may ask for payment of a fee to lock in the rate while you wait for the loan to be approved and closing to be scheduled. Consider the cost of any lock-in option when you compare one mortgage to another, and don't be shy about asking a lender to reduce the fee or eliminate it completely in order to get your business.

■ OBTAINING AN "A" MORTGAGE

An "A" or prime mortgage is the best deal offered by institutions lending to consumers: the best interest rates, costs, and terms. (Note that "prime" does not mean a loan that is based on the prime rate; in this usage it means "best.") In order to be considered prime enough for such a loan, you'll have to fit into a lender's pretty rigid definition of its perfect client. That definition usually requires:

■ A fit within specified ratios of housing expenses to income, and total indebtedness to income

■ A credit and savings history that demonstrates the likelihood you will be able to repay the loan

■ A verified work history, based on recent pay stubs, and an indication from your employer of your chances for continued employment

■ A down payment of at least the minimum specified amount

■ A reserve, typically at least equal to family expenses for three months or more, after the down payment is made

■ A home that is appraised to at least the value of the loan amount plus the down payment

■ A loan amount that conforms to the limits of the particular source of funding

And in most cases, the best mortgage programs are reserved for buyers who intend to occupy the home as a principal residence.

In years past, most lenders would have an approval committee that would review all applications, going over them line by line and ending up with a rating from A+ on down through A, A–, and ending up at an uncreditworthy D. Today, though, most lenders place the greatest emphasis upon a computerized score such as FICO (which is explained later). In general, to receive a prime loan, a borrower needs a credit score of about 700 or above. Some programs might extend to someone with a score of 660 and above.

■ DOCUMENTING YOUR INCOME

In order to receive a preferred interest rate on a loan, lenders want to see verifiable, consistent streams of income. If you're a salaried employee of a corporation, you've got the simplest case. Lenders will want to see your most recent federal tax forms and a current pay stub. If you receive bonuses or commissions, you may need to provide some evidence of the likelihood of receiving them again in future years.

It gets more complicated if you are self-employed. The lender will want to look at several years' worth of tax forms and will base its decision on your taxable—not gross—income. If your income varies greatly from year to year because it is based on commissions or royalties, your case for a loan will be stronger if you can present a long history of tax forms and some indication of future prospects.

Lenders also prefer to see a stable history of employment with the same company or in the same industry. If you have changed jobs to improve your position and salary, that's a plus. If your resume shows a more random hopscotch between jobs and employers, the lender may not want to make a loan.

You are not required to include child support or alimony payments as part of your income. However, if such payments will help establish your ability to make mortgage payments, you'll probably have to provide copies of court decrees or agreements that indicate the terms of the payment. If child support is not included on your tax returns—in general, it is not considered income for tax purposes—you may be required to verify receipt of support with bank statements or copies of checks.

The Self-Employed Dead-End

One red flag for many lenders is an applicant who is self-employed. Some will turn you away immediately, while others will decline to write a prime mortgage. If you own your own business or otherwise work for yourself, you can expect to be asked to provide several years' worth of personal and business federal tax filings. You can bolster your case by presenting signed audits or statements by an accountant attesting to your ongoing business operations. You can also present copies or summaries of ongoing contracts and business arrangements you have that will be the source of future income.

Among the problems faced by many self-employed workers is that not all of their income comes in the form of a paycheck. They may make contributions to a Keogh or other retirement fund, deduct depreciation and home office expenses, and build up equity and goodwill in the business they own.

One option available to self-employed applicants is a **no-documentation** or **low-documentation** mortgage. This is a loan that is based on a sworn statement by the borrower that the information provided in the application is accurate. That doesn't mean you can claim more income than you actually receive. If the lender later determines that the basis of the approval was falsified, the loan can be canceled and other penalties applied. And there is a price for this special consideration and convenience: No-documentation mortgages typically carry a higher interest rate and may require extra prepaid points and a larger down payment.

As an example, at press time the premium for a nondocumented income mortgage was about 1.75 percent. On a $200,000 conventional thirty-year loan, the cost of stating your income rather than proving it worked out to about $84,000 over the full term of the loan. That's a lot of money to pay for convenience. You should only consider a nondocumented income mortgage if that is the only way your application will be approved.

A low-documentation loan may come at a slightly better price. This sort of application requires easy-to-obtain information such as a credit report and bank and investment statements.

HOW LARGE A LOAN CAN YOU OBTAIN?

Among the most important numbers a lender will look at when considering the size of a mortgage is the relationship between your income and your scheduled debt payments. Most lenders actually compute two ratios, sometimes called a **monthly housing ratio** (also called a front or top ratio) and a **debt-to-income ratio** (also called a back ratio). The monthly housing ratio compares your proposed monthly mortgage payment (principal, interest, taxes, and insurance—abbreviated as PITI) to your monthly gross income. PITI also includes any homeowners association dues or condominium assessments. The debt-to-income ratio compares your proposed monthly PITI *plus* any other monthly outstanding debt to your monthly gross income. (Other outstanding debt includes auto or student loans, credit card payments, alimony, and child support. Most lenders include only obligations that will continue six months or more beyond the application date.)

The standard ratio requires that monthly mortgage payments should be no more than 28 percent of gross income, while the debt-to-income ratio should be no more than 36 percent of income. Other lenders may have stricter guidelines, presented in the form of lower ratios. FHA's guidelines, which generally also require the purchase of mortgage insurance, set the two ratios at 29 and 41 percent of gross income respectively.

Let me stop here for a moment to emphasize that the ratios are based on gross income—your salary and other income (including interest, dividends, child support, alimony, trusts, bonuses, and commissions) *before* taxes. And it is also important to consider that your monthly debts include any outstanding loans or lines of credit (including automobile loans, credit cards, and student loans), plus any alimony or child support payments you are obligated to make.

Here's how to calculate your monthly housing and debt-to-income ratios:

Calculating Monthly Housing and Debt-to-Income Ratios

There are four steps to calculating your front and back ratios:

1. Determine your total monthly gross income. (Include the income of any coborrower. Divide any annual income by 12 to yield monthly income).

Monthly gross salary (before tax)		_____
Monthly bonuses and overtime	+	_____
Other monthly income	+	_____
Monthly alimony received	+	_____
TOTAL MONTHLY GROSS INCOME	=	_____[A]

2. Determine the proposed monthly housing cost. (Divide any annual charges by 12 to yield monthly costs.)

Principal and interest on mortgage		_____
Property taxes	+	_____
Homeowners association fees	+	_____
Homeowners insurance	+	_____
TOTAL MONTHLY HOUSING COST	=	_____[B]

3. Determine your total monthly debt payments. (Divide any annual charges by 12 to yield monthly costs.)

Proposed total monthly housing cost		_____
Minimum monthly credit card payments	+	_____
Monthly car loan payments	+	_____
Student loans	+	_____

Other loan obligations	+	_____
Alimony or child-care obligation	+	_____
TOTAL MONTHLY DEBT PAYMENTS	=	_____[C]

4. Calculate the ratios.

Monthly Housing Ratio = B ÷ A

Total Monthly Debt Ratio = C ÷ A

Interpreting your Monthly Housing Ratio	
25 percent or lower	Generally considered a reasonable debt load.
26 to 29 percent	An acceptable level, but with little or no margin for additional debt.
30 percent and higher	At risk for financial difficulties. Lenders may not be willing to issue mortgages at the level you want.

Interpreting your Monthly Debt Ratio	
36 percent or lower	Generally considered a reasonable debt load.
37 to 42 percent	An acceptable level, but with little or no margin for additional debt.
43 percent and higher	At risk for financial difficulties. Lenders may not be willing to issue mortgages at the level you want.

We've explored the way a lending institution will look at your application to see if you qualify for the amount of mortgage money you've asked for. Now let's look at the same process from the other direction, estimating the amount of PITI a bank or lending institution would consider acceptable based on your income. The ratios used in this example (28 percent for allowable monthly housing cost and 36 percent for allowable monthly debt) are those employed by Fannie Mae and a number of other government-sponsored lenders, as well as other agencies and lenders. FHA and other HUD loans typically use percentages of 29 and 41 respectively. You may find a lender who is willing to make a loan based on more liberal ratios. In that case, adjust the two percentages used in the formula:

Allowable Monthly Total Housing Expense =
(Total Monthly Gross Income [A]) multiplied by 0.28 or 0.29

Allowable Monthly Total Debt Payments =
(Total Monthly Gross Income [A]) multiplied by 0.36 or 0.41

Here's an example of the calculation. Let's say that as a family you have an annual gross income of $75,000, including overtime and bonuses, and have no other regular income. Divide that amount by 12 to yield a monthly gross income of $6,250. To determine a typical allowable total housing expense, multiply $6,250 times 0.29 to yield a figure of $1,812.50 for PITI. To determine a typical allowable total debt payment, multiply $6,250 times 0.41 to yield a figure of $2,562.50 for the total of PITI plus any other scheduled debt.

THE ADVANTAGES OF PREAPPROVAL

Getting preapproved for a loan—before you even begin your search for a new place to live—is one of the smartest things you can do as a homebuyer. To begin with, you can find out ahead of time if there are any blemishes or questions on your credit report and deal with them. For example, you may find out that you have several credit cards and lines of credit open but unused. Closing lines you don't need will increase your credit rating and make it possible for you to obtain preferred rates. You may also find errors in your report that may take a few weeks to clear up.

Assuming your credit score is good, the bank or lending institution will be able to tell you how much you can expect to borrow and give you the time to consider various types of mortgage plans. Even a preapproval letter, though, usually includes a few contingencies: The home you seek to purchase must be appraised at a high enough value to meet the details of the loan, and the approval will be withdrawn if there is a material change in your financial situation, such as the loss of your job. Finally, any preapproval will have an expiration date. That doesn't mean the approval will be withdrawn, but it might require a re-examination of your finances and current mortgage rate trends.

With a preapproval letter in hand, not only will you be able to shop for homes with precise knowledge of the maximum you can spend—the loan amount plus down payment and costs—but you will also become a much more attractive bidder. Consider the following set of bids:

- $205,000, contingent on receipt of appropriate bank financing for $175,000 plus $30,000 from the seller in a carry-back mortgage, with closing in sixty to ninety days
- $200,000, contingent upon sale of a previous home and receipt of appropriate bank financing for a new mortgage, with closing in sixty to ninety days
- $198,000 from a preapproved borrower, with closing in thirty days

As the seller, which one would you want to accept? The highest bid gives you less cash up front and should make you worry about the creditworthiness of the buyer. The $200,000 offer will fall through if the buyer can't sell a previous home or is unable to obtain a mortgage. The lowest offer is the surest bet, going to closing quickly and with a minimum of loose strings. Most sellers would opt for the $198,000 and sleep better until closing day.

As the buyer, if you are offering $254,000 for a home, it might weaken your hand if you accompany your bid with a preapproval letter that says the bank is willing to lend you as much as $270,000. A seller—and the agents who work directly or indirectly for the seller, and who would be bound to point out the extra money on the table—will likely counter somewhere around $269,000. Some lenders will issue you a letter that states that they are ready to write a mortgage at the indicated interest rate, up to a particular amount when a specified down payment is made. This sort of a general offer may suit your purposes well, but if you are able to establish a good relationship with your would-be lender, it might be better to obtain a preapproval letter that matches your offer for a home. In the previous example, ask the lender to fax you a preapproval letter in the amount of $254,000. You already know the lender is ready to go to $270,000.

■ PREQUALIFICATION FOR A LOAN

Prequalification is a step in the right direction but not the same thing as preapproval. A lender may accept your application in person, over the telephone, or over the Internet and inform you that *based on the information you have provided* you would be qualified for a loan. The lender will state, though, that approval for the mortgage is dependent upon verification of the information provided. As the applicant, if you know that the information you have provided is correct and verifiable, a prequalification letter will help you to shop for a home, but it is not the same as a preapproved loan, even with contingencies.

YOUR CREDIT SCORE

Lenders don't make decisions on the cut of your clothes or the title on your business card. Most lenders decide whether to loan you money on the basis of a credit rating that is based primarily on your past history and current assets and liabilities. The most commonly used credit scoring system is called FICO, developed by a company called Fair, Isaac. More than 70 percent of the one hundred largest financial institutions use FICO scores to make credit decisions, including more than 75 percent of mortgage loan originations and a similar percentage of auto loans.

FICO scores range between 300 and 850. The higher your credit score, the more likely you are to be approved for loans, and the more favorable rate you are likely to be offered. Depending on the lender, the best loans are offered to borrowers with scores above 700. According to Fair, Isaac, the median score is about 725, with about 50 percent of all U.S. consumers with a score below or above that point. A score of 800 is held only by the top 10 percent of the population.

The rating is believed to be statistically tied to the known histories of borrowers. According to Fair, Isaac, each range of scores can be tied to a predicted delinquency rate for the following two years, defined as the percentage of borrowers who fall ninety or more days past due on a major loan, file for bankruptcy, or otherwise cause a lender to write off a loan as unreceivable.

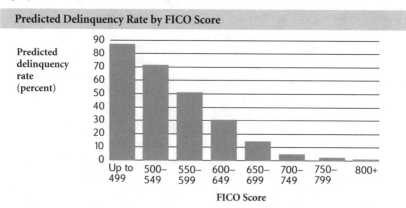

Predicted Delinquency Rate by FICO Score

The scores are based on statistical models that analyze electronic credit files that record previous applications, loan history, and other information. If you've ever applied for a credit card or a loan, chances are there is a file in your name at one or more of the major credit-rating services. The credit report includes any reported late payments, bankruptcy filings, and state and local records of tax liens or monetary judgments against you. You can also post your own statement of dispute to comment on entries you feel are incorrect or misleading. Most scoring schemes look at the following:

- Whether you have made payments on time
- The total amount of money you owe, across all open accounts
- The ratio of your total outstanding balance to the total credit line across all open accounts
- How often and how recently you have applied for new credit cards or lines of credit

Your score will be damaged if there have been more than three voluntary inquiries about your credit in the past six months. (A voluntary inquiry is one that results from your own requests for credit, such as when you apply for a loan and authorize the lender to check your credit. An involuntary inquiry is one that is initiated by a credit company looking for business—that's the reason you likely receive all of those unsolicited credit card offers in the mail. FICO scores are supposed to be designed in a way that your score is not lowered because of your own examination of your credit or because of multiple requests to check your credit when you shop around for a single auto or home loan.)

Lenders like to see a healthy credit history. They look approvingly on a would-be borrower who has had numerous lines of credit and revolving credit accounts over the years, with good payment history. If your past is a blank slate, the lender may consider you an unknown risk and therefore less than prime.

Although consumers have had the ability to read the contents of their credit reports for a number of years (and request corrections), the FICO score used to be restricted by Fair, Isaac to its clients, which included the three largest national credit bureaus: Equifax, Trans Union, and Experian. In 2001, though, legislators at the national and state level began to draft laws to require access to the scores, and Fair, Isaac decided to open its files. To obtain your FICO score, go to www. myfico.com or www.equifax.com. In 2002 a Score Power report cost $12.95, delivering an Equifax credit report on-line, a current FICO score accessible for thirty days, plus an explanation of the key reasons for your score and recommendation on actions you can take to raise your score. A year-long subscription was also available.

How much difference does a high FICO score make on a home loan? According to Fair, Isaac, here was the range for a few typical loans in mid-2002:

FICO score	500–559	560–619	620–674	675–699	700–719	720–850
Thirty-year home loan interest rate	9.742%	9.098%	8.243%	7.093%	6.555%	6.430%

For a typical $200,000 loan over thirty years, borrowers with scores in the low 500s could end up paying more than $166,389 in extra interest compared to a borrower with a score near 800. (Of course, you could hope to improve your credit score over time and refinance at a lower rate.)

■ CAN YOU IMPROVE YOUR STATUS?

If there is a mistake in your credit report, you should be able to have it fixed or, at the least, have your explanation attached to the file. Similarly, if the report shows you have too much in outstanding lines of credit—even if you are not using them—you can contact lenders and ask that the accounts be closed. Unfortunately, it can take several weeks to repair a problem in your report. For that reason, you should examine your credit report several months before you begin the mortgage application process and attempt to make corrections at that time.

If you have a large amount of outstanding debt, you should pay it off, if possible. The debt may reduce your FICO score and also affect the debt-to-income ratio lenders will calculate for your proposed mortgage. You can also accompany your application with a letter explaining past difficulties. For example, your credit history may show you had serious problems three years ago but none since. Did you lose a job, suffer the breakup of a marriage, have to deal with a one-time significant financial loss, or other problem? Provide as much detail and substantiation as you can.

Remember that lending companies are in the business of making loans—they don't want to accept a bad risk, but they're always looking for a reason to put their funds to work.

■ CORRECTING ERRORS IN YOUR REPORT

Under the Fair Credit Reporting Act, if you notify a credit bureau that you disagree with an item in your credit file, your complaint must be investigated. However, the negative information will be removed only if an investigation determines it's incorrect. You may still be able to attach your own dispute of the information on your report. If you want to check your credit report or file a complaint about information you find there, contact the credit bureaus that maintain this data:

Equifax, Inc., 1600 Peachtree Street NW, Atlanta, GA 30309, (800) 685–1111, www.equifax.com

Experian, P.O. Box 2104, Allen, TX 75013–2104, (888) 397–3742, www.experian.com

Trans Union Corporation, Consumer Disclosure Center, 2 Baldwin Place, P.O. Box 1000, Chester, PA 19022, (800) 888–4213, www.transunion.com

For assistance in resolving an error you find on your credit report, you can contact:

Federal Trade Commission, Division of Credit Practices/Consumer Response Center, Sixth Street and Pennsylvania Avenue NW, Room 130, Washington, DC 20580, (202) 382–4357, www.ftc.gov

STUCK IN SUB-PRIME TERRITORY

What if you are unable to climb out of sub-prime territory? Unless you have an especially bad credit history or have lost your job without any prospects for new employment, you should be able to find a lender willing to offer you some level of funding. You can expect sub-prime mortgage rates to be anywhere from one to three or four points higher than those offered to the best prospects, and the lender may require more of a down payment. Finally, the lender may decide to offer less money than you were seeking for the purchase. In the past, one solution here was to seek to take over an assumable mortgage held by the seller, adding cash or a wraparound mortgage to pay any amount above the outstanding balance on the old loan. In today's market, though, relatively few mortgages are assumable by a new buyer, and even those that can be transferred may require that the new borrower meet its criteria for a prime mortgage.

SHOULD YOU SEEK A COSIGNER FOR A LOAN?

If your own history or resources are not enough to get a lender to offer you a mortgage on reasonable terms, you can consider bringing a cosigner to the table. Anyone can fit the bill: family, friends, or business associates among them. A cosigner needs to be qualified for the loan with or without you.

The cosigner will not necessarily be asked to help with the down payment or pay some or all of the monthly payment—that is something between you and the person helping you. As far as the lender is concerned, the role of the cosigner is someone who will be ultimately responsible for the loan if you end up in default. In a worst-case scenario, a cosigner would be called upon to make payments—or be subject to a lawsuit for payment of costs—if you were to go into default on a mortgage.

Now comes the question: Why would someone put their own finances and credit history at risk to support your purchase of a home? If the cosigner is a relative, the answer may be out of family loyalty. Business associates might expect some form of payment for the risk and the effect cosigning the loan has on their own ability to obtain credit.

One way to convince another person to cosign your loan is to draw up an agreement that gives the cosigner an ownership position in the property. The cosigner might be promised a specified percentage of the profit when the home is sold or paid a fee when the mortgage is refinanced in just the borrower's name. If the cosigner's name is placed on the deed along with the principal borrower (something some lenders will require), the cosigner may be able to get back any payments made in the event of default by selling the property. As the borrower, you also want to make sure that any agreement with a cosigner does not give that person the right to take over your interest in the property without your approval except in circumstances spelled out in the agreement.

Be sure to involve a real estate attorney in the drafting of any agreement with a cosigner to protect the interests of both parties.

FULL DISCLOSURE TO THE BORROWER

The federal **Real Estate Settlement Procedures Act (RESPA)** was passed to help prevent abuses by lenders, including kickbacks and exorbitant fees. In a transaction that's on the up-and-up, it helps applicants understand their part of the mortgage bargain. The act is administered by the U.S. Department of Housing and Urban Development's FHA and applies to nearly all mortgage loans and lenders, not just FHA-insured mortgages.

At the time of a loan application, the lender must give the buyer an FHA-approved information booklet that contains consumer information on various real estate settlement services, a Good Faith Estimate of settlement costs, and a Mortgage Servicing Disclosure Statement that tells the buyer whether the lender intends to keep the loan or to transfer it to another lender for servicing and gives information about how the buyer can resolve complaints. (You can see an example of a Good Faith Estimate in appendix H.) Depending on their operating plans, some lenders are required to include two additional disclosures as part of the Good Faith Estimate given to applicants. One will inform the borrower whether or not the company you are dealing with will service the mortgage once it is issued. (As I've noted, despite all the warm and fuzzy promises by banks and lending institutions about how they take care of their customers, in many cases mortgages are sold to secondary lenders once they are written.) The other disclosure form states whether any of the entities involved in the closing process—including escrow agents, title insurance companies, and inspectors—have a business affiliation with the lender. In most cases you are not required to use these companies for you mortgage. You can make an informed decision about whether to accept the lender's recommendations or find your own agents.

After the application but before closing, the lender must provide an Affiliated Business Arrangement Disclosure if any of the services to be used at settlement are entities with which the lender has any kind of business connection, such as common ownership. A borrower usually cannot be required to use a company affiliated in any way with the lender. If the borrower requests it twenty-four hours before closing, the lender must provide a preliminary copy of a HUD-1 Settlement Statement. The form provides estimates of all settlement charges that will need to be paid by the buyer and seller.

At the closing itself, the lender has to provide a final version of the HUD-1 Settlement Statement, showing the actual charges at settlement. At closing or within forty-five days afterward, the lender must give an Initial Escrow Statement, itemizing the estimated taxes, insurance premiums, and other charges that will need to be paid from the escrow account during the first year of the loan.

After the loan is in force, RESPA also mandates that the mortgage originator or servicer provide an Annual Escrow Loan Statement, summarizing all escrow account deposits and payments during the past year. The statement also notifies the borrower of any shortages or surpluses in the account and tells the borrower how these can be paid or refunded. If the loan has been transferred during the year, the borrower must also receive a Servicing Transfer Statement.

RESPA also prohibits a number of egregious business practices for loans related to a federal program, including:

■ Kickbacks, fee splitting, and unearned fees. No one connected with any mortgage can demand, give, or accept something of value in exchange for referrals for any settlement service.

■ A seller-required title insurance company. The borrower must be free to use any title insurance company.

■ An over-funded escrow account. The lender must establish a reasonable limit to the amount of money held in escrow to pay property taxes and (on some loans) homeowners insurance and other fees, such as dues for homeowners associations. Once a year, the lender must provide an accounting of any shortage, or excess, and refund overages of $50 or more.

CHAPTER TWELVE

DOWN PAYMENTS AND PREPAID POINTS

THE INEXPERIENCED BORROWER focuses just on one number: the interest rate. Over the long term—thirty years, for example—the interest rate is generally the most important element of a mortgage. But in the short term, it is also important to pay attention to a pair of other components of a loan for the purchase of a home: prepaid points and the down payment.

Some of the most successful investors and business people have made their fortunes by using OPM: other people's money. If you want to be more formal about it, it's called *leverage.* Consider the following situations:

▪ You purchase a home for $200,000 in cash. After four years, you sell the house for $250,000 after paying a real estate commission. You've made a nice profit, 25 percent on your investment of $200,000. In the meantime, you've lost whatever you might have earned on the money had you invested it. In this example, the net profit may be slim or none.

▪ You purchase a home for $200,000, taking out a mortgage with a down payment of $20,000. After four years you sell the house for a net of $250,000. In this case you've made a $50,000 profit on an investment of $20,000, or 250 percent. That's the sort of impressive return on our money most of us would be thrilled to get.

I've simplified this example a great deal, excluding the cost of the loan and interest and a brokerage commission to the real estate agents involved in the sale. But you get the idea: OPM.

THE THEORY OF DOWN PAYMENTS

Why does a lender want you to make a substantial down payment? It's not because the institution wants to lend you less money—lenders are in the business of making a profit on the interest they charge for loans. The reason is to reduce the risk of default. A down payment, the theory goes, helps the lender in two ways:

- The fact that the borrower has invested tens of thousands of dollars or more in the home makes it less likely that he or she will walk away from the home in default.
- The down payment forms a cushion that protects the lender from losing money in the event of a default.

Here's how that second part works. Let's assume you are purchasing a home valued at $200,000. In a typical conventional loan, the lending institution will ask you to put down 20 percent, or $40,000, and issue a mortgage in the amount of $160,000. The lender has first claim on the property in the event of default, taking possession and reselling it if necessary.

In this example, the lender knows that if the borrower defaults on the property and he is forced to foreclose, the lender stands a good chance of recovering most or all of the money loaned. If the house has somehow declined in value, the borrower bears the cost of the first $40,000. The lender is also protected against the expenses of litigation and resale.

Before you despair of ever coming up with a 20 percent down payment, take solace from the fact that there are a number of mortgage offerings that require smaller down payments and some that will loan the full value of the home with zero down. These plans make use of mortgage insurance or guarantee plans, in which the borrower will pay a few percent per month or per year for the cost of protecting the borrower from the loss of an amount equivalent to a typical down payment.

■ THE RELATION OF MORTGAGE INSURANCE TO THE DOWN PAYMENT

Private mortgage insurance (PMI) underwrites a portion of the mortgage loan against default by the borrower. Put another way, this is insurance that protects the lender, not the borrower. If your down payment is below a lender's loan-to-value ratio, you will likely be required to take out mortgage insurance. You can avoid this expense by raising the amount of your down payment.

Most PMI programs cover as much as 25 to 30 percent of a loan. Although this is not the same as a down payment by the borrower for that amount, lenders feel that the insurance compensates for the added risk of a very high loan-to-value ratio.

Insurance premiums vary but are based on a percentage applied to the mortgage balance. Typical charges run from about one-quarter to one percent of the mortgage amount. Some companies require payment of a full year's coverage or more at closing, while others collect the premium each month.

Federal regulations require current mortgages to automatically cancel PMI coverage (and end collection of premiums) once the outstanding balance declines to the point where your equity reaches 22 percent (or 20 percent in the case of Fannie Mae or Freddie Mac guaranteed loans). Lenders, though, can continue to require PMI if you have a history of late or missed payments.

Credit Life Insurance

Another form of insurance offered by some lenders and third parties is credit life insurance. This is something that is not required and not a very good idea. Credit life insurance promises to pay the outstanding balance on your mortgage in the event of your death. The payoff declines as the principal does.

"What if you were to die suddenly?" the pitch goes. "Do you want to leave your family with a sudden bill for $200,000 to pay off the house in their time of grief?" Well, of course you don't want to do that. But you also don't want to waste your family's money on a bad deal for insurance.

Although the concept of life insurance is a good one for most people with families, credit life insurance is almost always a very bad deal. It is almost always much less expensive to buy a term life insurance policy. In addition to saving on the cost of insurance, having a term policy rather than a credit life policy allows your family to decide what to do with the proceeds of the insurance. It might not make sense to pay off the mortgage. The only reason to consider credit life insurance or credit disability insurance (which makes payments for you if you are disabled and unable to work) is if you are unable to buy any other form of life insurance because you have a serious medical condition.

Here's the bottom line: Credit life insurance is *not* required by the lender or state law. If a lender puts it into the deal without your permission, ask that it be taken out. If you haven't already done so, purchase a term life insurance policy to protect your family against debts.

■ RAISING FUNDS FOR A DOWN PAYMENT

One of the advantages of owning a house is the opportunity to build up equity, in a combination of your original down payment, the portion of your monthly payment that is applied to the principal, and the appreciation that historically adds to the value of real estate over time. Most homeowners use some or all of the equity in their home as the down payment on later homes they buy as they trade up or move to a new neighborhood. But for first-time buyers, the choices each come with costs. You can satisfy a lender's requirements by:

■ Coming up with the cash for a down payment from savings and investments, which depletes your emergency cushion and possibly results in lower return on your investment

■ Taking out a loan without making a substantial down payment through use of mortgage insurance, which adds to the cost of the loan

■ Tapping into your savings in an IRA account

■ Borrowing against life insurance

- Having the seller "take back paper" on the sale, issuing a separate loan for a portion of the purchase price
- Seeking a loan from friends or family for the down payment
- Accepting a gift from friends or family

Because lenders base their lending ratio on your total amount of indebtedness, they will take into account any loan you receive from an insurance company, the seller, friends, or family. They will likely ask to see copies of any loan agreement, including interest costs. If you accept a gift, most lenders will require that you provide documentation that proves that you are not required to repay the funds.

Do you have to disclose a private loan agreement you have made? This sort of loan is not likely to be reflected on you credit report and usually does not include an interest in property you own, which would require notification to local government offices. So, the chances of the lender finding out about such a loan is rather remote . . . unless you end up in a dispute with the lender or with one of the people with whom you have a private agreement. And if that happens, you could end up in default on your mortgage and subject to prosecution for fraud.

Although some experts advise against tapping into retirement funds as a source of a down payment, this may be a worthwhile gamble if you expect the value of your home to rise at a rate comparable to or greater than you would have received in the retirement account. Withdrawals can be made from a traditional IRA account at any time, but a 10 percent penalty is imposed by the IRS on withdrawals made before the magic age of fifty-nine years and six months. There are some exceptions when withdrawals can be made without being subject to penalty, including use of the funds for significant unreimbursed medical expenses, qualified higher-education expenses, and funds used to pay for a first-time home purchase, subject to a lifetime maximum of $10,000 for an individual or $20,000 when taken from the separate holdings of a husband and wife. There are also some very complex provisions that allow for penalty-free, tax-free distributions from a Roth IRA account. Be sure to consult with your tax advisor before touching any of your retirement accounts.

■ SOURCES OF DOWN PAYMENT ASSISTANCE PROGRAMS

There are a number of plans available under the sponsorship of the Federal Housing Administration, the Veteran's Administration, and some state housing authorities that permit first-time and low- and moderate-income homebuyers to obtain a mortgage with low- or zero-down payment. (For a discussion of first-time and low-income buyer programs, see chapter 8, which includes a list of state housing finance agencies.) The U.S. Department of Agriculture's Rural Housing Service also offers a program, which is intended to encourage low- and moderate-income buyers in rural areas. For information call (202) 720–4323 or consult www.rurdev.usda.gov/rhs.

THE THEORY OF POINTS

To lenders, the interest rate is just one element of the profit they make on a loan. They look at the total "yield" on a loan, including interest received, prepaid points, and markup on services they may provide. Each point is equal to 1 percent of the mortgage amount. For example, 1 point on a $200,000 loan would be $2,000. In most cases, prepaying 1 point of interest shaves one-eighth of a percent off the mortgage interest rate.

If you pay points on a loan, not only are you giving the lender some immediate income, but you are also increasing the yield. If you pay $3,000 in points on a $200,000 loan, you are in effect receiving only $197,000 from the lender even though your monthly payment (and outstanding balance) will be based on the full amount of $200,000. This differential can be seen in the APR, which adjusts the stated interest rate to take into account additional costs to the borrower.

■ DEDUCTIBILITY OF POINTS

In most loans, points are tax-deductible in the year they are paid for the borrower because they represent prepaid interest. If you are in the 30 percent tax bracket, $4,000 in points will only cost you $2,800 when you include the tax savings. IRS regulations say that the amount of the points must be typical for the region the loan was obtained and must be clearly indicated on the settlement statement used at closing. In order to obtain a full deduction for points and mortgage interest costs, you must be purchasing a home for your own use. (Different regulations apply to homes bought as an income property or as a vacation residence.) Be sure to consult with your tax advisor before making decisions based on tax consequences of a mortgage.

■ ZERO-POINT LOANS

A mortgage with zero points sounds very attractive, but remember that there is no free lunch—or free loan, either. Lenders try to make about the same amount of profit on any of the mortgage products they offer. If you pay points, your interest rate is going to be lower than it would be for a zero-point loan.

Here's an example of two thirty-year fixed-rate loans for $200,000, one with a hefty amount of prepaid points, and one requiring zero points up front:

Loan Principal	Prepaid Points	APR	Monthly Payment
$200,000	3.181	5.75	$1,167
$200,000	0	6.375	$1,215

In this example, the first loan requires an up-front payment of $6,362 in points. If you hold both loans through maturity in thirty years, the loan with prepaid points will cost about $30,000 less. The break-even point comes after five years and two months, assuming you're in a typical tax bracket. Assuming you have the cash to pay the points when you first took out the mortgage, this analysis shows that if you hold on to the house for more than five years, you're ahead of the game and will remain so until the mortgage is paid off.

If you expect to stay in your home more than a few years, it is usually worthwhile to pay a few points to reduce the monthly cost of the loan. The break-even point typically occurs between four and seven years down the road, and after then you will be ahead of the game. For a rough estimate of the break-even point when you compare two mortgages, use the following process:

1. Determine the difference in monthly payment between the higher **Loan 1** (**zero points**) and **Loan 2** (**with points**).

2. Determine the closing costs for Loan 1 and Loan 2. Include the cost of points plus closing costs, and subtract any credits the lender might offer as an enticement for one or the other mortgage. Subtract the costs for Loan 1 from Loan 2 to yield the net difference in closing costs.

3. Divide the net difference in closing costs by the difference in the monthly payment. The result will be the number of months it will take to pay off the extra up-front charges.

ZERO-COST MORTGAGES

Some lenders will offer a loan in which closing costs are "free." We know better than that, of course. The lender recoups the costs through a higher interest rate or by financing them as part of the principal.

You can apply the same sort of analysis used for other loans to a zero-cost or "cash-saver" loan to determine the break-even point when you compare two loans. The differential between a zero-cost mortgage and one that charges several points up front plus closing costs would likely result in a shorter time to break even than you would find comparing a zero-point loan to one with points.

■ SHOULD YOU GO FOR A ZERO-COST LOAN?

It sounds very attractive: move into this house without a down payment and pay no points at closing. The good news, of course, is that you don't have to come up with tens of thousands of dollars from savings or in loans from relatives. The bad news, though, is that the monthly payment and the ultimate total cost of the mortgage are going to be much higher. And if you sell the house in the first ten years or so of the term, you will have very little equity in the home to use as down payment on a new dwelling. You can hope, of course, that the home itself will appreciate in value in the time you have owned it; however, in many cases the appreciation on a house will be eaten up by the additional cost of a no-down-payment mortgage.

As an example, as this book was written a typical thirty-year, $200,000 conventional loan based on a standard 20 percent down payment was available for 6.75 percent interest. Paying a hefty 3.816 points plus the down payment would reduce the rate to 5.75 percent. If instead you chose to seek a no-down-payment loan with no points, the rate rose to 8.5 percent. Remember that if you make a down payment, you will lose the opportunity to make interest on that money. In the following example, I will assume you could earn 5 percent on the money. Here are the comparative numbers on those three loans:

Loan A: $200,000 for thirty years	
Down payment	0
Points	0
Interest rate	8.5 percent
Monthly payment (P&I)	$1,538
Total cost after thirty years	$553,037
Amount of interest paid in five years	$81,975
Amount of interest paid in ten years	$160,704

Loan B: $200,000 for thirty years	
Down payment	$40,000 (20 percent)
Points	0
Interest rate	6.75 percent
Monthly payment (P&I)	$1,038
Total cost after thirty years	$374,175
Amount of interest paid in five years	$51,668
Lost interest on down payment in five years	$14,168
Amount of interest paid in ten years	$128,688
Lost interest on down payment in ten years	$32,350

Loan C: $200,000 for thirty years	
Down payment	$40,000 (20 percent)
Points	3.816 ($7,632)
Interest rate	5.75 percent
Monthly payment (P&I)	$933.72
Total cost after thirty years with points	$344,160
Amount of interest paid in five years	$43,770
Lost interest on down payment in five years	$14,168
Amount of interest paid in ten years	$84,499
Lost interest on down payment in ten years	$32,350

So which is the best deal? (To begin with, it should be obvious that you have to do the numbers in order to make an informed comparison.) As I've demonstrated, there is usually a significant cost to buying leverage, especially since mortgage lenders raise their interest rates, require mortgage insurance, or both when the borrower puts down little or no down payment. But if you can get a no-down-payment loan for a rate that is nearly the same as for one requiring 10 or 20 percent down, go for it. Any appreciation in the house will be based entirely on other people's money. But if the cost of a no-down-payment loan is a few extra interest points, the cost of the loan will be significantly higher over the full term. The lowest-cost loan is usually one that requires both a standard down payment of 20 percent plus a significant amount of prepaid points, as in Loan C. The break-even point on the prepaid points usually comes somewhere in the first ten to fifteen years of the thirty-year loan.

If you are buying a house as an investment, your business plan should indicate if it makes sense to pay a higher cost for the mortgage for the privilege of keeping your own money out of the deal. But for most people, buying a house is mostly a matter of owning shelter. We hope for appreciation over time, but that is not the reason that makes us want to become a homeowner. If that's the way you look at the process, it often makes sense to make a substantial down payment to reduce the monthly payment for the life of the loan.

Although it is impossible to accurately predict interest rates for years to come, it is also true that over the past few decades houses in many parts of the country have appreciated in value at a slightly higher rate than other investments. So, for example, if you expect your home to grow in value by 8 percent per year and your money market or mutual fund accounts are earning 6 percent, you're probably ahead of the game by putting money into the equity of the house. Remember, too, that as much as $500,000 of profit on the sale of a home is tax-free to a couple who files jointly.

HOW TO CHOOSE

If you expect to hold on to a home, or the mortgage on the home, for only a few years, it probably makes sense to seek a zero-point or low-point mortgage and pay the slightly higher interest rate during the term of the loan. On the other hand, if you expect to keep the home for an extended period and can afford to pay points up front, the monthly payment will be more manageable from the start, and the net cost of the loan will be much lower once you cross the break-even point.

CHAPTER THIRTEEN

BIWEEKLY PAYMENTS, EQUITY LOANS, AND REVERSE MORTGAGES

WHEN MOST PEOPLE THINK of a mortgage, they envision a relatively straightforward transaction: a lender gives you money to buy a home, and you pay it off over time in monthly installments. But there are also some interesting spin-offs of the traditional home loan that offer certain advantages to some borrowers. In this section we'll look at biweekly or extra-payment mortgages that allow you to pay off your loan years quicker and for thousands less in a relatively painless manner; home equity and second mortgages that allow you to tap into some of the value of your home without selling it; and reverse mortgages, which call for a bank or other institution to pay you the value of your home without the need to sell it.

BIWEEKLY OR EXTRA-PAYMENT MORTGAGES

Why in the world would you want to pay more money on your loan than you are required? The answer: because doing so is one way to save thousands or tens of thousands of dollars on the cost of the mortgage in a way that many borrowers find to be all but painless. The trick here lies in the nature of a standard amortization schedule for a mortgage. In the early years of a loan, almost all of your payment is for interest costs. The principal of the loan is reduced very gradually. But if you were to add extra money, or an extra payment, those funds could be directed to reduce the principal. The net effect is to shorten the term of the loan and to reduce the total interest paid.

For example, on a thirty-year conventional mortgage for $200,000 at 7 percent interest, the monthly payment for principal and interest would be $1,330.60. In the first year, about $1,160 would go for interest and just $170 toward reducing the outstanding principal. Six years into the loan, the situation is not much better: about $1,095 per month to pay interest costs and $255 to reduce the principal. Not until the twentieth year of the loan would the payment be split evenly between principal and interest.

Someone out there is going to point out that an unwanted effect of shortening the term of a loan is that you will lose a few years of tax write-off of interest costs. That is true, but as I explained, the greatest proportion of your interest cost comes in the early years of the loan. And once you pay off your mortgage you can always buy another property or refinance your existing home to tap the equity.

The key to paying off the loan ahead of schedule is the right of the borrower to prepay. This is usually—but not always—permitted. Under some loans there is a penalty for prepayment beyond a specified percentage of the amount borrowed in the early years of the agreement. Be sure you understand the fine print of your mortgage agreement.

There are several ways to go about making extra payments on your loan:

- By adding extra money to your monthly payment.
- By adding a larger amount of money to your payment once a year. (For example, you could apply some or all of your tax refund, or your Christmas bonus.)
- By signing up for a biweekly mortgage payment.

Discuss with your lending institution how best to express your intentions for the extra money paid. Most lending institutions include a line on the payment coupon where you can indicate that extra money is to be applied to the principal of the loan.

Here is an example of the benefits of making extra payments, figured with the aid of a calculator available at www.bankrate.com and on other Web sites. Let's assume we have a new thirty-year conventional mortgage for $200,000 at 7 percent. If you were to make the regular monthly payments for principal and interest, the loan would be paid off in full after 360 payments, or thirty years. The total cost of the loan would be $479,017 ($200,000 in principal and $279,017 in interest.) Now let's look at the same loan and include an extra $100 per month directed to payoff of the principal. The loan would be paid off in twenty-four years and four months, and the total cost would be $415,709. You would be paying the same amount in principal, but your interest cost would be reduced by $63,308. Or, you could make one extra payment of $1,200 each December, directed at payoff of the principal. The loan would be paid off in twenty-four years and six months, and the total cost would be $225,640. (One thing to watch out for: Your extra payment at the end of the year could be credited to the next payment due instead of as a reduction to outstanding principal.)

Be sure to check that your payments are properly applied to principal. Some lending institutions report the amount of principal owed on the monthly bill you receive, while others wait until the annual recapitulation statement. Either way, you should see an indication of the extra principal you paid. As with shorter-term mortgages, you will also lose the tax write-off of interest payments earlier in the term of the loan.

■ SETTING A BIWEEKLY PAYMENT SCHEDULE

Some lenders will be happy to set up a conventional mortgage right from the start that requires payment on a biweekly schedule instead of monthly. Each payment is calculated at half the amount that would be due under a monthly schedule. Because there are fifty-two weeks in the year, you will end up making the equivalent of a thirteenth monthly payment each year. The extra money is applied toward reduction of the principal.

This sort of scheme works well for some borrowers who are paid biweekly. (Some plans have called this sort of schedule a "paycheck mortgage.") If you are self-employed or receive your income on a less-regular basis, a biweekly payment mortgage may cause problems.

If you have an existing mortgage with a monthly payment schedule, ask the lending institution if it can be converted to a biweekly payment. If that can't be done (or if there would be a significant fee), you can achieve the same effect by adding one-twelfth of the monthly payment each time you make a payment, designating the extra money to reduce the principal. You may be contacted by financial companies that offer to set up a biweekly or extra payment schedule and work out all the details with your lender . . . for a fee that can amount to hundreds or even thousands of dollars. There is no reason to pay a company to set this up for you. In addition to charging for something you can do on your own for free, a handful of these companies have crossed the line into fraud. There have been instances where the companies have done nothing more than hold on to your biweekly payment for a few weeks and make your payment on time . . . or not at all.

HOME EQUITY LOANS AND SECOND MORTGAGES

Although it is comforting to own your home free and clear of debt, or to be far enough along in a mortgage to see the day when you can burn the loan papers in a backyard ceremony, there is also the problem of being house poor: having a large part of your net worth tied up in an asset you cannot easily tap. Two solutions are to take out a home equity line of credit or a second mortgage. These are loans that are secured by an interest in the portion of your home that you own. As such they are generally offered at a lower interest rate than an unsecured loan. In most cases, the interest cost on the loan is deductible from your taxes, which reduces the cost of the loan. (Ordinary consumer loans are not tax-deductible.)

You can use a large portion of the equity in your home for repairs or maintenance, college education, travel, purchase of a car, health care, or other purposes. The most important thing to keep in mind, though, is that an equity loan or line of credit must be repaid, and a default could put your home at risk. Under a line of credit, you are allowed to take out funds up to a specified amount over the course of the loan term. Some plans allow you to write checks to access the line of credit or use a special credit card linked to the loan, while others require requests for transfer of funds into the line.

A second mortgage also taps into the equity of your home, but unlike a line of credit, the lender will issue a check or credit for a specific amount or term. In most plans, the second mortgage calls for repayment of the borrowed amount over the term of the loan.

The process of obtaining an equity loan begins with an appraisal of the value of the home and a calculation of the outstanding balance on any existing primary mortgage. Most lenders will offer credit based on a proportion of the value of the home minus the outstanding balance. Here's an example of an equity loan calculation:

Appraised value of home and land		$250,000
Loan to value percentage	×	0.75
Maximum equity loan amount		$187,500
Balance owed on existing mortgage	−	$125,000
Equity loan offered		**$62,500**

In addition to looking at the present and future expected value of the home, the lender will also consider your ability to repay the loan through an examination of your income and debts.

A typical equity line of credit has a fixed term of five to ten years. Some loans require full repayment by the end of the agreed-upon period—either in monthly payments or a lump sum "balloon" payment—while others permit renewals of the credit line with the permission of the lender.

As with any other mortgage, the most important figures in a loan are the annual percentage rate and the closing costs, which typically include an application fee, credit report and appraisal charges, and sometimes up-front loan origination fees (points). Some equity loan agreements also include an annual administration fee or a transaction fee each time you use the line of credit.

Many equity lines of credit are based on variable rather than fixed interest rates. The APR is usually tied to an independently calculated index, such as Treasury bill rates, plus a specific "margin" above the index. It is important to read the loan agreement to find out how often the interest rate on the line of credit can be adjusted by the lender and the specifics of a "cap" that sets a limit to how high the rate can rise during the term of the loan.

Some lenders promote their loans with an artificially low rate—sometimes called a "buy-down"—for an introductory period such as the first year of a multiyear deal. For example, as this book was written many lenders offered an introductory rate set at 1 percent below the prime rate for the first six months of the loan. After the introductory period, the interest rate was set to rise to prime rate plus 1 percent.

If you are making monthly payments on the loan, a change in the APR will result in an increase or decrease in the interest portion of the payment. If the loan is structured as a balloon mortgage, a change in the APR will increase or decrease the total amount due at the end of the loan term. Depending on market conditions, you may also want to consider fixed-rate mortgages to take advantage of a particularly attractive rate. And some variable rate mortgages allow you to "lock in" at a fixed rate during the course of the loan.

Under most equity loan agreements, if you sell your home, the loan must be paid in full immediately. The amount due will likely be subtracted from the proceeds of the sale at the time of closing and paid directly to the lender.

When you compare the cost of one equity line of credit to another, or one second mortgage to another, consider the APR and other costs. However, you cannot directly compare an equity line of credit to a second mortgage because the APR is calculated differently. The APR for a second mortgage loan is calculated in the same way as a first mortgage, including the interest rate charged plus points and other finance charges. The APR for a home equity line of credit is based entirely on the periodic interest rate and does not include points or other charges.

REVERSE MORTGAGES

The focus in this book has been on buying a house with a mortgage premised on rising equity and falling debt. Over time, borrowers pay off the outstanding balance and build up a larger percentage of ownership of the home and land. That's the dream of most homeowners, especially younger ones. A paid-off mortgage means that the home—with its increased value over the years—becomes a major asset.

Now consider the situation faced by an older, retired couple. Let's say the mortgage has been paid off, and they are living on their retirement funds and Social Security. Although their home is worth several hundred thousand dollars, it's not an asset they can use without selling the place where they live. There are three common solutions:

- Sell the home and move to a less-expensive home or a rental property
- Take out an equity loan, which requires monthly repayment of the amount borrowed
- Agree to a reverse mortgage, which is a loan against the full value of your home that does not have to be paid back as long as the owners live there

A **reverse mortgage,** as its name suggests, turns the ordinary mathematics of a mortgage on its head. Another name for such a plan is a **home equity conversion mortgage.** In essence, the owners sell their house to a bank or lending institution over time, receiving a lump-sum payment or a monthly payment. Under this scheme, the owners experience declining equity and rising debt. The money paid to the owner becomes a loan with interest that must be paid back when the last surviving borrower dies, sells the home, or permanently moves away. The repayment of the loan can be made from the sale of the home. A great advantage of a reverse mortgage is that you do not need to have an income. The value of the home itself will be used to repay the loan.

During the term of the reverse mortgage, the amount you owe will grow larger because of the disbursements to you and the interest on the loan. But the mortgage agreement is set up so that you can never owe more than the home's value at the time the loan is due to be repaid. (And if your home appreciates in value, as most do, you or your estate will likely receive some funds when the home is sold, even after the cost of the loan is subtracted.) During the course of the loan, the owners are responsible for property taxes, insurance, and repairs and upkeep to the home.

In addition to the appraised value of the property, the lender will also take into consideration the age of the owners in deciding how much money to loan. Like it or not, older borrowers presumed to have a shorter life expectancy will receive more money than younger borrowers who are likely to accrue many years of interest costs under the reverse mortgage.

In general, a reverse mortgage must be a "first" or primary mortgage against your home, meaning that there can be no other debt secured by the value of the home. If you have an outstanding balance on a conventional mortgage, in most cases you will need to pay off that loan before you get a reverse mortgage or pay off the loan with some of the proceeds you receive from a reverse mortgage.

Borrowers have to pay the same sort of fees that an applicant for a standard mortgage or refinancing would face, including an application fee, appraisal fee, and credit costs. The terms of a reverse mortgage may include an origination fee, points, insurance, and other charges. The closing costs can generally be included within the loan balance.

The U.S. Department of Housing and Urban Development operates the Home Equity Conversion Mortgage (HECM) plan, insured by the FHA to protect lenders against loss if amounts withdrawn exceed equity when the property is sold. The program is open to participants age sixty-two and older and living in the property as their principal residence. To help protect against possible fraudulent practices against elderly clients, participants must receive free counseling from a HUD-approved agency before applying for a reverse mortgage.

The total income that an owner can receive through HECM is calculated with a formula based on the age of the owner or owners, the interest rate, and the value of the home. In recent years, for example, a sixty-five-year-old could borrow up to 26 percent of the home's value, a seventy-five-year-old could borrow up to 39 percent, and an eighty-five-year-old up to 56 percent. HECM borrowers can be paid by a monthly payment from the lender for as long as the borrower continues to occupy the home as a principal residence; monthly payments for a fixed period selected by the borrower; a line of credit, which allows withdrawals at any time up to a maximum amount; or a combination of the various options.

Under the federally insured plan, the borrower remains owner of the home and can sell it at any time, keeping any proceeds that exceed the mortgage balance. The borrower cannot be forced to sell the home to pay off the mortgage, even if the mortgage balance grows to exceed the value of the property. When the loan must be repaid, the borrower or his or her heirs will owe no more than the value of the property, even if the mortgage amount exceeds the value of the property.

HECM plans require payment of two mortgage insurance premiums: an up-front premium of 2 percent of the home's value and a monthly premium of 0.5 percent of the mortgage balance. The up-front charge can be financed by the lender. In addition, the lender can assess a loan origination fee. For information call HUD's toll-free housing counseling information line at (888) 466–3487.

In addition, a number of reverse mortgage programs are offered by state and local governments, often through housing authorities. These programs are sometimes limited to specific purposes such as home repairs and improvements, while reverse mortgages offered by banks and lending institutions can generally be used for any purpose.

If you participate in such a program, be sure to consult with your tax advisor. In general, loan advances are not considered to be income for tax purposes; however, the funds might affect your eligibility for other programs such as SSI or Medicaid.

PART IV

LAND

CHAPTER FOURTEEN

BUYING LAND

—

DOWN PAYMENTS FOR LAND are often higher than those for home purchases because lenders want to make certain that buyers will remain financially attached to the property while they are not living there. Similarly, interest rates for land are usually slightly higher than those for homes. In most cases, you'll need to obtain a short-term construction loan to pay the builder at specified points in the contract. Because the bank or its appraisers become involved in checking the progress of construction, these loans usually function like a line of credit and carry interest rates above those for already-built homes.

CHOOSING A PIECE OF LAND

Before you decide you want to own the view from horizon to horizon, consider the following:
- Who is going to mow the lawn?
- Are you prepared to erect and maintain fences and no-trespassing or no-hunting notices?
- Have you considered the cost of bringing utilities to a remote site?
- Do you really want to be that isolated from neighbors?

Not all land is equal: A heavily wooded acre may be much more private than three acres of flat land in a development, and a small plot of land with an uninterrupted view of the water or mountains may be much more attractive than a much-larger hidden spread. The beauty of a piece of property is often in the eye of the beholder, although it helps a great deal to be a fully informed beholder.

Some people dream of living on top of a mountain, with views in all directions. Others would find that isolation terrifying and the hassle of getting to the supermarket unacceptable. Some would love to be in a well-tended gated community, while others would run away from the idea of conformist suburbia with putting-green lawns and gleaming sidewalks.

■ STOP, LOOK, AND LISTEN

There is no right and wrong when it comes to fulfilling your dream—although you do need to keep your eyes wide open when it comes to finding out about zoning of the land and nearby properties. Here are some questions to ask yourself or your real estate agent:

- Spend an hour on the site and get a feel for the atmosphere. Stop, look, and listen. What do you see? What do you hear? Is there an active road or train line nearby? Is the property beneath the flight pattern of an airport?
- Will the house of your dreams fit on the land and blend in properly with the surrounding landscape and other homes in the area?
- Where on the property is the likely location for the house? Where are the nearest utilities?
- Is there a stream, pond, or marsh on the land? Is there a history of flooding in the area? Does water drain properly, away from the home site?
- Locate the northern (shaded) and southern (sunlit) exposures and consider the orientation of a home on the site. Do you want particular rooms facing sunrise or sunset?
- Is the site heavily wooded? Will clearing trees for construction ruin its appeal to you?
- Is the property level? If not, what will the builder have to do to fit the home into the slope? In snow country, is the driveway too steep to keep clear of snow and ice? If the property is built into a slope, is the hill stable against slides?
- Is there an access road and driveway in place? If so, is it sufficient for the home and for the construction vehicles?
- What kind of landscaping will be required once the home is built?

■ EVALUATING A LOT

Whether you are buying raw land to build a home or moving into an existing home, spend the time to see how comfortable you are with the property. Depending on your personal preferences and the climate, you may want to extend your living room out onto the deck, the backyard, or the front porch. Ask yourself:

- Is the lot large enough for the uses you have in mind? Is it regularly shaped—rectangular or square—or does it have an unusual form that may make it hard to use, landscape, and resell?
- Are there existing decks or porches? If so, are they shaded or directly in the sun? Is there a barbecue pit or a platform for a grill?
- Is the lot on a slope? A hillside may be attractive to some buyers, but it also presents some construction difficulties that can increase costs and reduce design options. A sloped lot can require a steep driveway—something that could present a great deal of difficulty when covered with snow or ice. And it may be difficult to maintain a lawn.
- Does water drain properly away from the house? The worst possible situation is to have a home located at the low point of a lot so that water drains into the foundation and basement. A properly engineered lot has swales or berms to

channel the water. Some properties include drainage pipes or French drains (a grating over a rock-filled well) to take water away from the home.

■ Is the lot landscaped to your liking? Some people prefer a simple lawn, while others invest thousands of dollars in plants and flowers that will require a lot of attention to maintain.

For a Land-Buying Comparison List useful for evaluating different lots, see appendix G.

RESTRICTIONS ON LAND USE

In most parts of the country, local municipalities create **zoning codes** that restrict the uses of land in certain areas. In most instances, this is to your benefit: You probably don't want an oil refinery or a fast-food restaurant arriving on the property next to yours. Some zoning codes require subdivisions to be of a minimum size so that houses are spaced apart from one another. Your real estate agent or attorney should be able to assist you in researching not just the current zoning status but also to advise on any expected changes, as well as the municipality's long-range land-use plans. (Consider the fact that many people living next to a new prison, a sewage treatment plant, or a superhighway did not know about allowable uses of adjacent land when they bought their own property.)

In some locations, zoning regulations may require certain types of construction or limit the number of structures or families on a piece of land. And in certain districts there may be design boards that must approve all new construction (and subsequent expansions and remodeling) to make certain new homes fit in with the local history. In addition to government regulations on land use, some developments and individual deeds include **restrictive covenants** that may set standards for types and designs of homes and other controls. (For example, a small development of expensive homes near mine requires whitewashed picket fences and architectural review of all construction.)

■ EASEMENTS

An easement is a right by another to cross your land or to make specific use of it. The easement may be as minor as a water pipe or electrical cable crossing a corner of your land en route to another property or may permit a neighbor to drive across your land. A major utility might hold an easement that permits eventual installation of a line of huge electrical towers with wires that cross over your home.

Any offer you make for purchase of land should be contingent upon your acceptance of any easements in the deed. Your attorney should assist you in reviewing the document for the land you are offering to purchase as well as surrounding property.

If access to the property is made from a private road, there should be a formal document dealing with ownership of the road and easement across it. In some instances, there will be a road-maintenance agreement that requires abutters to the road to contribute to its upkeep.

CONTINGENCIES ON A LAND OFFER

A contingency is an escape hatch you can place into an offer, allowing you to cancel the deal or open it to renegotiation if a particular event occurs or fails to occur. For example, you can make an offer contingent upon:

- Acceptance of any previously undisclosed easement or restrictive covenant found by your attorney or title insurance company before closing
- Approval of sewer or septic permits from a municipality
- Receipt of financing for the purchase
- Approval by a review board of your home design plans

Some offers to purchase land are less than precise about the total number of acres involved, sometimes stating "approximately" XX number of acres or making reference to a previous survey. You can make the amount of your purchase offer contingent upon the result of a new survey, which may be necessary for a mortgage, by offering a specific amount per acre as found in the survey.

FINANCING THE PURCHASE OF LAND

Mortgages for the purchase of land are more difficult to obtain than those for a home. Major lending institutions and banks often view land purchase as speculation and are unwilling to take on the risk when they can just as easily lend funds to a homebuyer.

Most loans for land purchase are made by small local banks or by the seller, and many require a substantial down payment of 30 percent or more. If you're buying land to build a new home, one good source of funds is an equity loan against the value of your present home. Interest rates are relatively low, and interest costs are tax-deductible. Whatever the source of the loan, it can later be refinanced as part of a construction loan or as financing for a home once completed on the land.

Many lenders used to assume that the land would represent about 25 to 30 percent of the final cost of the property and dwelling. That number may still be apt in some areas, but land values can vary greatly. In a very competitive resort community, land value can be much more than the house that stands on the property. In some areas where land is very inexpensive, the home's cost can represent 90 percent or more of the overall worth.

CONSTRUCTION COSTS

Your real estate agent and local builders associations should be able to tell you the average cost per square foot for typical construction. Rates will vary based on the location of the property—if it is very isolated or far from a main road, for example. Other factors that will raise the cost include features of the land, including hills and bodies of water that may require nonstandard construction techniques. The design of the house also affects the cost. An unusual roof line or a compound roof (one with multiple sections and angles), special features like dormers or cupolas, skylights and unusual windows, and elaborate kitchens and bathrooms can all contribute to the cost.

In general, it costs less to build up rather than out. A two-story home should be less expensive to construct than a ranch house of the same square footage because the foundation and roof are smaller, and plumbing and heating systems are simpler and more efficient to install. Depending on local conditions, including annual weather patterns and the type of soil, the house may require a basement, which costs more to construct than a crawlspace or a slab.

The cost of hooking up to utilities can be major if the nearest wires and pipes are hundreds or thousands of feet from the home site. If the property requires a well and septic system, you'll need to obtain an estimate for their construction. The cost of building a driveway or access road to the property can also be significant.

PART V

NEW HOMES

CHAPTER FIFTEEN

BUYING A BRAND-NEW HOME

LET'S GET SOMETHING out of the way right away: I'm not going to tell you how to build your own home from a truckload of lumber and a box of nails, and I'm also not going to explain how to find, hire, and supervise a contractor and dozens of subcontractors. Not that there's anything wrong with doing it yourself. It's just very, very complicated and fraught with peril. It's the sort of thing you should never do for the first time. (If you do want to go ahead with arranging for the construction of a home by yourself, I'd suggest you try to find a few people who have done it before and seek referrals to reliable contractors. You should also contact an area builders association and the Better Business Bureau in search of recommendations and warnings.) Instead, in this section I will concentrate on buying a house from a tract or production builder, an individual or corporation that creates subdivisions small and large. Then I will open the door just a bit toward becoming a contractor, exploring factory-built modules that arrive on a truck to be bolted into place on a foundation. Finally, I'll discuss ordering home plans from a catalog.

TRACT OR PRODUCTION HOMES

A builder who is developing a subdivision is essentially setting up an assembly line. In most cases the builder subcontracts out much of the work, hiring a framing crew that moves from home to home, followed by plumbers and electricians, Sheetrock hangers, finish carpenters, and so on. The developer can lower costs by making bulk purchases of supplies and obtaining better rates on construction crews who can be guaranteed regular work across a number of homes. There are also savings to be had on the cost of installing utilities and roads to serve the new homes.

Some developers maintain their own sales force, ready and waiting to meet with buyers who arrive in their showroom: a model home. Although there will likely be a "list" price for each house in the development—with some adjustments for particularly desirable lots plus optional upgrades or allowable changes—that doesn't mean that prices aren't open to some level of negotiation.

If you arrive at a subdivision with your real estate agent, the builder will usually have to pay that agent's half of a standard commission. In some cases, the builder may have a separate arrangement with real estate agents, paying them what amounts to a finder's fee for delivering buyers. You should ask your agent about such arrangements before visiting a new development. In some cases, a builder may be willing to cut prices on a home—or throw in some upgrades or changes—if you arrive without an agent. However, there is no guarantee that a sharp buyer's agent wouldn't be able to help you negotiate a better price.

Here are some things you can do to improve your bargaining position with a developer:

■ Get prequalified for a loan and make an offer without any contingencies. Builders can easily have millions of dollars tied up in loans for property, supplies, and unsold homes.

■ Buy early. If you're among the first buyers in a development, the builder may be very anxious to sell a few homes and start to recoup the investment. Prices may be a bit more negotiable or perhaps not quite as marked up as they may be when the project is nearly sold out.

■ Buy late. By the time there are just a few homes left to sell, most successful builders are already at work on their next development. They want to close out the books and move their salespeople and foremen on to somewhere else. In a buyer's market, you may be able to pick up one of the remaining homes for a bit less than your neighbors paid.

■ Buy in a yet-to-be-built phase. In a large development, the builder often works on the project in discreet phases to avoid a patchwork of finished homes and raw land. By putting down a deposit on a later phase, you're helping the builder with long-term plans.

■ Buy a model home. When a development is near completion, the builder will accept offers on model homes. Be sure to evaluate the home as if it were previously occupied, bearing in mind that hundreds or thousands of people have traipsed though it.

■ SHOULD YOU BUY EARLY?

Early residents may have to deal with muddy roads, power outages, and the near-constant noise of construction while the rest of the development is completed. You're essentially moving into a construction site. Area services may not be fully in place in the early stages of a development. A large subdivision will eventually lure convenience stores, gas stations, and other services.

You may have a bit more leverage with the builder to have punch lists completed and repairs accomplished while the development is still under way. The developer doesn't want to have an unhappy homeowner spoil new sales. (If you are ready to go to war with the developer, you could consider putting a sign on your lawn inviting shoppers to ask you about the builder. Believe it or not, though, some developers put restrictive covenants in their deeds banning such signs—the ban may not stand up to a First Amendment challenge.) Finally, there is always the risk that a developer will go bankrupt, leaving uncompleted roads and unfinished homes.

■ EVALUATING A MODEL HOME

In theory, a model home will be built with the same components and in the same manner as new homes for sale. However, in most cases the model home was built before production homes were started. You can bet that the model home was very carefully checked for problems before it was opened to the public. Nevertheless, you should check the construction of the model home. If you find sloppy work here, you have little reason to expect that subsequent homes will be better built. If you can, visit homes that are under construction or that have been completed for actual buyers. If you have any doubts about the quality, bring along a knowledgeable friend or a home inspector on your tour.

FACTORY-BUILT HOUSING

When most of us envision the construction of a house, we think of what builders call a "stick-built" structure—one put together piece by piece by carpenters, roofers, and other tradespeople. The vast majority of homes are still built in that way, although an increasing number of structures are now assembled at least partly out of modules built elsewhere.

At the simplest level, you can expect to see things like prebuilt roof trusses, manufactured flooring joists, and panelized walls, including wallboard on the interior, insulation, and exterior plywood or particle board. The components arrive by truck and are fitted into place on the foundation and stick-built structural supports. In the most advanced form, virtually the entire house is built in sections in an indoor weatherproof factory. They are called **factory-built homes** or **modular homes.** Large modules include exterior and interior walls, flooring, ceilings, electrical wiring, and plumbing fixtures. Each of the modules is engineered to fit on a large flatbed truck for transport to the site. Homes are assembled from two to six or more modules.

Don't confuse modulars with **manufactured homes,** which have historically been known as **mobile homes.** Manufactured homes are built in compliance with the national HUD Code and are sometimes called HUD houses. They are usually simple structures of just one or two sections (a "double-wide"), and most are built on steel-frame trailers that remain in place under the house even if it is installed on a foundation. A factory-built home is built to comply with the generally more substantial Unified Building Code (UBC) or other national building codes that apply to stick-built homes.

Modulars are generally equal in quality of construction to stick-built homes and are sometimes built to even higher standards. In many cases the modular designs can be customized at the factory, and additional touches and trim can be installed at the home site. There are four significant advantages to putting to-gether a home with modules:

■ The cost of construction is usually less than that of a stick-built home, gener-ally 10 to 15 percent less expensive. The more customization on site, the less sav-ings. The homes are built on an assembly line, allowing efficient use of materials and labor. There are no delays because of bad weather, theft, or vandalism at the construction site.

■ In some respects the quality of a modular home can be superior to that of one built on site. Lumber and supplies are protected from the elements during con-struction, and tools and patterns can be held to finer tolerances in the factory. Some elements of structural design are sturdier in a module since it must be transported by truck and lifted in place on the site.

■ Modular homes can often be erected and be made ready for use in a matter of weeks, instead of six months to a year for a typical stick-built home.

■ In most cases it is much easier to maintain a tight grip on the budget with a modular home. The agreement with the factory sets a firm price for the con-struction of the modules and usually also includes the cost of delivery and in-stallation. The homeowner or the contractor handling the site work is responsible for preparing the land, putting into place a foundation that precisely matches the specifications set by the module maker, and connecting electrical, plumbing, telephone, and cable services to the attachment points of the mod-ules. Depending on the design, local contractors will install decks, porches, garages, and other add-ons. In theory, there is little reason for a cost overrun at the site.

One potential down side to modulars, though, is the limitation imposed by the dimensions of the building-block modules themselves. A home built from scratch can be built to virtually any dimensions, but manufactured homes get their length and width from the sizes of the modules. The typical width of a module is 14 to 18 feet. Modern computer designs allow modules to be stacked and offset to permit construction of complex two- and three-story homes.

In some parts of the nation, modular housing makes up a significant portion of new housing starts—nearly 25 percent of all new single-family homes in re-cent years. Done properly, a modular home should look no different than a stick-built equivalent.

BUYING A HOUSE FROM A CATALOG

In our modern economy, there is not much you can't buy from a catalog or, even more so, from an Internet Web site. You can buy clothing, food, appliances, hard-ware, cars, books . . . and houses. Before I go much further, I should point out that Sears, Roebuck and Company began selling building materials in their cat-alog in 1895, and by 1908 a reader could order an entire home by mail, with prices starting at about $695. The pieces, and a set of instructions, would arrive at the nearest railroad terminal. Today there are several national and regional

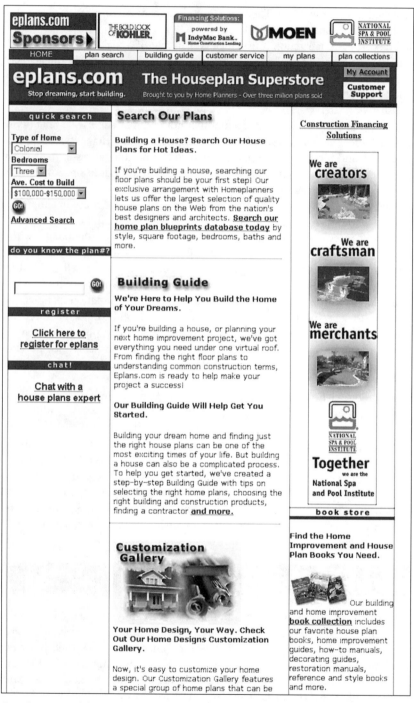

eplans.com
Sponsors

THE BOLD LOOK OF KOHLER.

Financing Solutions: powered by IndyMac Bank. Home Construction Lending

MOEN

NATIONAL SPA & POOL INSTITUTE

HOME | plan search | building guide | customer service | my plans | plan collections

eplans.com The Houseplan Superstore

Stop dreaming, start building. Brought to you by Home Planners - Over three million plans sold

My Account

Customer Support

quick search

Type of Home
Colonial

Bedrooms
Three

Ave. Cost to Build
$100,000-$150,000

GO!

Advanced Search

do you know the plan#?

GO!

register

Click here to register for eplans

chat!

Chat with a house plans expert

Search Our Plans

Building a House? Search Our House Plans for Hot Ideas.

If you're building a house, searching our floor plans should be your first step! Our exclusive arrangement with Homeplanners lets us offer the largest selection of quality house plans on the Web from the nation's best designers and architects. **Search our home plan blueprints database today** by style, square footage, bedrooms, baths and more.

Building Guide

We're Here to Help You Build the Home of Your Dreams.

If you're building a house, or planning your next home improvement project, we've got everything you need under one virtual roof. From finding the right floor plans to understanding common construction terms, Eplans.com is ready to help make your project a success!

Our Building Guide Will Help Get You Started.

Building your dream home and finding just the right house plans can be one of the most exciting times of your life. But building a house can also be a complicated process. To help you get started, we've created a step-by-step Building Guide with tips on selecting the right home plans, choosing the right building and construction products, finding a contractor **and more.**

Customization Gallery

Your Home Design, Your Way. Check Out Our Home Designs Customization Gallery.

Now, it's easy to customize your home design. Our Customization Gallery features a special group of home plans that can be

Construction Financing Solutions

We are **creators**

We are **craftsman**

We are **merchants**

NATIONAL SPA & POOL INSTITUTE

Together we are the **National Spa and Pool Institute**

book store

Find the Home Improvement and House Plan Books You Need.

Our building and home improvement **book collection** includes our favorite house plan books, home improvement guides, how-to manuals, decorating guides, restoration manuals, reference and style books and more.

At eplans.com, visitors can search a large database of available home plans and consult a building guide with tips on choosing land, selecting a plan, and hiring a builder. *Published by permission of Home Planners, LLC*

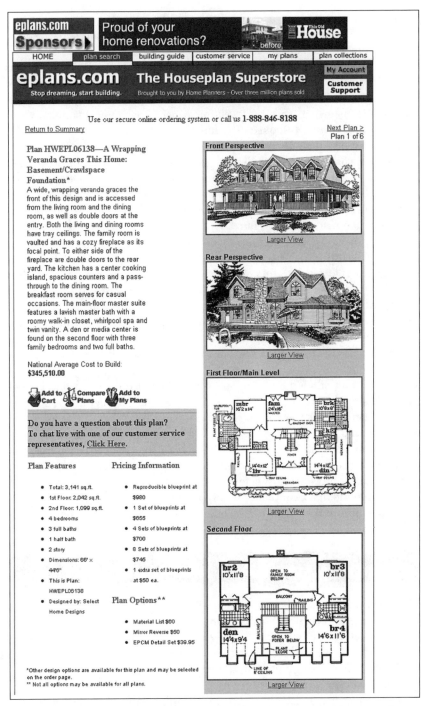

An example of an on-line display of a home design at eplans.com. Once you choose a plan you can order sets of blueprints and a list of materials. *Published by permission of Home Planners, LLC*

companies that sell plans, materials lists, and blueprints for construction of a wide range of home designs. You can select your home from a catalog available in bookstores or from a Web site.

Depending on the source, a building package of eight sets of blueprints plus a materials list sells for about $500 to $1,200. Some companies customize the materials list to include estimated costs for your region. Among the best are: **Creative Homeowner,** www.creativehomeowner.com; **Home Planners,** www.eplans.com; and **Sunset Books,** www.sunsetbooks.com.

Choosing the home design is the easy part. More complex is finding a buildable lot (see chapter 14) and finding a reputable contractor. The construction of a home from a set of plans requires a capable and experienced builder. As I suggested earlier in this chapter, seek advice from others who have worked with contractors and look for recommendations and warnings from area building associations and Better Business Bureaus.

Once you have found a group of possible contractors, meet with each of them, provide them with a copy of the construction plan and materials list, and ask for written formal bids for construction. Make sure you compare equivalent bids that include all of the components on the materials list and brand names and specifications for appliances and heating and cooling systems. You should expect that prices will be within a relatively narrow range. If one bid is much lower than others, you should ask for an explanation and check to see that nothing in the plans has been overlooked or that specifications have not been downgraded in quality.

Be very wary of a bid that proposes the job be billed on a cost-plus basis—generally a markup of the costs of materials and time for everyone working on the job. There is little way to control the final cost of such a process. Even on a fixed-price bid, you can expect to be billed for each and every change that is made during the course of construction. If you ask for a door to be moved or for an upgrade in quality of a component, insist that a change order be written up and that you approve the cost before work is done.

Keep in mind that a contractor is only as good as the subcontractors that will be used. Find out the names of major subcontractors and check the quality of their work.

TAKING POSSESSION OF A NEW HOME

As your new home is built, you should visit the site as often as possible to check that upgrades and changes have been installed as promised. When the home is near completion, the builder will set a closing date. You may want to consider hiring a home inspector to check the work. In any case, you should walk through the house before closing and create a "punch list" of work that needs to be completed.

The builder may finish off all remaining work before the closing or agree—in writing—to finish the items on the punch list in a reasonable period of time. In some contracts you—or an escrow agent—will be able to withhold a percentage of the purchase price until the job is completed. Typical items on a punch list include landscaping—the builder may want for adjacent homes to be completed before putting in lawns and trees—as well as some special-order items such as unusual lighting fixtures. Your bank or lending institution, though, is not likely to allow you to go to closing without all of the windows and flooring in place and critical appliances such as heating, cooling, and kitchen equipment installed. The possibility of having a punch list uncompleted at closing is one reason why you might want to have a real estate agent represent you in the purchase of the production home.

■ CLOSING DATE FOR NEW HOMES

It is generally very difficult to get a developer to commit to a particular completion date for new construction, especially in a subdivision. Very few builders have crews of their own, instead being dependent upon the work of various subcontractors. They are also subject to delays because of weather and problems with suppliers. If it is a buyer's market, you may be able to make your offer for a home under construction contingent upon completion within a window of sixty or ninety days. If the home is not ready, you would be able to withdraw the offer and receive a refund of your deposit.

PART VI
CONDOS, CO-OPS, AND TIME-SHARES

CHAPTER SIXTEEN

CONDOMINIUMS AND CO-OPS

EARLIER IN THIS BOOK I extolled the benefits of owning your own piece of earth and the structure that stands upon it. For many it's the American Dream, but for others the thought of mowing the lawn, painting the eaves, and maintaining the furnace is a nightmare. It is possible to have it both ways: to own your own property at the same time as you avoid full responsibility. The most common solutions are condominiums and cooperatives.

BUYING A CONDOMINIUM

The concept of a condominium refers to the theory of ownership, not the physical design of the high-rise, town house, or other structure. Participants in a condo agreement do not individually own the apartment or unit where they live. In essence, they own—with a deed—the air space within the walls, ceiling, and floor. The physical structure is instead commonly owned by all of the residents. This includes the walls, floors, and roof, as well as heating, cooling, and plumbing facilities; elevators and stairs; lobbies; and land. In addition to any mortgage and real estate expenses for their living space, residents are assessed a monthly or annual fee for maintenance, repair, and insurance for the commonly owned property. Owners typically are billed for real estate taxes by the municipality.

Be sure you understand the assessment process. Larger units or those with special features should be asked to bear a larger portion of the maintenance fee than smaller units, for example. Find out how much of the assessment goes to a manager or management company.

In some cases, finding a loan for a condominium can be trickier than doing the same for a home. To begin with, lenders often include maintenance fees in their calculation of an allowable loan amount, which could result in a lower loan. And some banks and lending institutions may not want to make a condominium loan for a structure that is not 70 percent or more sold. If you are considering moving to a complex that has just recently begun the process of becoming a condominium (or a new structure built specifically for such a plan), you may need to seek special financing. Some builders or management companies will arrange short-term or long-term financing during this early period.

BUYING INTO A COOPERATIVE

A cooperative is similar to a condominium except that residents don't own real estate. Instead, they purchase shares in a corporation that owns the building. The shares allow them to lease a unit from the corporation. The lease typically includes maintenance, repairs, and property taxes. In most cases the shares can be resold to the corporation or directly to a new buyer, and therefore they can appreciate in value just as an actual piece of real estate might. Because the corporation pays real estate taxes on the building, that expense is passed along in the monthly payment.

Cooperatives usually have boards made up of residents who are charged with screening potential residents to make sure they meet financial and other criteria. They are not supposed to discriminate on the basis of race or religion, although such bias is hard to prove. The boards, though, can reject an individual or a family if it is felt there is not a good fit of personality or character.

Not all banks or lending institutions will make loans for cooperative shares, and some boards require that applicants pay cash from their own resources, which is one way to ensure a certain type of resident lives there.

Cooperatives are not all that common across the country but exist in large numbers in some big cities, including New York, Washington, D.C., and Chicago.

■ ADVANTAGES OF CONDOS AND CO-OPS

In most cases the purchase price of a condo or co-op is less than buying a home with the same amenities, location, and view. (The trade-off, though, is that even in a market where individual homes are increasing in value there is no guarantee that a condo deed or the shares of a co-op will rise at the same rate or be easily sold.) The primary advantage of buying a condominium or a co-op is that it relieves you of much of the upkeep involved in owning a home. The homeowners association or co-op board arranges for mowing the lawn, repairing the roof, and—depending on the design of the structure—maintaining the heating, cooling, and hot-water systems. Condos or co-ops may have swimming pools, docks, health clubs, and other amenities owned in common.

■ DISADVANTAGES OF CONDOS AND CO-OPS

For most people the primary disadvantage of a condo or co-op is the loss of privacy and some elements of lifestyle involved in common ownership. You will be sharing exterior walls and sometimes floors, ceilings, lobbies, hallways, and extra structures with others—as you would if you rented an apartment. And depending on the homeowners association or co-op board, you may face limitations on how you can use your home. You may not be able to have pets or children as residents or visitors, and you may not be able to make permanent changes to the interior and exterior of your unit.

Be sure to read the by-laws and deed restrictions of a condominium or co-op before you consider buying there. As a new resident, you should not expect to be able to change the rules or seek an exception to them. And like it or not, many co-op boards require all new residents be approved by all current residents or by a substantial majority.

You may find that financing for a condominium or co-op may be more difficult to obtain, more expensive, or require a larger down payment. Expensive and highly exclusive co-ops may require buyers to put down most or all of the purchase price in cash. And there may be limitations on your ability to resell the unit.

Finally, the owners of a condominium or participants in a co-op are jointly responsible for major upkeep of the structure and amenities. The charges need to pay for insurance as well as maintain a fund for projects such as replacing the roof and repairing shared heating, cooling, plumbing, and electrical systems. Depending on the structure, the association or board may have to pay for major repairs such as elevators, pumps, and expensive equipment related to swimming pools and health clubs. Brand-new condominiums or co-ops may expect fewer maintenance costs at the onset but may be less experienced in budgeting for ongoing costs and major repairs.

It is worthwhile to request a copy of the most recent financial statement of the homeowners association or co-op board. Check to see if the group is in debt because of previous expenditures. You'll want to know if you are going to be asked to help pay off expenses already incurred.

■ TAX CONSIDERATIONS OF A CO-OP SHARE

In most states a co-op board pays property taxes and manages a "blanket" mortgage for the whole building or development. As such, shareholders in the co-op may not be able to deduct the cost of taxes and mortgage interest from their personal tax returns. There is a way, though, for boards to structure their shareholder agreement in a way that allows residents to deduct that portion of their payment that goes for property taxes and interest. Consult your tax advisor to see if the board has done so.

TOWN HOUSES AND DUPLEX DEVELOPMENTS

Another form of home ownership grew up in some inner cities and has been transplanted to suburbs. Town house developments allow residents to own their home but share walls and sometimes roofs and basements in common. The concept grew out of the row houses and brownstones of New York (and London).

The deed to such a home spells out the individual and joint obligations of owners who share parts of a structure. In some developments homeowners must join or take part in an association to share the costs of repair to common structures. In some plans the association takes care of landscaping and exterior maintenance.

CHAPTER SEVENTEEN

VACATION HOMES AND TIME-SHARES

LOCATION IS EVEN MORE IMPORTANT in a vacation home, which is typically sold to fulfill someone's dream—not the mere necessity to have a roof overhead. A home on the lake is much more attractive (and expensive) than one across the road. A place on the golf course or the ski trail is prime real estate, while one that requires you to drag your clubs or your skis from the parking lot is not.

In some parts of the country vacation homes are attractive year-round. Elsewhere, they are mostly used seasonally, such as at a ski resort, a golf course, or a summer community. You'll get the most utility, and the best appreciation on your investment, with a home in a multiseason resort. For example, many ski hills promote themselves as golf and tennis resorts in the summer.

YOU'VE GOT TO KNOW THE TERRITORY

When you move to a town, you should spend the time to investigate the local economy and government to make certain you are coming into a stable community or one on the upswing. You don't want to buy property at the peak of its value and watch its worth tumble. The same applies with vacation property: If you are buying a home at a resort, you should investigate the financial condition of the business. A beautiful home along the fairway of a bankrupt golf course or on the trail of a shuttered ski resort will hold little value.

Be sure you understand the long-term plans at a resort community. Is the resort completely built out, meaning there are no plans (or better, there is no more available land) for more homes? Are there plans to construct a huge expansion of homes at the resort, greatly expanding the competition when it comes to resale? Are there plans for a new resort 10 miles up the road? Will this increase values at the older community or reduce them?

■ TAXES ON VACATION PROPERTY

Be sure to consult with your tax advisor about the deductibility of interest costs and property taxes on the mortgage for a vacation home. If you buy the home entirely for your own use or rent it out for only a few weeks a year, the expenses are generally deductible. If you rent out the home for a substantial part of the year, you'll need to work with your advisor to come up with a tax strategy that balances the income against expenses.

If your vacation home is a second home, one you use just for yourself and never rent out, the IRS lets you deduct interest and property taxes just as you do on your principal dwelling—up to a point. (If you have the income—and tax liability to support it—a second home can even be a motor home or a boat with living and sleeping quarters. Interest on a boat loan is not deductible if you are subject to the alternative minimum tax.) The tax break applies only to a first and second home, and only on the first $1 million of mortgaged debt. Property taxes are deductible on all homes you may own. There are a few other wrinkles worth discussing with your tax advisor. For example, prepaid points on a mortgage for a vacation home are not fully deductible in the year paid, but instead are apportioned over the full term of the loan.

A vacation house is still considered a personal residence if you use it yourself (or if it's used by family members or by others in a non-cash swap or donation) for at least fourteen days or 10 percent of the total number of days it is rented each year. If you rent the house for fourteen days or less per year, the proceeds are tax-free. If you rent for more than fourteen days, you must report rental income to the IRS, but you also qualify to deduct rental expenses from the income.

The distinction between personal use and rental use becomes important when it comes to accounting for losses incurred. Active owners involved in managing the property, dealing with tenants, and overseeing maintenance are operating a business, and a proportion of the losses can be deducted from your income. The higher your income, the less you can write off. If you're not in the business of renting vacation property, any losses are considered "passive." These year-to-year losses can be used to offset any profit you receive when you resell the property, or as an offset against other income.

TIME-SHARES AND FRACTIONAL OWNERSHIP

One of the more popular vacation trends in recent years has been time-sharing or fractional ownership of a property, in which you buy the right to use a home for a specified portion of the year or a certain number of weeks. The idea—to buy just enough of a vacation home to meet your needs—is appealing. Salespeople will make all sorts of attractive pitches, comparing the price of ownership to the cost of renting a motel room and all but promising appreciation on your investment. A word of warning, though: Not every time-share resort works out to be a good investment. Many owners find that it is very difficult to resell their ownership or are offered prices well below what they paid for their share.

The difference between a fractional ownership and a time-share is summed up in the names. Fractional buyers own a physical share in a home, while time-share buyers own a block of time. Under a time-share you may not use the same unit or home in a development each time you visit. A fractional ownership generally passes along interest costs and property taxes to the owner as a deductible expense; time-shares generally do not.

Under fractional ownership, buyers own calendar shares—quarter (thirteen weeks), tenth (five weeks), and the like. There are various schemes, including a fixed schedule each year and schedules that vary from year to year. A quarter share may require you to use all thirteen weeks in a row or be split into a few weeks each season. Buyers are able to use the weeks themselves, rent them to others (sometimes with the assistance of the management company, which will charge a fee), or trade the week for a week at another time-share or fractional ownership resort.

A fixed-week ownership gives you the right to use, trade, or rent a specific week and unit. A floating or flex ownership gives you a deed to a specific week and unit, but you will need to request particular weeks of use each year. A fixed week would be more valuable at a ski resort, where you want to make certain you get to visit while there is snow on the hill, or at a summer resort, for which you would need to coordinate school vacations. Floating weeks are appealing to people who find it difficult to commit to time off every year at the same time.

Time-shares are typically sold in periods as short as one week. Buyers are offered both fixed and floating weeks. At many resorts, buyers are not promised a specific unit in a development.

Under either scheme, owners are required to pay a proportionate share of maintenance and repair costs. And if you ask the management company to rent out the unit or clean up after a tenant, you will have to pay for that service.

Finally, there is the matter of how to buy a time-share or fractional ownership property. When first opened to the public, shares are usually sold directly by the developer, with most units and periods sold at list price. Early buyers may get to choose the exact unit and time period they want, but they will also be called upon to pay the construction and marketing costs of the developer. Once most of the units have been sold, prices are set by supply and demand on the resale market—prices may be above or below those paid earlier.

As I said in the introduction to this section, salespeople for the developer will all but promise appreciation on your investment. In truth, that is not always the case. Unless a development is especially attractive—with demand exceeding supply—time-shares and fractional ownerships often resell at a significant discount from their original price. All you need to do is to check with real estate agents who specialize in resale of time-shares. Once a development has been open for a few years, in most areas you'll find a pretty good selection of time-share or fractional ownership resales. There are also Internet Web sites that post offerings. At one place I visited, a huge billboard sat just outside the gates of the development advertising shares for resale.

In some cases, buyers of units directly from the developer receive perks, such as membership in an "awards" program shared by multiple sites. Buyers of resale units may be excluded. You'll have to assess the value of any special offer from the developer versus the generally lower prices on the resale market.

PART VII
GOING TO CLOSING

CHAPTER EIGHTEEN

CLOSING THE DEAL

I'VE BEEN TO ENOUGH CLOSINGS in my life to anticipate the universal advice given by the attorneys and real estate agents: bring a pen, proof of your identity, and your checkbook. But to that list I've learned to add one more thing: bring an understanding of the process. The closing is an orchestrated orgy of paper passing, notarized signatures, and exchange of checks between and among the buyer, seller, attorneys, title insurance companies, and real estate agents. Nothing you see at the closing should be a complete surprise to you. Lenders are required to give you a copy of a detailed Good Faith Estimate of closing costs within three days after you apply for a loan, and you can request an updated version of the form a few days before the actual closing. (For an example of a blank Good Faith Estimate form, see appendix H.)

Examine the estimate carefully, checking the numbers against your own notes and expectations. If you have any questions about the figures and costs, do not hesitate to call your attorney if you are using one for the closing, your real estate agent, or the lending institution. The best time to raise questions is *before* you are seated at the desk with a stack of papers in front of you and a room full of lawyers and lenders. Even at the closing, don't sign anything you don't understand—ask for an explanation. And never sign an incompletely filled-out form, missing such things as a date or the name or names of parties to the agreement.

As part of a closing you'll be asked to confirm some of the information you first provided on your application, and you may be asked to allow the lender to check with the IRS to verify your recent tax filings. The lender and its agents are within their rights to check anything and everything you have claimed on your application, including your tax filings, employment records, and investments. But as the borrower you should make sure that any papers you sign that permit the lender to check on your personal data is appropriate to your application, is limited in time, and provides proper protection to your privacy. If the beginning or ending date on a form is blank or extends out for more than a few months, or if the names of the parties given permission to check up on you are missing or include a company or individual not known to you, it's time to raise the red flag.

If you've hired an attorney to represent you at the closing, seek advice. Similarly, if your real estate agent is at the table, ask for help—keeping in mind the fact that the agent is primarily there to pick up a commission check and wants the closing to happen without a hitch. In most cases the seller will deal with your objections and fix the forms to your satisfaction. Again, at this point in the process he wants the closing to happen. But if he refuses, you may have to decide whether to stick to your position or cave. One halfway measure: If the representative of the lender makes any oral statements about how the form will be used ("We left out the name on the form because we will be reselling the mortgage immediately. We can notify you of the name and send you the amended form within ten days."), ask for the same promise in writing.

UNDERSTANDING CLOSING FEES

Here are some of the charges you can expect to see on a closing statement. In the following, the numbers before the names of the fees refer to HUD's codes used on a Good Faith Estimate (see appendix H). Some estimates may use slightly different language to describe the charges.

■ 800: ITEMS PAYABLE IN CONNECTION WITH LOANS

801: Origination Fee. Some lenders tack on an origination fee of as much as one point to pay commissions to their own sales staff or a mortgage broker. However, the origination fee is nothing more than additional profit on the loan. (A mortgage company principally makes its money on the interest it collects.) If the loan was brought in by a mortgage broker, that person or company may make its profit exclusively from an origination fee paid by the lender. (A loan origination fee is not the same as prepaid interest and is not tax-deductible.) The lender might try to justify this charge by pointing to the cost of the services provided, the fancy leather chairs in the office, and the television and Internet advertising that brought you to that lender. In any case, there is no reason not to ask for a reduction in a loan origination fee or to look for a lender that does not add it to the cost of closing.

802: Discount Fee (Points). This is a fee paid to the lender to increase its immediate profit on the loan or as a commission to a mortgage broker. Each point is equivalent to 1 percent of the amount of the loan. For example, if the lender charges 1.875 points on a $200,000 loan, you would have to pay $3,750. As a rough estimate, you can figure that each prepaid point should reduce the interest rate on a thirty-year, fixed-rate mortgage by one-eighth of a percent. When the annual percentage rate (APR) is calculated for a loan, the cost of the points is included for the first year—or the full term of the loan if the points are financed—increasing the interest rate over the nominal or stated interest rate.

Prepaid interest for purchase of a home is deductible in the tax year in which it was paid, while prepaid interest on a refinanced mortgage must be spread over the entire term of the loan.

803: Appraisal Fee. A lending institution will generally require that the current fair market value of your home be determined by an independent appraiser or someone on its own staff.

804: Credit Report. The lender will pay a fee to one of the national credit reporting services to check on outstanding loans and obligations and your history in repaying previous mortgages and other loans. The charge may be due at closing or up front in a loan application fee.

805: Lender's Inspection Fee. Usually associated with new construction, this pays the expenses of sending a representative of the lender to check the new home to see that it has essentials such as flooring, roofing, and certain utilities and appliances. Other inspections for pest infestation, radon, and other hazards are covered under line 1302.

807: Assumption Fee. If the mortgage is permitted to be assumed by a new borrower, the lender may be entitled to a fee to cover the cost of the paperwork. Check the language included in the existing mortgage.

808: Mortgage Broker Fee. If an independent mortgage broker is involved in the process, her fee is listed here if one is due at closing.

810: Tax-Related Service Fee. The buyer is usually charged for work performed to change tax records from the original owner's name.

811: Loan Application Fee. This charge may bundle together fees for essential services such as obtaining a credit report, an appraisal, and an inspection—and includes a bit of pure profit. Some lenders may bill individually for these services, and it may be required that the charges be paid at the time of applying for the mortgage. You should ask for an itemization of fees and look for ways to save. For example, you can offer to pick up documents or have them mailed to you rather than paying for couriers or overnight service.

■ 900: ITEMS REQUIRED BY LENDER TO BE PAID IN ADVANCE

901: Interest from ___ to ___ days at $___. The borrower is usually required to pay the cost of interest from the date of closing until the first regularly scheduled monthly payment is due. Nearly all mortgages in the United States have payment due dates of the first of the month, and interest payments are calculated in arrears, based on the previous month. For example, if you close your loan on April 15, your first mortgage payment will be due on June 1 and will cover interest costs for the month of May. At closing, though, you'll have to pay the interest cost on the loan from April 15 through April 30. If you don't need to move immediately, you should attempt to adjust the closing date as close to your needs as the seller and the bank will allow.

902: Mortgage Insurance Premium. Depending on the type of loan and the down payment, a lending institution may require the borrower to purchase and maintain mortgage insurance. This policy benefits only the lender, ensuring that it will be paid if the borrower defaults on the loan. You may see this abbreviated as MIP (Mortgage Insurance Premium) on a conventional loan or MMI (Mutual Mortgage Insurance) for government plans.

Mortgage insurance is usually required if the down payment is low, usually less than 20 percent. Certain government-backed loan programs also require the insurance, which typically adds about 0.25 to 0.5 percent to the interest rate. If you are required to have mortgage insurance, be sure to find out the equity level at which it is no longer required and cancel the coverage once your monthly payments have raised your interest in the home to that percentage. The premium may be a lump sum for the entire life of the loan or collected annually.

903: Hazard Insurance Premium. Borrowers are required to protect the lender's interest against loss. Depending on the lender, the borrower will either have to bring evidence of a paid-up first year's policy or purchase such a policy through the lender at closing. It is almost always considerably less expensive to provide your own insurance. Your insurance agent should assist you in selecting a level of coverage that protects you as well as the lender.

904: County Property Taxes. In some localities, the lender will require payment of local property taxes at closing or evidence that you have done so on your own.

905: Flood Insurance. If the lender requires the purchase of flood insurance, you will need to bring evidence of a paid-up policy or purchase it through the lender.

■ 1000: RESERVES DEPOSITED WITH LENDER

Depending on local custom or regulation, you may be required to pay in advance the cost of homeowners insurance, mortgage insurance, assessments for local government or homeowners associations, and local property taxes. The funds are accumulated as escrows or impounds by the lending institution and then paid directly to the insurance company or taxing authority on your behalf. The lender is looking out to protect its own interests, making sure that insurance is in place and that taxes are current. Some lenders have more stringent requirements for loans with a lower down payment, on the theory that homeowners with little or no equity in a home may be more likely to walk away from their obligation in the event of financial difficulty.

Watch out for an excessive requirement for the impound. Add the annual cost of insurance and the expected property tax. Your monthly payment to the escrow account should be about one-twelfth of the total. The initial deposit is usually two months' worth of payments.

1001: Hazard Insurance. _____ mo. at $_____ per month.

1002: Mortgage Insurance. _____ mo. at $_____ per month.

1004: Tax and Assessments. _____ mo. at $_____ per month.

1006: Flood Insurance.

■ 1100: TITLE CHARGES

1101: Closing or Escrow Fee. Depending on local custom, an attorney or a real estate broker may be chosen to hold on to all payments—from the borrower to the lender for charges, from the lender to the seller for closing, and from the borrower or lender to various providers of services related to the transaction—until the closing is completed. In some parts of the country—principally the West and Midwest—lenders use the services of an independent escrow company, which typically extracts a fee for its presence at the closing. If there is a fee listed here, be sure it is reasonable for the service provided. You may be able to arrange for a different escrow company or agent at a lower cost.

1102: Abstract or Title search. The cost of uncovering all extant titles and transfers on a piece of property may be listed as a separate charge or included within the cost of title insurance.

1103: Title Examination. Similarly, the cost of having an attorney or other expert check available titles for defaults and other problems may be listed as a separate charge or included within the cost of title insurance or attorney's fee.

1105: Document Preparation Fee. In addition to paying an attorney, you'll also likely be charged for the preparation of the stack of documents necessary for the closing. Many years ago this might have required a day of typing and calculating, but today the documents zip out of a computer after a few keystrokes. In any case, this is somewhat like being charged for the cost of printing out a receipt for your purchases at the supermarket—it's a cost of doing business, and it's all there on the computer anyway. It is not at all unreasonable to ask for this charge to be removed. You won't be the first to ask, and you just might get what you asked for.

1106: Notary Fee. A notary is legally licensed to swear that she witnessed a particular person sign a document. There are notaries in nearly every lawyer's office and bank. Unless a notary has to be brought in from outside, there is no excuse other than corporate greed for a charge to be levied here. You should bring a passport, photo ID, driver's license, or other government-issued identification to prove you are the person signing the document.

1107: Attorney Fees. Most lenders will require you to pay for the services of a real estate lawyer to protect its interests in the closing. Under some agreements, the seller will pay for attorney's fees. Depending on local custom, regulation, or your preference, you may want or need to hire an attorney of your own.

1108: Title Insurance. This is a one-time policy that protects the lender against most defects in the title, including liens, that have not been disclosed by the seller and previous owners. Depending on state law or custom, the policy may be the responsibility of the seller or the buyer. The buyer can also purchase a title insurance policy to protect against loss up to the full value of the home, including down payments and accumulated equity. It may be possible to lower the cost of title insurance a bit if the previous owner has only held the title for a short time and no claims were made against the title since the last time a search was performed. In this case, a company may be willing to quote a reissue rate.

Another way you may be able to reduce the premium is to use the same title insurance company for the policy that protects the buyer and the lender. Some companies are willing to reduce the cost because only one search need to be performed for both policies. The separate costs of the lender's and buyer's policies are sometimes listed under items 1109 and 1110.

■ 1200: GOVERNMENT RECORDING AND TRANSFER CHARGES

Depending on the locality, there are usually a number of fees associated with transferring and recording a deed. The buyer may also have to purchase city, county, or state tax stamps. Under some sales agreements, the seller agrees to pay these charges.

1201: Recording Fees. This is a fee for the process of recording documents at municipal, county, state, or federal offices to indicate that a mortgage has been paid off or initiated, a deed modified, and other necessary paperwork. The fees are charged to the party on whose behalf the work was done, meaning that both buyer and seller will incur expenses here.

1202: City/County Tax/Stamps. Included here are charges for recording the deed, new mortgage, and mortgage release for the previous loan.

1203: State Tax/Stamps. Some states levy similar charges for deeds and mortgages, as well as other charges to cover a municipal lien certificate that shows that all previous tax and assessment obligations have been paid.

1204: Intangible Tax. In some states and localities, residents must pay a tax on intangible property—ordinarily defined as stocks, bonds, and interests in limited partnerships, but in some states also including promissory notes and mortgages. Consult an attorney and tax advisor with any questions about charges here.

■ 1300: ADDITIONAL SETTLEMENT CHARGES

1301: Survey. The lender often requires that a surveyor check the property to make sure that the home meets local zoning requirements for things like percentage of land cover, setbacks, and side yards. A survey may also discover that a neighbor's driveway is on your property or that the fence on your property encroaches on another's land. The fee is usually paid by the buyer, although in some cases the seller agrees to pay this charge.

1302: Pest/Termite Inspection. Most lenders will require that a qualified inspector check the home for signs of infestation by termites, rodents, or other pests. Some inspectors also check for wood rot and water damage at the same time. Depending on local custom or regulation, the fee may be paid by the seller or the buyer.

1303/1304/1305: Other Inspections. Depending on the area, some closings include the cost of inspections for lead paint, radon, formaldehyde insulation, and other hazards. The seller may agree to pay for these inspections.

NEGOTIATING CLOSING COSTS

Let's back up a bit and consider a way to save some money when you are applying for a mortgage in the first place. After you've negotiated the purchase price of a home, save a little bit of energy and time to work on reducing some of the costs of closing. Almost every element of the closing costs is subject to negotiation. We've already explored such things as seeking a better interest rate or reducing prepaid points—a pair of interlinked elements of the mortgage itself.

Once you've decided on the terms of the mortgage, discuss the closing costs themselves: things like attorney's fees, title insurance, appraisals, inspections, document preparation, and the like. If you see a cost that seems out of line, ask for a justification. In times when there are more loans than applicants, the lender may be willing to remove or lower some charges to get your business. Make your requests for a better deal on closing costs *before* you sign your mortgage application and hand over the application fee. Your leverage is greatest before the bank begins the process of verifying your application and seeking underwriting approval.

When you compare the monthly payments, interest rates and prepaid points of various lenders, you should also find out the estimated closing costs charged by each. Get as much detail as possible. Some lenders will give you a copy of a typical Good Faith Estimate of closing costs even before you apply for a loan.

Here are some areas where you may be able to get the lender to reduce closing costs:

- **Application fee.** This is nothing more than additional profit to the lender for something that is an ordinary cost of business. If other lending institutions in town (or over the Internet) do not charge a fee for making an application, bring this to the attention of the officer you are dealing with and ask for a reduction or elimination of the fee.

- **Underwriting fee.** This is another charge for ordinary business expenses. Ask for a reduction if the fee is out of line with costs at another lender.

- **Appraisal.** In most situations the lender will hire a qualified real estate appraiser to come up with an estimate of the market value of the home. A lender doesn't want to (knowingly) issue a loan for more than the expected current resale value of the home, or for more than a particular loan-to-value ratio. The appraiser works for the lending company, but in most cases you'll get the bill. Rates for appraisals, typically about $150 to $400, vary by location and the type of home. If you think the price is out of line (check out the costs listed by other lenders and ask your real estate agent to help you compare charges), ask for a reduction and make it clear to the lender that you are aware that other institutions charge less for this service.

- **Attorney's fee.** The lending company is likely to hire an attorney to look after its interests at closing. Remember that this lawyer does not represent you. In most cases the lender will charge you for the attorney's fee, sometimes $1,000 or more. Ask for a justification of this charge, and include the cost in your comparison among companies.

In some cases you may be able to reduce the attorney's fees by agreeing to pick up and deliver certain documents rather than paying for overnight delivery or courier service. You may also be able to reduce the cost by scheduling the closing at the attorney's office rather than at a location more convenient to you.

If you hire your own attorney to represent your interests—a good idea, but not all that common in every part of the country—expect to pay that lawyer a fee in the range of about $500 to $1,000.

- **Document preparation.** In addition to the fee for the attorney (and bear in mind that much of the work is probably done by secretaries and paralegals), you may be charged for the preparation of the legal documents for the closing.

This may have made sense twenty years or more ago when the primary office tool was a typewriter, but in this modern age of computers, the preparation of documents is a push-button operation. Ask for a reduction or elimination of this charge.

■ NO-CLOSING-COST LOANS

Some high-volume mortgage institutions promote "no closing cost" loans. If they absorb the cost of closing, and the interest rate and points are equal to or better than the loans offered by another institution, you are ahead of the game. If they add to the prepaid points or boost the interest rate to cover the cost of closing, this is generally a bad deal. Boosting the points merely transfers the cost from one place to another, while even a very small increase in interest rates will cost many thousands of dollars more than the original closing costs.

Even a so-called no-closing-cost loan may actually be a no-lender-fee mortgage. Under such a program, the lender does not charge fees for application, underwriting, commitment, document preparation, and the like but does pass along charges for appraisal, title insurance, and mortgage recording fees.

TITLE INSURANCE

Do you really own the land that lies beneath your dream house? Yes, the seller presented you with a deed, and the town clerk is willing to accept the transfer of the property from the previous owner to you. But are you certain that every transfer of the land, going all the way back in some cases to colonial days, was properly performed? Has there ever been a lien filed against a previous owner that was not properly paid off? Are you aware of every claim to access of the property by utilities or government agencies?

Chances are your purchase or sale of property will proceed completely without hitch. Your attorney will check town or city records as part of the drafting of a deed, and recent liens and claims should be listed there. But the remote chance that a dusty claim or an as yet undiscovered error or fraud could invalidate ownership of property is something that should scare anyone about to go into hundreds of thousands of dollars of debt. And the bank holding your mortgage will simply not stand for any uncertainty about the security of its interest in the land.

The solution is something called title insurance, a policy that protects against financial loss because of defects, forgery, missing heirs, and recorded liens or encumbrances on the land. Title insurance companies arrange for their own search of the history of the land and issue a policy that indemnifies the buyer (and the lending company or bank). Certain issues are not protected in a standard title insurance policy, such as unrecorded easements or liens, unrecorded utility rights of way, public or private roads, community driveways, and other types of encumbrances.

The lender will require you to purchase a policy protecting it from loss because of an unforeseen claim that disputes the legality of the transfer of the property. (You may want to purchase your own policy to protect whatever down payment and equity you hold in the property.) Although the lending institution or its lawyers may have a favorite title insurance company—and may receive commissions or other payments for delivering business to it—you may be able to find a better deal on insurance through another company. Again, check with other lenders to determine their customary charges for title insurance and ask your real estate agent or your own lawyer for advice. You should also be able to save on your own title insurance by piggy-backing on the lender's policy, saving the cost of a separate search of the title. The lending institution's attorney should be able to assist you here.

Policies are available to protect owners, purchasers, and mortgage issuers. Each party generally needs its own policy, although you as the purchaser may be required to pay for your own as well as one for the lender.

Title insurance will remain in effect for as long as the ownership does not change again, and a single premium is collected at the time the policy is first issued. If you refinance or otherwise make changes to your ownership of the land, you'll need to start over with a fresh title insurance policy.

Much less valuable is a certificate of title issued by a lawyer who has researched the history of a piece of property, including the chain of ownership, easements, wills, and anything else that affects its provenance. The lawyer can produce an abstract and opinion about the validity of the title. This is good information to know, but it is by no means a guarantee that there will not be a challenge to your ownership.

TAKING TITLE

When you buy a house and property, you take the old name off the deed and put yours in its place, right? How complicated can that be? Well, consider a few of these very real possibilities:

■ The old title might be based on less-than-permanent markers like river banks, trees, and old structures long gone. Which cherry tree marks the southern boundary?

■ A single woman offers a home for sale, but the title shows the home was purchased with her former husband. Does she have the right to sell the home?

■ A divorced man sells a house but neglects to tell you that his former wife is contesting his right to the proceeds.

■ The children are selling the house, but their parents' names still appear on the title. Is there a will that properly describes how they wanted the home disposed of?

■ A disgruntled contractor gave up trying to collect money from the former owner, his former clients, but not without filing a workmans or mechanics lien on the home. As the new owner, are you now responsible for payment?

■ The former owner is several years overdue on back taxes, and the IRS has a lien on the property. How will this affect your claim to ownership?

- The surveyor finds that a shed sits too close to the property line to meet the local building code, or a fence installed by a neighbor actually sits on the property of the home you're ready to buy.
- The current owner expanded the house without seeking approval from the building department, resulting in a structure that takes up too much of the available acreage. Also, the new bathroom violates the town's restrictions on sewer use. Does this matter?

Like it or not, the answer to all of these questions involves the services of a real estate attorney and, in most cases, a title insurance company. If you are buying a piece of property directly from the seller, be sure to hire your own attorney to examine the proposed new title. If you are buying through a mortgage, the lender's attorney will examine the title with an eye on protecting the lender's interests. The best way to protect yourself is to hire your own attorney.

■ TYPES OF DEEDS

Depending on local custom and law, your property may come with one of several different types of deeds. Be sure you understand the type used in the transfer, and enlist your attorney if you need an explanation. The following are the types of deeds:

- **Mortgage deed or deed of trust.** A lender will ask for this type of deed, which gives it an interest in the property until the loan is paid off.
- **Warranty deed.** This is a promise by the seller to protect the buyer against any future claims over ownership of the property.
- **Quitclaim deed.** This is a document signed by the seller and any other parties in which they release any rights they have to the property. This does not protect from claims from others, though.
- **Owner's affidavit.** This is a sworn statement by the seller that there are no problems with the title or outstanding liens. The document does not protect against claims, although the signatory to the affidavit could be held liable in a lawsuit.

■ IN WHOSE NAME?

If you're buying a home by yourself, you'll most likely list the ownership of your home in your name. If you're married or otherwise buying a home with another person, the legal phrasing of the title becomes a bit more complex. Be sure to seek the advice of a real estate attorney or a licensed real estate broker if you have any questions about the manner in which the title of your property will be held.

The most common form of joint ownership for a married couple is joint tenancy with the right of survivorship or tenancy by the entirety. The two forms are similar. In either case, if one owner dies, the other is automatically granted ownership of the property without the need to go through probate. If the home or the overall estate is especially valuable, a tax or estate attorney may suggest that the home be titled in just the husband's or wife's name. A lender, though, might balk at this if earnings to support the mortgage are coming from the other spouse.

If you are buying a property with someone who is not your legal spouse, in some states the title can be set up as joint tenancy, with the property automatically passing to the partner in the event of death. Another form of title is tenancy in common, which divides ownership in a property according to an agreement between the parties; one or the other tenant can sell or otherwise dispose of an interest in the property. In the event of death, the disposition of one person's interest is dictated by the terms of a will, or absent a will, according to state law.

Another solution, one that works well with unmarried partners as well as those who jointly own a property as an investment, is to create a partnership that will take the title. The investors own the partnership and have an agreement that covers their right to sell their interest and the disposition of their ownership shares in the event of death. It is important to include a provision that allows one or another partner to withdraw from the deal. Contracts generally require the partner to offer the shares to the other participants in the partnership first.

PART VIII

INSURING YOUR HOME

CHAPTER NINETEEN

HOME INSURANCE AND HOME WARRANTIES

THERE'S NOT REALLY MUCH OF A CHOICE as to whether you *need* insurance for your home. First of all, if you take out a mortgage, the lender (who in effect owns the home until you finish paying off the loan) will require that you protect it against the loss of its interest in the home. If the home is worth $300,000 and your outstanding balance on the mortgage is $125,000, in theory you only need to insure for $125,000.

Note, too, that except in very unusual circumstances you need to cover only the cost of structures. The land itself does not need to be insured since it is not expected to go away. (Possible exceptions include land along ocean shores or in known active slide or earthquake zones.)

Most importantly, you owe it to yourself to protect your large investment in your home. Fires, floods, explosions, and other unhappy events do occur, and this is not a case where self-insurance makes sense. You also need to consider protecting any unusual possessions you have: an irreplaceable stamp collection, jewelry, artworks, and the like. The liability you have as a homeowner also needs to be considered. What happens if your dog bites a neighbor, the FedEx guy trips over your kid's bike in the driveway, or someone falls into your pool?

So, the real questions are not *whether*, but instead *what kind* and *how much?*

THE LENDER'S REQUIREMENTS

Because the lender requires that its interest in your home be fully protected from loss, it will be listed on your insurance policy as having an interest in the property. In most cases, if you fail to make payments on the insurance policy, the lender will be notified and you will receive a notice demanding that you reinstate coverage. If you don't respond quickly, some lenders will purchase coverage for the home and apply the premiums—usually much more expensive than coverage you can obtain on your own—to the outstanding balance of the mortgage. In a worst-case scenario, the lender could declare the mortgage in default and begin foreclosure proceedings. You may have made a late payment to the insurance company, there may have been an error at the company, or you may be in the process of changing from one insurance carrier to another. In any case, be sure to respond to any such notice from the lender and involve your insurance agent if necessary.

STANDARD HOME INSURANCE COVERAGE

Insurance companies offer seven basic packages of insurance coverage for homes in most every state. The classes are:

- **HO-1: Basic Homeowners.** This covers the dwelling and most types of personal property against losses caused by fire or lightning, windstorm or hail, explosion, riot or civil commotion, aircraft, vehicles, smoke, vandalism or malicious mischief, theft, damage by glass or safety glazing material that is part of a building, and volcanic eruption.
- **HO-2: Basic Homeowners Plus.** This covers the dwelling and most types of personal property against the HO-1 perils plus falling objects; weight of ice, snow, or sleet; certain types of water-related damage from home utilities or appliances; and electrical surge.
- **HO-3: Extended or Special Homeowners.** This covers perils of HO-1 and HO-2 plus all other perils except for flood, earthquake, war, or nuclear accident.
- **HO-4: Renters Coverage.** This covers personal property from perils of HO-1 and HO-2.
- **HO-5: All Risk Coverage.** This covers all risks for the building and personal property and is not commonly available.
- **HO-6: Condominium Coverage.** This covers personal property from HO-1 and HO-2 perils as well as that part of the building in which the unit owner has an insurance interest or exposure.
- **HO-8: Basic Older Home.** This covers the dwelling and personal property from HO-1 perils, but instead of paying to rebuild, it offers coverage for repairs of the actual cash value of a home, which may be higher because of historical value.

One state that has slightly different regulations is Texas, where home insurance packages are:

- **HO-A:** This offers extremely limited actual cash value coverage of the dwelling and its contents. Only the types of damage specifically listed in the policy are covered.
- **HO-A Amended:** This offers more extensive coverage than the base HO-A policy.
- **HO-B: Replacement Cost Coverage:** This protects against most types of damage, except those specifically excluded in the policy.
- **HO-C:** This is the most extensive coverage.

Texans can also purchase certain policies from national insurance companies that provide packages of coverage similar to those in other states.

■ PROPERTY COVERAGE

Most insurance policies do not insure the "market value" of your home—the amount of money you would expect to receive in a sale—but instead for the cost to rebuild it using modern methods if the house were destroyed. Depending on the age of the home and local conditions, the cost of rebuilding may be higher or lower than the market value—but in either case, you will regain your home. The one situation where market value is more important than rebuilding cost is if you own a historic or notable home worth much more than the cost of the wood and nails that hold it together.

Be sure you understand any deductible or coinsurance that may apply under your policy. For example, if you have a policy with a $500 deductible and a 20 percent coinsurance on a house with a value of $100,000, in the event of a total loss you would receive only $79,500 from the insurance company (80 percent of the value of the dwelling, minus the $500 deductible).

When it comes to covering the contents of the home, the insurance company will want to know about locks and alarms. All policies exclude certain types of expensive property, including artwork and other collectibles, valuable jewelry, and many home electronics. You'll need a "rider" to specifically cover these items or a separate policy on them. Equipment related to a home-based business also will not be covered at a reasonable level in a homeowners policy. A separate commercial policy is needed.

A standard policy provides coverage for your possessions at a level equal to 50 percent of the value of your home. That may or may not be sufficient for the contents of your home. If your home is especially valuable but your possessions are not, you do not need to increase coverage here. Otherwise, you can purchase additional coverage.

A standard policy covers freestanding structures such as garages and sheds up to a value equal to 10 percent of your dwelling. Most policies will also pay for replacement of trees and shrubbery up to an amount equal to 5 percent of the coverage on your home. If you need additional coverage, you can purchase more.

Depending on the policy, contents are either insured for their actual cash value (ACV) or their replacement costs. Under ACV, your five-year-old television set has lost most of its value, and you would receive only its depreciated value in the event of theft or fire. Under replacement cost coverage, your destroyed or stolen 21-inch TV would be replaced by a payment sufficient to purchase an equivalent new model.

Standard policies will also recompense homeowners for the loss of use of their home while it is being rebuilt or repaired. The money can pay for rental of a home or hotel room. Typical coverage can be as much as 30 percent of the insurance on your home.

Most policies also offer a level of protection for your possessions when you are out of your home. A theft from your hotel room or car, for example, may be covered by homeowners insurance. Homeowners policies may also protect possessions you purchase while traveling, as well as those you ship to your home.

■ LIABILITY COVERAGE

The typical policy provides coverage for liability in the range of $100,000 to $300,000. That may sound like a lot of protection until you consider the multi-million-dollar jury awards for death or injury cases. Is there a backyard pool or other "attractive nuisance" that increases the exposure to liability? Do you conduct a business from the home or rent rooms or the entire house to others? The insurance company will probably rate you a higher risk.

The higher the value of your personal assets, the more exposure you have to attorneys in search of "deep pockets" in a lawsuit. Although you may be able to purchase additional liability coverage as part of your homeowners policy, for most people the better route is to buy an "umbrella" liability policy that adds coverage for your home, your automobile, and other exposures.

■ EXCLUSIONS

As we have already seen, various types of insurance policies offer differing levels of covered perils. The most common policy, HO-3, covers the most common problems, including fire, explosion, theft, and damage from failure of a heating or hot-water system, but it specifically excludes other perils, including:

- Earthquake damage
- Flooding
- Settling or shifting of the foundation
- Ordinary wear and tear on your home and insect infestation over time
- Freezing damage to patios, swimming pools, fences, and other outbuildings
- Damage from frozen pipes in an unoccupied building
- Theft or vandalism from a building under construction or one that is vacant for more than thirty days
- Property belonging to tenants
- Losses resulting from your failure to protect your property after a loss

Also specifically excluded from coverage is any loss due to war or a nuclear accident. In today's unfortunate circumstances, most insurance companies have declared terrorism to be an act of war and do not fully cover any loss that can be blamed on such acts.

Even if a particular peril is covered, the insurance company will always be happy to find a way to shift the risk back to the homeowner. You must maintain your home and its systems properly. For example, although you are covered for water damage to your home and property loss caused by a burst pipe, the insurance company could deny the claim if you left the house unheated or failed to reasonably care for the heating system.

The failure of the heating system, a clothes washer, or dishwasher is not covered by the policy itself, although damage they cause to your property may be—again, if the equipment has been properly maintained. If your roof leaks, damage to the interior of your house is ordinarily covered, although repairs to the roof itself are considered ordinary wear-and-tear expenses and are not. However, if the roof is damaged in a storm or because a tree falls on it, this casualty loss and associated property damage is covered. Flood damage is not covered by ordinary homeowners insurance. Special policies, underwritten by the Federal Emergency Management Agency (FEMA), are available in most communities.

Be sure to read the policy to understand your responsibilities in the event of a loss. Typically, these include promptly notifying the insurance company or its agent, protecting the property from further damage and making any temporary repairs necessary for that purpose, preparing a detailed list of damaged or destroyed items with purchase and replacement costs, and cooperating with the insurance company's appraisers.

HOW AN INSURANCE COMPANY EVALUATES YOUR APPLICATION

As expensive as homeowners insurance is—$1,000 to $2,000 per year for a typical median-value house—look at the equation from the other side for a moment. The insurance company is on the line for several hundred thousand dollars. Although major claims are relatively rare, insurance companies can suffer huge, multi-billion-dollar losses from hurricanes, wildfires, and floods. Like it or not, insurance companies look to find reasons to reject your application for coverage. They are looking to only cover "good risks." As the homeowner, you are betting something is going to go wrong while you're hoping that you're not right. The insurance company is betting the other way.

Insurance companies will decide whether to issue a policy based on the location and construction of the house, as well as personal information about you as an applicant. Among the information they'll request is your date of birth and other identifying information, occupation and employment history, marital status, and previous addresses. The company will check for criminal or civil judgments and history, examine your credit report, and consult a database to determine whether you have made any unusual insurance claims. If your previous policy was canceled, you'll need to provide an acceptable reason. You're off the hook if your previous carrier had withdrawn from your state or stopped writing a particular type of policy.

Then there is your home. Is it located in a flood plain, near the coastline, in an earthquake-prone area, in an urban area with high crime rates but nearby fire and emergency services, or in a rural setting without fire hydrants or a full-time fire department? How old is the house? What kind of construction was employed? Other factors include the number of rooms and the type of heating system. Is there a smoke detector? Does the house include a fireplace or woodstove?

Finally, how much would it cost to rebuild the home in the event of a fire or other serious damage?

■ FILING A CLAIM

A claim on your home or its contents is a big deal to you but just a minor consequence of doing business for the insurance company. That may or may not make a difference in the quality of the service you receive. In some circumstances, a major insurance company with a well-oiled claims and adjustment department may be easier to work with than a smaller one. If you are working with an insurance agent rather than directly with the company, you should assure yourself that the agent will stand by to assist you in the event of a claim. Here are the steps you should follow:

1. Promptly notify your insurance agent or the company in the event of a loss. Make notes on the date and time of your notification and anything you are advised to do.

2. Review your coverage with the agent or company to make sure you take advantage of all of the policy's features. For example, most policies will pay for emergency housing and living expenses if your home is unlivable.

3. With the approval of the insurance company, arrange for any temporary repairs necessary to prevent further damage. For example, if your roof or a window is damaged, you should contract for temporary patches to keep rain and wind out of the house and protect against theft. Do not, though, make permanent repairs before an insurance adjuster approves them.

4. Make sure the insurance adjuster knows how to reach you, either directly or through a friend, relative, or business associate.

5. Try to meet with the adjuster during the inspection of your home. Point out any hidden damage and special conditions. Keep full notes on the meeting.

6. Maintain a log with date, time, and notes on all conversations you have with the adjuster, the insurance company, and police or emergency responders.

7. Create a detailed description of the damage, along with lists of any damaged, destroyed, or stolen items. Your case will be bolstered if you can produce receipts and other documents. A photo or video survey of your home taken before the incident can be very helpful.

8. In general, stay away from "public" or "independent" adjusters who may approach you after a loss with promises to help you collect. Their services should not be necessary, and you will have to pay them for their work or give up a percentage of your check form the insurance company.

9. If you are dissatisfied with the claim offer from the insurance company, ask for a review. You can submit your own estimates for repair submitted by a reputable contractor and ask that the adjuster meet with the contractor. If you are unable to resolve differences with the insurance company, you can hire an independent adjuster or an attorney and pay a fee based on a percentage of any money recovered that is more than the amount offered by the insurance company.

10. Once you have accepted a claim payment from the insurance company, seek out bids from more than one contractor for the completion of the repair or restoration. Judge both the cost and the quality of the work by the contractor. In most cases you'll do better to give the work to a local contractor with roots in the community.

SAVING MONEY ON HOMEOWNERS INSURANCE

In most states the broad outlines of insurance rates are set by state agencies. Competition between companies also helps keep prices from various companies relatively close to each other. However, there are some things you can do to reduce the bottom line of your insurance bill.

The first step is to consider accepting a higher deductible—the amount of money you must pay before insurance coverage kicks in. A change from a $250 deductible to $500 or $1,000 may reduce the annual premium by 20 to 30 percent. For most homeowners it's a worthy gamble—you'll make up the difference in the deductible after just a few years.

Be sure you are insuring the value of your home and not the land. Except in the case of war, flood, or earthquake—events generally not covered by standard insurance policies—your land is not likely to disappear. Your policy needs to protect the replacement value of the structure, not the land it stands upon.

Other ways to reduce the cost of homeowners insurance include:

■ Some companies offer package discounts to clients who have multiple policies for homes and cars.

■ Take advantage of special discounts based on your age (some companies reduce rates for persons fifty and older) and your membership in associations (including alumni groups and AARP). Some carriers offer reduced rates if no one in your home smokes because of a reduced chance of fire.

■ Improve the security systems in your home with smoke alarms, fire alarms, burglar alarms, and deadbolts, and notify the insurance company or your agent. Some companies will also give credit for outdoor lighting systems.

■ Review your policy annually with your agent or the insurance company. Ask for suggestions on ways to reduce cost, and be sure to ask your agent to compare available policies from other companies.

If you have a high net worth—more than a few hundred thousand dollars—you should also consider purchasing an umbrella policy that extends your automobile and homeowners or renter liability coverage for most risks, including auto accidents, incidents in your home, and many other types of claims. An umbrella worth $1 to $3 million in additional coverage typically costs a few hundred dollars per year. Umbrella policies don't begin to pay until after the basic liability insurance in your homeowners policy has been used. Insurance companies can offer the high amounts of coverage because such peaks are rarely reached.

RENTERS INSURANCE

If you rent a house or apartment, the owner of the structure bears the risk of loss to the structure itself. Their insurance coverage, though, does not cover your belongings. Conversely, renters insurance you may purchase will protect your possessions but not the building they are housed within.

The basic home insurance policy, categorized as HO-4, protects *possessions* against the same seventeen perils covered in a homeowners HO-3 policy. A similar policy for condominium owners is HO-6. Other components of a renters policy usually include loss of use that pays for housing and living expenses if your apartment cannot be used due to a covered loss, and payment for medical expenses for minor injuries sustained by others in your residence.

Renters receive a package of liability coverage as well, protecting against accidents to a visitor or worker in your apartment, for example. And there are some unique liability exposures for renters. For example, a policy may provide coverage for damage caused to a neighbor's apartment by a burst waterbed in your quarters. (Some landlords may require you to purchase renters insurance for just that reason, to protect other tenants and the owner.)

Because a renters policy is not tied to the value of the structure, the amount of coverage for your possessions will be specified. Be sure it is sufficient, and consider purchasing additional riders for expensive items such as jewelry or computers that may not be otherwise covered.

CONDO AND CO-OP INSURANCE

As the owner of a condominium or cooperative apartment, you have an interest in the building itself as well as your own possessions, but the insurance company treats the two as separate issues. The various members of the condominium association or cooperative board contribute through monthly fees to pay for an insurance policy on the structure, which generally covers the foundation, roof, and structure, as well as common areas such as hallways, walkways, staircases, and elevators. In order to protect your possessions, you'll need to purchase a policy of your own—usually based on HO-6 language.

Your personal policy, similar to renters coverage, includes liability for accidents within your residence and generally provides for temporary living expenses if you are unable to remain in your condo after a covered loss. Some HO-6 policies may help protect you against damage to the structure that is not sufficiently protected by the association's coverage and is passed along to members as an assessment.

FLOOD INSURANCE

If your home is in a flood-prone area, you may be able to purchase special coverage under the National Flood Insurance Program (NFIP), which falls under the umbrella of the Federal Emergency Management Agency—the nation's disaster-relief department.

If your home is in a designated Special Flood Hazard Area, NFIP coverage is required in order to receive and maintain federally guaranteed mortgages. Otherwise, coverage is voluntary, although homeowners who receive federal disaster assistance from one flood must purchase federal flood insurance to protect themselves from future losses. The insurance covers the structure and contents separately, with a $500 minimum deductible.

Your local insurance agent should be able to tell you if your community participates in the program. For more details you can also consult www.fema. gov/nfip or call (800) 427–4661.

HOME WARRANTIES

A home warranty is an extended guarantee—or more accurately, a service contract—on particular systems of your home. You can purchase a policy to protect refrigerators and other major appliances, heating and air-conditioning systems, plumbing, and electrical wiring. Other warranties protect the structure itself against ordinary failures (as opposed to perils covered by insurance).

Systems have to be in working order when the policy is first issued. Some warranties (much like health insurance plans) do not cover preexisting problems or may require a waiting period before they take effect. Most policies require a co-payment toward the cost of repairs, and you'll generally have to use a repair company authorized by the warranty company. Some policies limit the amount of money paid toward a particular system.

Keep in mind that warranties work together with homeowners insurance but don't replace coverage. For example, if your home's hot-water heater were to break and flood the basement, the warranty would pay for repairs of the boiler while the insurance would pay for damages to the room.

The cost of a home warranty varies depending on term, the size of the house, and the particular type of appliances and systems that are covered. Prices range from about $250 to $500 per year for an older home. You can also purchase a contract for a new home at a lower annual rate.

Your service contract is no better than the company that issues it. Ask for references from other customers and from real estate agents who may have clients who have purchased a plan. And be sure to read the contract itself before you sign on the bottom line. Here's an example of the sort of the restrictions you'll find:

This contract is only valid if your covered products have been maintained in accordance with the manufacturer's specifications. Keep copies of all receipts; proof of maintenance may be required when you file a claim.

You must obtain approval prior to having work performed that may be covered by this contract. If you believe the failure may be covered by this contract, you must call the administrator before the work is performed.

We provide service only. We will not provide reimbursement if you use your own contractor or complete unauthorized repairs without our prior approval.

Selling Power

Home warranties are a valuable tool when it comes to selling your home. Buyers may feel reassured about the uncertainties of buying a used home if it comes with a policy.

Warranties issued by a homebuilder for new construction usually require that most repairs be done by the builder, with the insurance company reimbursing the cost where necessary and compensating the homeowner in the event of non-performance by the builder. In other words, you will be, first of all, relying on the builder to construct a house of good quality and then again to make repairs during the course of a warranty that can run for as long as ten years.

The bottom line: Many experts consider home warranties to be a bad investment, suggesting instead that you put aside the money you would otherwise spend on the policy and use the funds to pay for necessary repairs. If a seller includes a warranty as an inducement to purchase the house, consider its cost and provisions as part of the value of the home.

PART IX
SELLING YOUR HOUSE

CHAPTER TWENTY

HOW TO GET THE MOST
FOR YOUR HOME AT RESALE

SETTING THE PROPER ASKING PRICE for your home is one of the most difficult of arts—it's most certainly not a science. There is no guaranteed right price, but there are many ways to make a costly mistake. The biggest mistake for many sellers is to set the price of your home on the basis of the profit you feel you need to buy another house. The price that you need is not related to the fair market value, and unless you are extraordinarily lucky, you are setting yourself up for a situation where your home becomes less attractive than others and less likely to sell.

Another common mistake is to add the cost of any major improvements—landscaping, a new kitchen, roof repairs, and such—to the purchase price and then add some profit onto that total. The fact is that very few home improvements are fully recovered by owners at the time of sale. A new kitchen makes your home much more attractive, but you may only receive back 80 percent of the money you invested in it. The improvements are worth even less if they result in making your home overpriced for the neighborhood. A good seller's agent will try to help you set a proper selling price. It doesn't benefit the agent—who in most cases has only a limited amount of time under the brokerage agreement—to inflate the price because it reduces the chances of a quick sale.

The best way to estimate the selling price is to examine comparable sales ("comps"). What you're looking for is a similar home in the same neighborhood that has sold in the current market environment. Comparables become harder to come by when the market softens—there are fewer houses being sold, and prices may decline.

The natural inclination is to set the listing price above the level you have decided is the minimum you will accept. That's a reasonable position to take since very few houses are sold without some negotiation of the listing price. Your real estate agent should be able to give you a feel for typical bargaining sessions. Most brokerages or MLS groups maintain statistics that indicate, on average, what percentage of the listing-price homes are selling for.

Real estate is marketable but rarely a liquid asset. Bean-counters consider an asset liquid when it can easily and quickly be converted to its cash value. In most cases, conversion of a piece of property into cash takes months—and only then once a buyer is found who is willing to pay the seller's determination of its value. I point this out because it is linked to the fact that a rushed or urgent sale of a piece of property generally results in a lower price or the acceptance of a lower-quality bid that demands special terms or seller financing. An essential step toward getting the best price for your property is to allow a reasonable amount of time for marketing it and qualifying would-be buyers.

HOW MUCH IS A HOUSE WORTH?

The most important question in the sale or purchase of a home is not something that can be determined by wishes, hopes, or guesses. The short answer is that a home is worth the highest bid from one or more qualified buyers at a particular moment in time. But before sellers accept bids, most want to have some sense of the value of their property. If expectations are too low, a seller could end up losing reasonable profits. If expectations are too high, it could result in the seller losing time and money waiting for an unreasonable offer.

In order to gauge the value of a property, there are two main tools used by professionals: a check of recent comparable sales and a more detailed evaluation by a licensed appraiser. As a seller, in most situations a real estate agent can perform a check of comparables and deliver a sense of the current market that can help you determine a realistic asking price for your home. As a buyer, you will likely be relying on the same information—at least until time comes to apply for a mortgage. Most lenders will require a professional appraisal of the home (paid for by the applicant) and may limit the amount of money they will lend based on the value determined by the appraiser.

In general, there is no need for sellers or buyers to obtain an appraisal on their own. However, there are some situations where the seller might want to do so:
- If the home or the land on which it is built, or both, are so unusual that there are no comparables to check
- If the market has undergone a significant change since the last time one or more comparable homes sold
- If you are selling the home without a real estate agent and are unable to come up with your own assessment of comparable sales

■ HOW TO HIRE AN APPRAISER
If you do decide to hire a professional to evaluate your home, start by making sure the appraiser is properly licensed by your state. If you are working with a real estate agent, the brokerage should be able to recommend capable local appraisers. If not, you may be able to get assistance from officers at banks or lending institutions.

The appropriate candidate should have knowledge of your local area. There are very few situations in which an appraiser can parachute in from hundreds of miles away and be expected to quickly and accurately assess the neighborhood and comparable sales. You should also determine what sort of sources will be used. Old-school appraisers used to spend a day leafing through the record books at the town or county hall, while modern practitioners work the Internet and other electronic sources, which may be much quicker and more inclusive.

Rates for appraisals of standard single-family homes are generally in the range of $300 to $500. You can expect to pay more for unusual homes or properties. Be sure you come to an agreement on price before the work begins and determine how quickly you can expect to receive the report—most appraisers can deliver within a week or two. You may be asked to pay a premium for a rush job.

THE DANGERS OF OVERPRICING

What happens if a buyer agrees to pay more than the appraised fair market price for a home? You may be happy with the extra money, and the buyer may feel he has paid what he had to get a much-desired home. But the buyer may run into problems with obtaining financing, sometimes to the point where the sale itself may be endangered.

As part of the mortgage application process, the lender will appraise the value of the home it is being asked to help purchase. Lenders calculate a loan-to-value ratio, structuring their required down payment and interest rates with that figure in mind. The lender is trying to assure that it is protected in case the borrower defaults on the mortgage payments. If the home is worth less than the amount of the loan, the lender is exposed to an unsecured risk.

If the lender's appraiser determines the value of the home to be significantly less than the price you have agreed to pay, the lender may limit the amount of money it will offer in a mortgage or require a higher down payment to accomplish the same thing. In some cases the applicant may be able to appeal for a higher appraised value, providing updated information about the market. As the seller, you run the risk of having a would-be buyer withdraw his offer because he is unable to obtain a mortgage. With the assistance of your real estate agent, you may be able to include language in the purchase and sale agreement that requires the would-be buyer to make a larger down payment in order to obtain financing.

PREPARING A HOUSE FOR SALE

Before you invite would-be buyers into your home, try to see the place as a stranger would. Come in the formal entrance and appraise the view. Do you see a clean, uncluttered, and well-maintained home, or is your view of the place distracted by cosmetic flaws like a dirty carpet, a worn-out paint job, and piles of junk in the corners?

On the one hand, it may be hard for you to justify spending money on your house in the months leading up to planting a FOR SALE sign on the front lawn. However, unless your home is extraordinarily appealing or you have already lined up a buyer, most experts advise you to spend some money on repairs and maintenance that is immediately apparent to a would-be buyer. This doesn't mean you should undertake a major renovation project—a new kitchen or bathroom, or the installation of a swimming pool. In most instances you will not recover anything near 100 percent of the cost. Instead, concentrate on spiffing up the place with a new paint job, making repairs to any obvious problems like broken windows or screens, and putting the place through a serious cleaning. Consider hiring a professional cleaning crew to go through the home before it is shown and to make return visits from time to time.

Here are some things you can do to make your home as attractive as possible:
- Paint the interior. Be sure to use neutral colors—off-white, beige, and the like. A new paint job in electric green and mauve will cause most would-be buyers to immediately discount the value of your home by the cost of a return to neutral.
- Repair cracks and holes in walls and ceilings.
- Paint or wash the exterior. Again, you don't want to impose your choice of colors on a buyer. If the exterior needs painting, choose a color that is in keeping with the neighborhood. One way to make a great first impression is to repaint the entry doors and polish up brass door knockers and address numbers. Straighten up and apply fresh paint to the mailbox.
- Patch cracks in the driveway and walkways. Apply a fresh coat of driveway sealer.
- Install new carpeting, again in neutral colors. If the existing carpeting is only a few years old, you may be able to get by with a good cleaning. Don't install carpeting over a well-maintained hardwood floor, though. A handsome wood floor should be buffed and polished instead.
- Clean out the gutters and wash the windows and shutters.
- Spruce up the exterior landscaping. Lawns should be mowed and plants pruned. In the proper season you might want to add a few colorful flowering plants. Depending on the region where you live, you might want to apply a fast-acting fertilizer to the lawn and plants to bring them to their peak condition as buyers arrive.
- Remove exterior clutter. Visit the dump with the old gas barbecue grill that hasn't been used in years and properly dispose of the old tires behind the garage. Throw away, or at least move to the basement, kiddie toys.
- Clear out the clutter within. Throw away stacks of newspapers and old mail. Open up some space in closets by throwing away (or better yet, donating to a good cause) old clothing. You can also pack up out-of-season clothing and rent a temporary storage space.
- Open up some space in the living room and bedrooms by throwing away or putting into storage unnecessary furniture, exercise equipment that now serves as a clothes hanger, and too many toys. Allow the would-be buyer to picture his or her household effects in their place.

■ Clean out the attic, basement, and hidden storage spaces. You'll want to show-case these areas as places for the new owner to keep stuff—don't make storage space seem too limited. Anything you can throw away or give away is something you won't have to pay to move to your new home.

■ Pay special attention to cleaning bathrooms and kitchens. Remove any mold, mildew, or stains in shower or bath areas. Don't draw attention to ant or insect problems by leaving traps or sprays in sight. The same goes for mouse or rat bait or traps.

■ Make sure that interior lighting shows off the home to its best advantage. Replace any burned-out light bulbs. Check the proper functioning of drapes and shades.

■ Pay attention to odors in the home. Many buyers can immediately detect cig-arette smoke or the fact that you have pets. You may be able to alleviate these odors by cleaning draperies and rugs and by placing potpourri and unobtrusive deodorants around the home. Some real estate agents will suggest that you bake bread or a turkey on the day of an open house.

You should also do what you can to enhance the value of the systems in your house. Here are some things to do:

■ Clean the stove, microwave, refrigerator, dishwasher, clothes washer, and dryer. If you plan to leave these appliances behind, you'll want the buyer to think of them as like new. Even if you plan to take some or all of these devices with you, their condition says a lot about the quality of the house.

■ Have a qualified maintenance person tend to any squeaks, rattles, or odd noises in the heating system, air conditioner, and plumbing. Make sure there is a fresh filter in any air-handling system.

■ Repair or replace leaking faucets and leaks in plumbing below sinks.

SHOULD YOU REMODEL?

Remodeling your kitchen or bathroom or repainting the outside of your house will almost certainly help you sell your home, but in most cases you will not re-cover every dollar you spend on fixing up the house. To help determine if you should remodel, separate out the various advantages of work performed on your house:

■ **Ordinary maintenance.** Fixing the furnace or repairing a leaky roof is an es-sential task, and this is the sort of problem that must be disclosed to a would-be buyer. If you are able to attract a serious buyer, you can expect that her offer will be sharply reduced below market value. And in any case, many lenders will not issue a mortgage to a new buyer if its inspector finds such serious problems.

■ **Sprucing up.** Painting the interior or exterior of the home or replacing worn or dirty carpeting will help make your property more attractive and is usually a worthy investment that helps you receive the full market value at resale.

■ **Major renovations or expansions.** Here the rewards are sometimes mixed. Done properly, a major renovation of a bathroom or kitchen will make your home more attractive and easier to sell, but you may not recover the full cost of the project at resale.

According to the National Association of Realtors, the average cost recouped at resale for a kitchen remodel is about 88 percent. A bathroom remodeling or addition typically brings in about 82 percent of the cost when it comes to resale. Another study, by Remodeling On-line (www.remodeling.hw.net), projects that the costs of adding a home office will only return about 54 percent at resale. You'll get back about 68 percent of the cost of replacing windows with improved models and 75 percent of what you spend on a new deck. This should not hold you back from spending money on your home. Keep in mind the enjoyment you will receive while you live there and the value of being able to sell your home a bit quicker when it is time to move on.

THINGS YOU CAN DO TO SPEED THE SALE

And then you wait. For many home owners that's the most difficult part about selling a home—sweating out the marketing, open houses, and tours while waiting for the one best offer. It's especially frustrating if you need the proceeds from the sale of your home to buy a new place to live. Here are some things you can do to grease the wheels:

■ Offer the buyer a rebate for redecorating or for the purchase of new appliances. There is no real difference here between a rebate or a reduction in the price, but buyers love to get something "on sale."

■ Have the house preinspected and offer a home warranty. A cautious buyer will still hire an inspector to check the house before closing, but your advance work will make your home stand out from others.

■ Offer help with financing. The seller can pay some or all of the points at the buyer's closing, which results in a "buy-down" of the interest rate. A buy-down is often better than a reduction in the selling price because it may help an otherwise unqualified buyer get a mortgage.

■ Offer short-term direct financing to help a buyer who has not yet sold a previous home. The loan can be a mortgage, or it can help the buyer come up with a necessary down payment for a commercial mortgage.

■ Increase the commission or offer a bonus to the agent who brings in a successful bid. The best way to get the attention of an agent is to increase the payoff she receives.

GUARANTEED SALES

An interesting promotion offered by some real estate brokerages and homebuilders is a "guaranteed" purchase of your home. The brokerage might promise that if it is unable to sell your home in the course of a listing, it will buy it from you. Similarly, a homebuilder may try to entice a buyer to sign a contract for a new home by promising to buy her current dwelling if it has not sold by the time of closing.

In theory, a guaranteed sale is attractive. However, you can expect that the purchase price will be below fair market value. You should only engage in such a deal if you are willing to accept the purchase price if need be.

You should do what you can to keep the details of your arrangement confidential. For example, you may be listing your house for sale at $350,000 but have agreed to a guaranteed sale price of $310,000. A buyer who finds out your floor price comes into a negotiation already knowing exactly how low you are willing to go, which may reduce the size of an offer.

HOMES FOR SALE BY THE OWNER (FSBOs)

There is no requirement that you hire a real estate agent—and pay as much as 6 or 7 percent of the selling price for the privilege. You can spiff up your home, plant a FOR SALE sign in the front yard, publish ads in the newspaper, and sit back and wait for the right buyer to walk through the door. Homes for sale by the owner—the real estate shorthand calls them FSBOs, pronounced "fiz-bohs"—amount for as much as 25 percent or more of the market in some areas.

FSBOs have begun to benefit from the growth of the Internet. A number of Web sites have sprung up to serve as marketplaces and referral sites for private homesellers. The sites can function as electronic classifieds, or they can go a step further and help qualify shoppers before they contact sellers.

The advantage of a FSBO transaction is that you don't have to pay a commission to selling agent. That's about it. The savings can amount to quite a bit, though: perhaps $18,000 on a $300,000 sale. You'll have to weigh that cost against the possibility that would-be buyers coming to your door will offer less than you would receive from a client brought in by an agent. Some buyers assume that a FSBO is willing to sell for less because he is not paying a commission.

On the other hand, there are a few disadvantages to a FSBO transaction:

- You will have to do your own research on comparable prices and set a reasonable asking price.
- You will have to pay the expenses for advertising the house.
- There is no one to prequalify buyers. You are subject to visits from the most casual—or the most nefarious—of shoppers.
- Unless you strike a deal to pay a commission to buyer's agents, there is no incentive for them to bring you a client.
- Once an offer is made, you will have to pursue it through to a closing on your own.

So, should you consider becoming a FSBO? In a word, maybe. I would only recommend attempting to sell your home by yourself in a very hot real estate market. You shouldn't have much trouble attracting shoppers. If you have multiple buyers bidding for your home, chances are the price they offer will be as good as you would receive with the aid of a seller's and buyer's agent.

In a weak market, you're asking for headaches. You're going to have to beat the bushes for buyers, and you can expect that offers will be much less than you

A True Story of an Unexpected FSBO

A number of years ago I accepted a new job that required me to move from a suburb of New York City to the Boston area. We knew we had to dispose of our existing home—one we had owned for just a few years—pretty quickly to allow us to stay together as a family. The real estate market was warm, not hot, and so we decided to interview real estate agents to find one to represent us.

We invited a neighborhood agent to meet with us around the kitchen table and listened to her pitch. We asked about the state of the market, an estimate of how much she thought the house would sell for, and how her company would go out and find the right buyer. We promised her we would get back to her soon, after we had spoken to another agent or two.

About an hour later, our doorbell rang. It was a neighbor. She had noticed the real estate agent's car with its logo parked in our driveway.

"You haven't signed with an agent yet, I hope," she said. "My niece wants to move to this neighborhood, and we'd like to make an offer on your house—and you won't have to pay a commission."

We named our price, and after just a bit of not-very-spirited back-and-forth, we had an agreement to sell. The next morning I hired an attorney and asked him to manage the sale and closing, and we made plans for our move to Boston.

You should be so lucky.

would want to accept. In such a case, you might as well share the pain with an agent.

If you do go ahead and sell your home by yourself, I would strongly recommend that you hire an experienced real estate lawyer or an agent to serve as an advisor for the closing. Have the lawyer or agent draw up the sales agreement, hold on to the deposit in an escrow account, and make sure that every required step is followed leading up to the closing and at the passing of the papers. The attorney will likely spend four to six hours on your case. You can expect to spend anywhere from $300 to $600 or so for the very valuable safeguard of your interests.

TAXES ON SALE OF A HOME

The best way to avoid tax when selling a principal residence is to follow the simple rules of Internal Revenue Code 121. It allows up to $250,000, or $500,000 for a married couple filing jointly, tax-free home-sale profits. A single filer can take as much as $250,000 in profit without taxes; a couple filing jointly can take $500,000. And the break can be taken again and again—there is no lifetime limit on profits. Of course, little is so simple when it comes to the IRS, and so there are a few rules to observe. In order to write off the profit, the home must be a personal residence, and you must have owned the home and lived in it for at least two of the five years leading up to the sale. If you are forced to sell your home after living in it for less than two years, the law permits a partial exclusion of profits if the sale is connected with a change of jobs, health issues, or certain other exceptional situations.

Prior to 1997, sellers were allowed to roll over their profits on the sale of a home into the purchase of a new one. If you were over the age of fifty-five, you were permitted a one-time $125,000 exclusion on the profit from the sale of a home. If you benefited from that exclusion in the past, you are still free to take advantage of the current, more generous law. Consult a tax advisor to see if current regulations require that rollover profit be subtracted from the tax basis of your current home.

■ TAX BASIS

If your house has gone through an extraordinary rise in income, either because you have owned it for many years or because of a sharp boost in local real estate values, you will need to maintain records to establish the tax basis for the home. You'll need to establish how much you paid for the home originally, plus the cost of any capital improvements over the years. Significant improvements to the home such as additions and new heating or cooling systems are included in the basis, but ordinary repairs and maintenance such as paint jobs are not. (To reiterate, this is the sort of happy problem not all homesellers will face. It only applies if a jointly owned home has gone up in value more than $500,000 over its original cost.)

One area in which the federal government will not be able to help is in the relatively rare instance where a homeowner sells a residence for less than the original cost plus improvements. Losses on the sale of a home are not deductible.

There are some tax wrinkles that might apply here if the home is converted to a rental property prior to sale. Losses incurred *after* conversion are deductible since the home is now a business.

■ PROFITS ON A HOME OFFICE

If you have deducted some of the cost of your home over the years for a home office, you cannot include the proportional profit on the home office in tax-free profit. For example, if you have written off 15 percent of the home, that same amount of profit plus depreciation is subject to taxes. You may be able restore your home to full residential use by ending the claim of home office deductions at least two years before you sell the house. Be sure to consult your tax advisor in order to stay on the right side of the law here.

■ MOVING EXPENSES

If you can establish that the reason for your move is related to a change in jobs, you may be able to write off the cost of moving your possessions and the expenses for travel and lodging. The IRS requires that the new job has to be at least

50 miles farther from your old home than your previous job was. This can bring up some unusual situations, such as changing from a job that was 30 miles east of your home to one that is 30 miles west—this would not qualify. You'll also have to work full time for at least thirty-nine weeks of the fifty-two weeks after your move. If you're self-employed, the time period doubles to seventy-eight weeks out of the first two years.

The tax write-off can be taken in the filing immediately after the move. If you end up not meeting the work requirement at your new location, you will have to file an amended tax return or report the amount of the previous deduction as income in the subsequent year.

PART X
MOVING

CHAPTER TWENTY-ONE

PREPARING FOR A MOVE

LIFE IS IN THE DETAILS, something you'll become very aware of as you prepare to move from one community to another. There are dozens of government agencies, companies, and friends and associates to notify, and then there is the entangling web of utilities and services that make up the modern life. If you have a choice, try to avoid moving in the summer—the busiest and most expensive time at moving companies.

Here's a checklist of a number of obvious and not-so-obvious steps to take.

One to Two Months Before Moving Day

❏ Keep copies of all expenses related to the move. You may be able to deduct some costs from your taxes.

❏ Gather legal, medical, insurance, and financial records in a safe place. Make a checklist of insurance companies, banks, and investment companies that will need to be advised on your change of address.

❏ If you are moving out of the area, contact your doctor and other medical providers to obtain copies of your records or arrange to have them sent to new providers.

❏ Notify magazine publishers, book clubs, and other regular shippers of your new address. Most require several weeks or more to change their records.

❏ Notify the IRS of your change of address to assure you will receive refunds and forms. The Postal Service will automatically notify the IRS if you file a change of address form, but to be on the safe side, file an IRS Form 8822 (you knew there had to be another form out there). You can find a printable copy of the form at www.irs.gov (search for "change of address"), or you can call the IRS at (800) 829–1040.

❏ If you lease or finance a vehicle, notify the lending company of your new address. Some leasing companies may object if you move out of state or require that you return the vehicle to the original state at the end of the lease arrangement.

❏ Collect or purchase a supply of boxes, tape, rope, and markers. Begin the process of packing items you know you will not need in the coming weeks—out-of-season clothing, for example. Mark boxes with a note about their contents and indicate where in the new house the box should be placed for unpacking.

❏ Throw away, give away, or sell anything you don't need. You're going to have to pay to pack up and move the items—why not convert them to cash? Consider the fact that many homeowners have their basements, attics, and closets filled with boxes of items never unpacked from their last move.

❏ Finalize arrangements with a moving company, or for the rental of a moving truck and equipment if you plan to do it yourself.

Two Weeks Before Moving Day

❏ Notify electric, water, gas, local telephone, and trash-removal services of your upcoming move. If you use oil or other fuel that is delivered to your home by truck, try to avoid buying much more than you will need before you move.

❏ Notify cable television and long-distance services far enough in advance of your move to avoid paying for service you will not use.

❏ Contact utilities at your new home and arrange for hookups and deliveries. If you are moving within the same region, you may be able to keep your old phone number. If you are moving out of the area, you may be able to transfer your long-distance service plan to your new number.

❏ File change-of-address forms with banks, insurance companies, and invest-ment firms. If you are moving out of the area, you may want to close out your bank accounts, although you can also do this by letter or telephone after you move.

❏ Notify credit card companies of your new address. Make arrangements to pay outstanding bills at on-line Web sites.

Five Days Before Moving

❏ File a change-of-address form with the post office. You can do so in person, or on-line at www.usps.com. The on-line service costs $1.00 for processing.

❏ If you are moving out of the area, empty the contents of any safety deposit boxes and close out the account. Store the contents in a safe container you will carry with you, not one that will be packed and out of your control.

❏ Collect any extra keys you may have given to neighbors or hidden around the home. Remove the garage door opener from your car and leave it for the new owner. Make sure the keys and opener don't get packed.

Packing Tips

❏ Mark boxes with a note about their contents and indicate where in the new house the box should be placed for unpacking. Give each box a number, and keep a notebook with the numbers and contents. This will help you find partic-ular items later and help account for all boxes.

❏ Don't overload boxes. Objects are more apt to break if the box is overstuffed, and overweight boxes can damage other containers.

❏ Use bubble wrap (available from moving companies or office supply stores) or other soft material to cushion fragile objects. You can also wrap breakables in items of clothing.

❏ If you are moving yourself, rent a hand truck to help move heavy items. Rental truck companies usually offer cushioning blankets to protect furniture.

❏ Be sure *not* to pack things you'll need for the trip—tickets, wallets, legal documents, and the like. Keep separate moving tools such as a pocket knife or box cutter, tape, markers, and tape measure.

After the Move

❏ Check the contents of boxes and your furniture for damage. If you used a professional mover, file any claims for damage immediately.

❏ Locate the nearest emergency services: fire call boxes and firehouses, police stations, and hospitals.

❏ Confirm hookup of utilities and accounts for telephone, cable, and other services.

❏ Contact local government for information on registering to vote, reregistering your motor vehicle, and obtaining a new license.

❏ If you have moved from a different area, arrange for a new doctor, dentist, and other medical provider. Give them copies of your records from your previous providers or arrange for shipment.

❏ Locate a new pharmacy, if necessary, and ask the pharmacist to arrange for transfer of any prescriptions that have open renewals.

❏ Transfer insurance policies to a new agent if necessary. Ask for a review of all current policies.

PART XI

REAL ESTATE IN CYBERSPACE

CHAPTER TWENTY-TWO

ENTER THE WEB

BY ONE ESTIMATE, there are more than 100,000 Web sites devoted to real estate and home loans. Even in the post–dot com bust, mortgage and real estate services continue to thrive. You can search for homes from the comfort of your keyboard, compare one community to another, investigate mortgage rates, and communicate with a real estate agent thousands of miles across the country. Once you have decided on a home, you can finalize the mortgage, arrange for a moving van, and forward your mail without leaving the den.

The advent of the Internet age has made all of these tasks more convenient, saving a great deal of time and making it easy to save thousands of dollars by comparing one loan or service against another. That said, there is generally no special cost advantage to performing any of these tasks on the Web as opposed to using the telephone or visiting an office.

I love the Internet as a source of primary research. There is hardly a single major purchase I make that doesn't begin with a check of prices, specifications, and recommendations on the Web. But I almost always follow up with a phone call to companies I don't see on-line. As an example, every mortgage lender in the country is aware of the existence of Internet sites, and they know that if they don't match their rates or deliver some other valuable advantage, they are not going to be in business for very long.

In this section I'll tell you about valuable Web sites for real estate research, mortgages, moving services, and more. But don't limit yourself to the sites mentioned here—the pace of change in cyberspace is so great that you're likely to find new services every time you browse.

HOW AN ON-LINE MORTGAGE APPLICATION WORKS

There are three principal conveniences to applying for a mortgage on-line:
- The mortgage site usually has arrangements with dozens or even hundreds of different lenders around the nation, making it a superstore where you can choose just about any combination of available interest rates, prepaid points, term, and type of loan (fixed rate, adjustable, balloon, and other forms). The sites allow easy comparison of total costs and the break-even point, which lets you decide whether it is better to pay additional up-front points to lower the interest rate.
- You can fill out a mortgage application on-line, making use of automated systems that check for errors and omissions.
- Most on-line sites are geared for quick approvals and closing, sometimes able to react weeks faster than traditional mortgage offices. They can do so because they have computer programs that analyze Web applications as they come in and automatic links to credit bureaus for electronic credit checks. Most of the loans offered on these sites are conforming loans sold on the secondary market, where there are very specific criteria for borrowers, making it relatively easy to make quick and firm decisions.

The potential disadvantage of these sites is the fact that you will most likely not have a local contact to deal with, and the company may not be familiar with—or willing to deal with—any properties or borrowers that do not fit their cookie-cutter approval process. The sites will generally assign you a loan manager, reachable by telephone or e-mail, but in most cases you will still have to travel to an office of the lender, an attorney, or an escrow company for the actual closing process. In major cities and highly populated urban areas, the closing location may be convenient; in other areas, using one of these national services may come at the cost of some inconvenience on closing day. Then again, if you save $20,000 in the process, driving a few hours to closing is not an unreasonable price to pay.

Make sure the Web site you are dealing with uses secure encryption for the information you send electronically. If you have any doubts, call the company by telephone.

■ THE ELECTRONIC MORTGAGE PROCESS

The major on-line lenders, including E-Loan, Quicken, and Lending Tree, work in similar ways. Here's an example of the process as promised by E-Loan:

1. Compare loans on-line, searching through hundreds of available mortgages for the one that matches your needs. E-Loan will recommend a mortgage its experts consider to be the best deal, but you can select any available offering.

2. Apply for the loan on-line, using encrypted transmission. The company promises that information will be stored in a secure manner once received.

3. Based on the information provided in the application, in most cases applicants will receive conditional approval within minutes and a final credit approval within twenty-four hours. Borrowers are assigned a loan consultant who will be the point of contact for any questions that arise. Once a loan is approved, the applicant can provide a credit card to pay for appraisals and other fees.

4. Once approved, you can lock in your rate on-line. Once a mortgage rate has been confirmed, E-Loan guarantees that closing costs will not change.

5. The underwriting process continues, with loan documents prepared and delivered to a title company or attorney. You can select a signing office from available sites, and an appointment for the closing is set.

6. Funding is delivered at closing.

REAL ESTATE PORTALS

In cyberspace, a portal is a point-and-click entry to myriad on-line adventures. A Web site operator gathers together information and services of its own design or strikes deals with other companies to create an all-in-one electronic supermarket. The following are a few real estate portals:

■ **Homestore,** www.homestore.com. A wide-ranging portal for all things real estate, including access to MLS listings of sister site www.Realtor.com and other information, including city comparisons and neighborhood reports, credit reports, and mortgages.

■ **MSN HomeAdvisor,** www.homeadvisor.msn.com. A financial planning site with calculators for home buying and mortgages plus links to home listings. You can also obtain information about recent sales of real estate in your area and link to mortgage lenders for loans.

■ **Realtor.com,** www.Realtor.com. The official site of the National Association of Realtors includes more than two million listings of homes offered for sale by Realtors. You can examine MLS listings by state, region, or ZIP code, collect interesting properties in folders for later follow-up, and contact agents around the nation to begin your home search from the comfort of your den.

HOME BUILDERS AND PLANS

If you're considering going it yourself, building a home from a plan, or dealing with a custom or tract builder, you can start your research at one of these sites:

■ **Creative Homeowner,** www.creativehomeowner.com. An on-line bookstore for books that bring together hundreds of plans for homes of all designs.

■ **Eplans.com,** www.eplans.com. A gateway to thousands of plans offered by Hanley-Wood, one of the largest sellers of plans on-line and in a collection of books. A sister Web site, www.homeplanners.com, leads to the same collection. You can search for homes by size, design, and estimated construction cost.

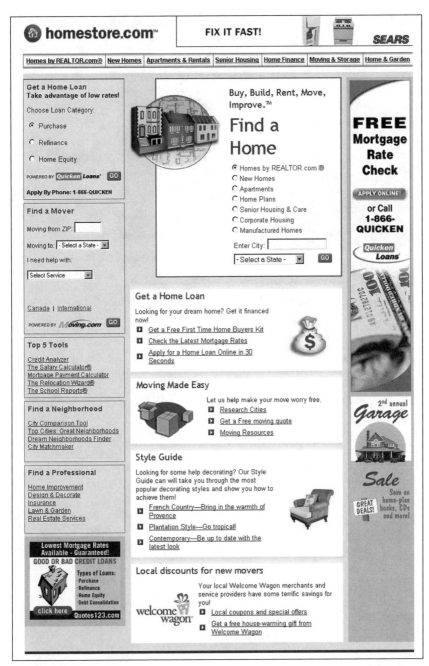

Homestore's home page includes access to MLS listings of Realtors around the nation as well as mortgage, insurance, and moving companies. *Published by permission of Homestore, Inc.*

An MLS link on Homestore yields full details on an available property in Vermont.
Published by permission of Homestore, Inc.

■ **HomeBuilder.com,** www.homebuilder.com. The official new homes site of the National Association of Home Builders features more than 100,000 new homes around the nation. The selection is spotty in some areas. The site also includes links to collections of home plans you can examine on-line and can put you in touch with custom builders.

■ **Sunset Books,** www.sunsetbooks.com and www.sunset.com/sunset/Sponsors /Home/HomePlans/HomePlanMain.html. Thousands of plans as well as the many home, garden, and entertainment books of Sunset.

MORTGAGE PORTALS

Financial services, including mortgage loans, are among the segments of the "old" economy that have adapted very well to the Internet era. The better sites, listed here, enhance the application process with specialized calculators and other research tools.

■ **E-Loan,** www.e-loan.com. This is one of the most complete and easiest to use of the mortgage portals: Answer a few questions about the sort of loan you want to consider, and the service will respond with as many as a dozen possibilities. Most mortgages do not require the payment of lender fees, and some loans are available with zero points and zero closing costs. E-loan also makes it easy to compare various mortgages. Among the information provided are charts showing the break-even point for loans that charge up-front points versus zero-point mortgages.

■ **Interest.com,** www.interest.com. A gateway to on-line mortgage lenders, the Web site also includes a solid collection of financial calculators that can help you choose your home buying strategy. Gathered together at www.interest.com/ calculators, the wizards can help calculate the monthly payment for a particular mortgage loan (www.interest.com/calculators/monthly-payment.shtml), calculate how much you have to make to afford the mortgage loan on a particular home (www.interest.com/calculators/earn-home.shtml), calculate how much mortgage loan you can afford to borrow (www.interest.com/calculators/afford-borrow.shtml), calculate if you should pay discount points on a mortgage (www.interest.com/calculators/discount.shtml), calculate how long it will take to recoup the costs of refinancing your mortgage loan (www.interest.com/ calculators/recoup.shtml), and calculate how much interest on your mortgage loan you will be able to deduct from your taxes (www.interest.com/calculators/ deduct.shtml).

■ **LendingTree,** www.lendingtree.com. This portal promises to electronically submit your application to a number of discount mortgage lenders. LendingTree has agreements with hundreds of lending institutions.

■ **Quicken,** www.quicken.com and www.quickenloans.quicken.com. This broad financial information and services Web site also includes a mortgage site. Once you receive a listing of available mortgages, you can customize the up-front points and see the effect on the interest rate and monthly payment.

Other lending institutions include the following:

- **Chase Manhattan,** www.chase.com
- **Countrywide Home Loans,** www.countrywide.com
- **Ditech,** www.ditech.com
- **North American Mortgage Company,** www.namc.com

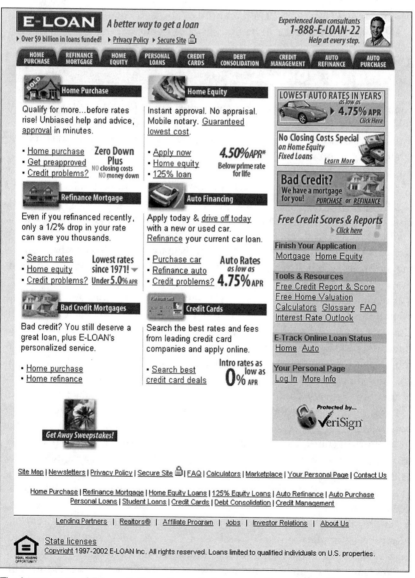

The home page of E-Loan is the gateway to home purchase, refinancing, and home equity mortgages. Tools and resources include a capable set of calculators and financial analyzers. *Published by permission of E-Loan.com*

| HOME PURCHASE | REFINANCE MORTGAGE | HOME EQUITY | PERSONAL LOANS | CREDIT CARDS | DEBT CONSOLIDATION | CREDIT MANAGEMENT | AUTO REFINANCE | AUTO PURCHASE |

Apply for a Loan | Search Mortgage Rates | Recommend a Loan | Mortgage Basics | Looking for a Home
Menu of Loans | Loan Process | Calculators & Tools | Free Credit Report | Free Home Valuation

Search and compare among hundreds of no lender fee loans in seconds.
No lender fees on all home loans.

Zero Down Plus!
• No money down
• No closing costs
• First-time owner eligible
• No mortgage insurance required

1. Your loan requirements

Loan amount:
$ 200000   *Example: 150,000*
(You can borrow more than 100% of the property value –up to 107%– in order to pay off existing debt or closing costs.)

Estimated property value (or purchase price if buying a home):
$ 450000   *Example: 175,000*

Property location:
Massachusetts ▾

Property use:
as a Home ▾

Property type:
a Single Family Residence ▾

Purchase Loans - indicate where you are in the homebuying process
○ found a home and made an offer
● looking for a property

Have you owned a home before?
● Yes
○ No

2. Your preferred loan type

○ Let E-LOAN recommend a loan for you.
OR
● Select your preferred loan type(s)

Adjustable Rate (30 Year Term)
☐ 6 Month Fixed (30 year)
☐ 1 Year Fixed (30 year)
☐ 3 Year Fixed (30 year)
☑ 5 Year Fixed (30 year)
☐ 7 Year Fixed (30 year)
☑ 10 Year Fixed (30 year)

Fixed Rate
☐ 15 Year Fixed (15 year)
☑ 30 Year Fixed (30 year)
☐ Zero Down Plus (30 year)

Special loans - qualify for more

3. Payment options and special considerations

Would you like to view rates for an interest only loan (vs. principal and interest) to lower your monthly payments? *(Available only on the 6 month, 5 Year, 7 Year, and 10 Year Adjustable Rate loans.)*

● View rates for **Principal + Interest** loans
○ View rates for **Interest-Only** loans

Will you consider a prepayment penalty in order to lower your rate?
(Not available in AK, DC, IA, ME, MA, NM, NY, SC, VT, WV)

● No

To see a list of mortgages appropriate to your needs, the E-Loan process begins with a simple search form. *Published by permission of E-Loan.com*

HOME PURCHASE	REFINANCE MORTGAGE	HOME EQUITY	PERSONAL LOANS	CREDIT CARDS	DEBT CONSOLIDATION	CREDIT MANAGEMENT	AUTO REFINANCE	AUTO PURCHASE

Apply for a Loan | Search Mortgage Rates | Recommend a Loan | Mortgage Basics | Looking for a Home
Menu of Loans | Loan Process | Calculators & Tools | Free Credit Report | Free Home Valuation

Today's Best Rates - 30 day lock period with impounds

1 **Choose a loan**
Click "Apply"
below or let
us help you ▸ GO

▶ **2** **Fast Approval**
Get pre-approved
in minutes

▶ **3** **Easy Close**
One-on-one
help at
every step

Rates assume use of an impound (or escrow) account.   [SEARCH WITHOUT IMPOUNDS]

💡 **Smart Tips** | Subscribe to our Market Outlook or Credit Management newsletters | Chris@ | [SUBSCRIBE]

☑ **Quick Apply**   Can't decide on a specific loan? Just apply now and a loan consultant
will help you select the right mortgage for your needs.
[APPLY NOW]   (Temporarily assumes 30-year fixed rate loan--you will be able to change this later)

Just a great rate!   **Rates for good-excellent credit current as of**
Friday, August 16, 2002 at 1:47 PM PDT   [Click here for details]

Good credit or bad, E-LOAN has the right loan for your needs. To perform   [CUSTOM RATE SEARCH]
a custom rate search based on your credit score click here.   by credit score

5 Year Fixed (30 year loan)   Questions: Call 1-888-E-LOAN-22

	Interest Rate SORT	Points or Credit* SORT	Payment SORT	APR	Margin SORT	Prepay Penalty	Closing Costs	Loan Details	Compare these loans
APPLY	4.500%	3.875%	$1,013	4.899%	2.750%	No	▸VIEW	▸VIEW	☑
APPLY	5.250%	1.900%	$1,104	4.667%	2.250%	No	▸VIEW	▸VIEW	☐
APPLY	5.750%	0.768%	$1,167	4.759%	2.250%	No	▸VIEW	▸VIEW	☐
APPLY	6.250%	No Points $464 Credit	$1,231	4.864%	2.250%	No	▸VIEW	▸VIEW	☐

❓ Help me choose a loan ▸ GO   See more **5 Year Fixed** loans ▸ GO.

10 Year Fixed (30 year loan)   Questions: Call 1-888-E-LOAN-22

	Interest Rate SORT	Points or Credit* SORT	Payment SORT	APR	Margin SORT	Prepay Penalty	Closing Costs	Loan Details	Compare these loans
APPLY	5.500%	3.648%	$1,136	5.345%	2.250%	No	▸VIEW	▸VIEW	☑
APPLY	6.250%	1.773%	$1,231	5.683%	2.250%	No	▸VIEW	▸VIEW	☐
APPLY	6.625%	0.836%	$1,281	5.853%	2.250%	No	▸VIEW	▸VIEW	☐

❓ Help me choose a loan ▸ GO   See more **10 Year Fixed** loans ▸ GO.

30 Year Fixed (30 year loan)   Questions: Call 1-888-E-LOAN-22

	Interest Rate SORT	Points or Credit* SORT	Payment SORT	APR	Margin	Prepay Penalty	Closing Costs	Loan Details	Compare these loans
APPLY	5.750%	1.746%	$1,167	5.959%	N/A	No	▸VIEW	▸VIEW	☑
APPLY	6.000%	0.807%	$1,199	6.123%	N/A	No	▸VIEW	▸VIEW	☐
APPLY	6.375%	No Points $1,082	$1,248	6.372%	N/A	No	▸VIEW	▸VIEW	☐

E-Loan presents a menu of available mortgages based on your criteria. You can ask
the intelligence behind the site to compare offerings or make recommendations.
Published by permission of E-Loan.com

HOME PURCHASE	REFINANCE MORTGAGE	HOME EQUITY	PERSONAL LOANS	CREDIT CARDS	DEBT CONSOLIDATION	CREDIT MANAGEMENT	AUTO REFINANCE	AUTO PURCHASE

Apply for a Loan | Search Mortgage Rates | Recommend a Loan | Mortgage Basics | Looking for a Home
Menu of Loans | Loan Process | Calculators & Tools | Free Credit Report | Free Home Valuation

5 Year Fixed vs. 30 Year Fixed

★ = superior	Product 1 5 Year Fixed		Product 2 30 Year Fixed	★	The 30 Year Fixed with 1.746% has lower total payments and interest costs over your hold period of 10 year(s).
Interest Rate (initial)	4.5%	★	5.75%		
Points	3.875%		1.746%	★	
Monthly Payment	$1,013		$1,167	★	
Prepay Penalty	no		no		To Apply for the 30 Year Fixed, click here.
First Adjustment	60 month(s)		N/A	★	
Lifecap	9.500%		N/A	★	
Index Type	One Year Treasury Bill		N/A		
Margin	2.750%		N/A	★	
Periodic Adjustment	12 month(s)		N/A	★	
Negative Amortization	None		N/A	★	

Mortgage Payment Comparison

Year	Product 1 5 Year Fixed	Product 2 30 Year Fixed	Difference (1 - 2)
1	$12,160	$14,006	-$1,845
2	$12,160	$14,006	-$1,845
3	$12,160	$14,006	-$1,845
4	$12,160	$14,006	-$1,845
5	$12,160	$14,006	-$1,845
6	$15,926	$14,006	$1,921
7	$16,496	$14,006	$2,490
8	$17,058	$14,006	$3,052
9	$17,626	$14,006	$3,620
10	$18,185	$14,006	$4,180
Points or (Rebate)	$7,750	$3,492	$4,258
Closing Costs	$2,471	$2,471	$0
	$156,314	$146,020 ★	$10,294

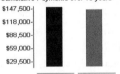

Cumulative Payments over 10 years

$147,500
$118,000
$88,500
$59,000
$29,500

5 Year Fixed   30 Year Fixed
146093   140057

Mortgage Interest Cost Comparison

Year	Product 1 5 Year Fixed	Product 2 30 Year Fixed	Difference (1 - 2)
1	$8,934	$11,433	-$2,499
2	$8,786	$11,281	-$2,495
3	$8,631	$11,120	-$2,489
4	$8,469	$10,950	-$2,481
5	$8,299	$10,769	-$2,470
6	$13,276	$10,578	$2,698
7	$13,812	$10,376	$3,436
8	$14,323	$10,162	$4,162
9	$14,825	$9,935	$4,890
10	$15,296	$9,694	$5,601
Points or (Rebate)	$7,750	$3,492	$4,258
Closing Costs	$2,471	$2,471	$0
	$124,871	$112,261 ★	$12,610

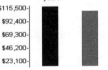

Cumulative Interest Costs over 10 years

$115,500
$92,400
$69,300
$46,200
$23,100

5 Year Fixed   30 Year Fixed
114650   106298

Compare the following two loans

5 Year Fixed with 3.875 points ▾   30 Year Fixed with 1.746 points ▾

over the next 10 years ▾

using a Basic ▾ comparison.

[Compare]

Your customized quote is for:
A loan amount of $200,000 on a property with an estimated value of $450,000. This loan will be used to purchase a property. The property is a single family home and is being used as a primary residence. The loan program quoted also assumes that you will use impounds, a 30 day lock and that you will document your income.

If any of this information is not correct, please return to the Search for Rates area and modify your search. You may be able to find a lower rate product than those shown above.

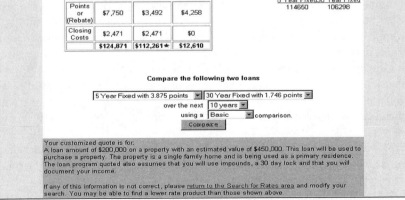

This example of a computerized comparison of a five-year ARM versus a thirty-year fixed-rate loan shows that the ARM is likely to cost $10,000 more over the first ten years of the agreement. *Published by permission of E-Loan.com*

GOVERNMENT AND GOVERNMENT-SPONSORED AGENCIES

They're from the government, and they're there to help you. Though those may be scary words in some situations, in the instance of government and government-sponsored agencies devoted to home loans, they are generally true. These sites promote home ownership without pushing a particular commercial interest.

▪ **U.S. Department of Housing and Urban Development,** www.hud.gov/buying. A noncommercial take on the home-buying process, including information on mortgages, fair housing laws, and the process of purchasing real estate. You'll also find mortgage calculators and various HUD and other government programs.

▪ **Fannie Mae,** www.fanniemae.com. General information about obtaining a mortgage, and the role of Fannie Mae in helping lenders obtain funds at advantageous rates.

▪ **Freddie Mac,** www.freddiemac.com. More information for would-be homebuyers, including surveys of current interest rates and types of mortgages.

▪ **Ginnie Mae,** www.ginniemae.gov. The government-owned mortgage-funding agency provides calculators and other resources for homebuyers.

MOVING SERVICES

Comedian George Carlin once famously defined a home as a place to keep your stuff, and as anyone who has moved a few times has discovered, it gets harder and harder to drag around all of that stuff with each repositioning. You'll find all sorts of tips and hints to lessen the pain at various sites maintained by professional moving companies and associations as well as a few portals devoted to the subject:

▪ **American Moving and Storage Association,** www.moving.org. This site provides information on how to choose a moving company, plan a move, and file a complaint if something goes wrong. Among specialized tips on the site are how to move computers, children, and pets.

▪ **Moving.com,** www.moving.com. This Web site is devoted to all things moving. You can estimate the total weight of your possessions, the number of boxes you'll need, and submit your information to multiple moving companies with the click of a mouse. Other features include tips and tricks on do-it-yourself moves as well.

▪ **Moving Center,** www.movingcenter.com. This is a portal to moving services. In addition to transportation you'll also find an apartment locator service, short-term housing, and storage companies.

▪ **U.S. Postal Service,** www.moversguide.com. This portal offers links to all sorts of moving services, beginning with an on-line change of address form, and also includes maps, community information, and links to moving companies, utilities, banks, insurance companies, and contractors.

■ OTHER MOVING RESOURCES

Major National Moving Companies

- Allied Van Lines, www.alliedvan.com
- Atlas Van Lines, www.atlasvanlines.com
- Bekins Moving, www.bekinsmoving.com
- Global Van Lines, www.globalvanlines.com
- Mayflower Transit, www.mayflower.com
- Metro Van Lines, www.metrovanlines.com
- National Van Lines, www.nationalvanlines.com
- North American Van Lines, www.northamerican-vanlines.com
- United Van Lines, www.unitedvanlines.com

Do-It-Yourself Rental Trucks

- Budget/Ryder Trucks, www.yellowtrucks.com
- U-Haul International, www.uhaul.com

Appendix A
HOME-BUYING COMPARISON LIST

	House #1	House #2	House #3	House #4
Address				
Asking price	$	$	$	$
Real estate taxes	$	$	$	$
Comparable sales in neighborhood	$	$	$	$
Property square footage or acreage				
Zoning class. Can home be expanded?				
Style of house (ranch, split, Cape Cod, other)				
Dwelling square footage				
Number of bedrooms				
Number of full baths				
Number of half baths				
Year built				
Construction (wood frame, wood and brick, brick, other)				
Number of floors				
Type of roof and condition				
Basement, crawlspace, slab? Finished or raw?				
Attic? Finished or raw? Properly insulated?				
Garage? Attached or free-standing? Number of spaces.				
Patio or deck?				
Fencing?				
Landscaping?				

	House #1	House #2	House #3	House #4
Heating system (gas, electric, oil, other)				
Distribution: forced air, convection, baseboard				
Annual heating bill	$	$	$	$
Age of furnace				
Air-conditioning? Central or room?				
Annual electrical bill?	$	$	$	$
Energy-conservation features: attic fan, extra insulation				
Age of heating system				
Age of hot water heater				
Annual water bill	$	$	$	$
Sewer or septic tank?				
Annual sewer bill	$	$	$	$
Sump pump or sewage lift pump?				
INTERIOR				
Fireplaces or woodstoves?				
Notes on living room				
Notes on dining room				
Notes on family room				
Notes on kitchen				
Refrigerator included?				
Stove included? Gas, electric?				
Dishwasher included?				
Laundry equipment included? Gas, electric?				
Burglar alarm installed?				
Deadbolts, other security features?				
Smoke detectors installed?				

	House #1	House #2	House #3	House #4
NEIGHBORHOOD				
Notes on neighborhood				
Condition of neighboring homes				
Street condition				
Sidewalks, lighting				
Distance to work				
Distance to schools				
Distance to shopping				
Distance to recreation				
Notes on school district				

Appendix B
RESIDENTIAL OFFER TO PURCHASE

This is an adaptation of the offer to purchase used in Wisconsin, complete with all sorts of bells and whistles. Do not use this in your own transaction. Consult a real estate agent or an attorney for advice on constructing an offer in your locality.

BROKER DRAFTING THIS OFFER ON _____ **[DATE] IS (AGENT OF SELLER) (AGENT OF BUYER) (DUAL AGENT)** [STRIKE TWO]

GENERAL PROVISIONS

The Buyer, _____ offers to purchase the Property known as [Street Address]_____ in the _____ of _____, County of _____, State of _____. Insert additional description, if any, at ADDITIONAL PROVISIONS/CONTINGENCIES, or attach as an addendum, on the following terms:

- PURCHASE PRICE: _____ Dollars ($_____.)

- EARNEST MONEY of $_____ accompanies this Offer and earnest money of $_____ will be paid within _____ days of acceptance.

- THE BALANCE OF PURCHASE PRICE will be paid in cash or equivalent at closing unless otherwise provided below.

- ADDITIONAL ITEMS INCLUDED IN PURCHASE PRICE: Seller shall include in the purchase price and transfer, free and clear of encumbrances, all fixtures, as defined under FIXTURES and as may be on the Property on the date of this Offer, unless excluded under ITEMS NOT INCLUDED IN THE PURCHASE PRICE, and the following additional items:_____

_____

- ITEMS NOT INCLUDED IN THE PURCHASE PRICE: _____

_____

ACCEPTANCE. Acceptance occurs when all Buyers and Sellers have signed an identical copy of the Offer, including signatures on separate but identical copies of the Offer. *CAUTION: Deadlines in the Offer are commonly calculated from* *acceptance. Consider whether short-term deadlines running from acceptance provide adequate time for <u>both</u> binding acceptance and performance.*

BINDING ACCEPTANCE. This Offer is binding upon both Parties only if a copy of the accepted Offer is delivered to Buyer on or before _____.
CAUTION: This Offer may be withdrawn prior to delivery of the accepted Offer.

DELIVERY OF DOCUMENTS AND WRITTEN NOTICES. Unless otherwise stated in this Offer, delivery of documents and written notices to a Party shall be effective only when accomplished by one of the methods specified in this section.

(1) By depositing the document or written notice postage or fees prepaid in the U.S. Mail or fees prepaid or charged to an account with a commercial delivery service, addressed either to the Party, or to the Party's recipient for delivery designated as Seller's recipient or Buyer's recipient below for delivery to the Party's delivery address in this section.

Seller's recipient for delivery (optional): _____
Seller's delivery address: _____
Buyer's recipient for delivery (optional): _____
Buyer's delivery address: _____

(2) By giving the document or written notice personally to the Party, or the Party's recipient for delivery if an individual is designated in this section.

(3) By fax transmission of the document or written notice to the following telephone number:
Buyer: ( ) _____. Seller: ( ) _____.

OCCUPANCY. Occupancy of the entire Property shall be given to Buyer at time of closing unless otherwise provided in this Offer under PRE/POST CLOSING OCCUPANCY. At time of Buyer's occupancy, Property shall be free of all debris and personal property except for personal property belonging to current tenants, or that sold to Buyer or left with Buyer's consent. Occupancy shall be given subject to tenant's rights, if any.

LEASED PROPERTY. If Property is currently leased and lease(s) extend beyond closing, Seller shall assign Seller's rights under said lease(s) and transfer all security deposits and prepaid rents thereunder to Buyer at closing. The terms of the (written) (oral) [STRIKE ONE] lease(s), if any, are _____
_____.

PLACE OF CLOSING. This transaction is to be closed at the place designated by Buyer's mortgagee or _____ no later than _____ unless another date or place is agreed to in writing.

CLOSING PRORATIONS. The following items shall be prorated at closing: real estate taxes, rents, water and sewer use charges, garbage pick-up and other private and municipal charges, property owner's association assessments, fuel, and _____. Any income, taxes, or expenses shall accrue to Seller, and be prorated, through the day prior to closing. Net general real estate taxes shall be prorated based on (the net general real estate taxes for the current year, if known, otherwise on the net general real estate taxes for the preceding year) (_____). [STRIKE AND COMPLETE AS APPLICABLE]

CAUTION: If proration on the basis of net general real estate taxes is not acceptable (for example, completed/pending reassessment, changing mill rate, lottery credits), insert estimated annual tax or other formula for proration.

PROPERTY CONDITION PROVISIONS

■ PROPERTY CONDITION REPRESENTATIONS: Seller represents to Buyer that as of the date of acceptance Seller has no notice or knowledge of conditions affecting the Property or transaction (see below) other than those identified in Seller's Real Estate Condition Report dated _____, which was received by Buyer prior to Buyer signing this Offer and which is made a part of this Offer by reference [COMPLETE DATE OR STRIKE AS APPLICABLE] and _____. [INSERT CONDITIONS NOT ALREADY INCLUDED IN THE CONDITION REPORT].

■ A "condition affecting the Property or transaction" is defined as follows:
(a) planned or commenced public improvements that may result in special assessments or otherwise materially affect the Property or the present use of the Property;
(b) completed or pending reassessment of the Property for property tax purposes;
(c) government agency or court order requiring repair, alteration, or correction of any existing condition;
(d) construction or remodeling on Property for which required state or local permits had not been obtained;

(e) any land division involving the subject Property, for which required state or local approvals had not been obtained;

(f) violation of applicable state or local smoke detector laws (note: state law requires operating smoke detectors on all levels of all residential properties);

(g) any portion of the Property being in a one-hundred-year floodplain, a wetland, or a shoreland zoning area under local, state, or federal laws;

(h) that a structure on the Property is designated as a historic building or that any part of Property is in a historic district;

(i) structural inadequacies that, if not repaired, will significantly shorten the expected normal life of the Property;

(j) mechanical systems inadequate for the present use of the Property;

(k) insect or animal infestation of the Property;

(l) conditions constituting a significant health or safety hazard for occupants of Property (note: specific federal lead paint disclosure requirements must be complied with in the sale of most residential properties built before 1978);

(m) underground or aboveground storage tanks on the Property for storage of flammable or combustible liquids, including but not limited to gasoline and heating oil, which are currently or which were previously located on the Property (note: state law contains registration and operation rules for such underground and aboveground storage tanks);

(n) material violations of environmental laws or other laws or agreements regulating the use of the Property;

(o) high-voltage electric (100 KV or greater) or steel natural gas transmission lines located on but not directly serving the Property;

(p) other conditions or occurrences that would significantly reduce the value of the Property to a reasonable person with knowledge of the nature and scope of the condition or occurrence.

■ REAL ESTATE CONDITION REPORT. State law requires owners of property that includes one to four dwelling units to provide buyers with a Real Estate Condition Report. Excluded from this requirement are sales of property that has never been inhabited, sales exempt from the real estate transfer fee, and sales by certain court-appointed fiduciaries (for example, personal representatives who have never occupied the Property). A prospective buyer who does not receive a report within ten days may, within two business days after the end of that ten-day period, rescind the contract of sale by delivering a written notice of rescission to the owner or the owner's agent. Buyer may also have certain rescission rights if a Real Estate Condition Report disclosing defects is furnished before expiration of the ten days, but after the Offer is submitted to Seller. Buyer should review the report form or consult with an attorney for additional information regarding these rescission rights.

■ **PROPERTY DIMENSIONS AND SURVEYS.** Buyer acknowledges that any land, building, or room dimensions, or total acreage or building square footage figures, provided to Buyer by Seller or by a broker, may be approximate because of rounding or other reasons, unless verified by survey or other means. Buyer also acknowledges that there are various formulas used to calculate total square footage of buildings and that total square footage figures will vary dependent upon the formula used. **Caution: Buyer should verify total square footage formula, total square footage/acreage figures, land, building, or room dimensions, if material.**

■ **INSPECTIONS.** Seller agrees to allow Buyer's inspectors reasonable access to the Property upon reasonable notice if the inspections are reasonably necessary to satisfy the contingencies in this Offer. Buyer agrees to promptly provide copies of all such inspection reports to Seller and to listing broker if Property is listed. Furthermore, Buyer agrees to promptly restore the Property to its original condition after Buyer's inspections are completed, unless otherwise agreed with Seller. An "inspection" is defined as an observation of the Property that does not include testing of the Property, other than testing for leaking carbon monoxide or testing for leaking LP gas or natural gas used as a fuel source, which are hereby authorized.

■ **TESTING.** Except as otherwise provided, Seller's authorization for inspections does not authorize Buyer to conduct testing of the Property. A "test" is defined as the taking of samples of materials such as soils, water, air or building materials from the Property and the laboratory or other analysis of these materials. If Buyer requires testing, testing contingencies must be specifically provided for under ADDITIONAL PROVISIONS/CONTINGENCIES or in an addendum. Note: Any contingency authorizing such tests should specify the areas of the Property to be tested, the purpose of the test (e.g., to determine if environmental contamination is present), any limitations on Buyer's testing, and any other material terms of the contingency (e.g., Buyer's obligation to return the Property to its original condition). Seller acknowledges that certain inspections or tests may detect environmental pollution, which may be required to be reported to the State Department of Natural Resources.

■ **PRECLOSING INSPECTION.** At a reasonable time, preapproved by Seller or Seller's agent, within three days before closing, Buyer shall have the right to inspect the Property to determine that there has been no significant change in the condition of the Property, except for ordinary wear and tear and changes approved by Buyer, and that any defects Seller has elected to cure have been repaired in a good and workmanlike manner.

■ **PROPERTY DAMAGE BETWEEN ACCEPTANCE AND CLOSING.** Seller shall maintain the Property until the earlier of closing or occupancy of Buyer in materially the same condition as of the date of acceptance of this Offer, except for ordinary wear and tear. If, prior to closing, the Property is damaged in an amount of not more than five percent (5%) of the selling price, Seller shall be obligated to repair the Property and restore it to the same condition that it was on the day of this Offer. If the damage shall exceed such sum, Seller shall promptly notify Buyer in writing of the damage, and this Offer may be canceled at option of Buyer. Should Buyer elect to carry out this Offer despite such damage, Buyer shall be entitled to the insurance proceeds relating to the damage to the Property, plus a credit toward the purchase price equal to the amount of Seller's deductible on such policy. However, if this sale is financed by a land contract or a mortgage to Seller, the insurance proceeds shall be held in trust for the sole purpose of restoring the Property.

FIXTURES. A "fixture" is defined as an item of property that is physically attached to or so closely associated with land or improvements so as to be treated as part of the real estate, including, without limitation, physically attached items not easily removable without damage to the Property, items specifically adapted to the Property, and items customarily treated as fixtures, including, but not limited to, all: garden bulbs; plants; shrubs and trees; screen and storm doors and windows; electric lighting fixtures; window shades; curtain and traverse rods; blinds and shutters; central heating and cooling units and attached equipment; water heaters and softeners; sump pumps; attached or fitted floor coverings; awnings; attached antennas, satellite dishes, and component parts; garage door openers and remote controls; installed security systems; central vacuum systems and accessories; in-ground sprinkler systems and component parts; built-in appliances; ceiling fans; fences; storage buildings on permanent foundations; and docks/piers on permanent foundations. **Note: The terms of the Offer will determine what items are included/excluded. Address rented fixtures (e.g., water softeners), if any.**

TIME IS OF THE ESSENCE. "Time is of the Essence" as to: (1) earnest money payment(s); (2) binding acceptance; (3) occupancy; (4) date of closing; (5) contingency deadlines [STRIKE AS APPLICABLE] and all other dates and deadlines in this Offer except: _____.
If "Time is of the Essence" applies to a date or deadline, failure to perform by the exact date or deadline is a breach of contract. If "Time is of the Essence" does not apply to a date or deadline, then performance within a reasonable time of the date or deadline is allowed before a breach occurs.

DATES AND DEADLINES. Deadlines expressed as a number of "days" from an event, such as acceptance, are calculated by excluding the day the event occurred and by counting subsequent calendar days. The deadline expires at midnight on the last day. Deadlines expressed as a specific number of "business days" exclude Saturday, Sunday, any legal public holiday under Wisconsin or Federal law, and any other day designated by the President such that the postal service does not receive registered mail or make regular deliveries on that day. Deadlines expressed as a specific number of "hours" from the occurrence of an event, such as receipt of a notice, are calculated from the exact time of the event and by counting twenty-four hours per calendar day. Deadlines expressed as a specific day of the calendar year or as the day of a specific event, such as closing, expire at midnight of that day.

THE FINANCING CONTINGENCY PROVISIONS IN THE FOLLOWING SECTION ARE A PART OF THIS OFFER IF THE CHECKBOX AT <u>FINANCING CONTINGENCY</u> IS MARKED, SUCH AS WITH AN "X." THEY ARE NOT PART OF THIS OFFER IF THE CHECKBOX IS MARKED N/A OR IS NOT MARKED.

❏ FINANCING CONTINGENCY: This Offer is contingent upon Buyer being able to obtain a _____
[INSERT LOAN PROGRAM] first mortgage loan commitment as described below, within _____ days of acceptance of this Offer. The financing selected shall be in an amount of not less than $_____ for a term of not less than

_____ years, amortized over not less than _____ years. Initial monthly payments of principal and interest shall not exceed $_____. Monthly payments may also include one-twelfth of the estimated net annual real estate taxes, hazard insurance premiums, and private mortgage insurance premiums. The mortgage may not include a prepayment premium. Buyer agrees to pay a loan fee not to exceed _____ % of the loan. (Loan fee refers to discount points and/or loan origination fee but DOES NOT include Buyer's other closing costs.) If the purchase price under this Offer is modified, the financed amount, unless otherwise provided, shall be adjusted to the same percentage of the purchase price as in this contingency, and the monthly payments shall be adjusted as necessary to maintain the term and amortization stated above.

CHECK AND COMPLETE ONE OF THE FOLLOWING TWO FINANCING PROVISIONS:

❏ FIXED-RATE FINANCING: The annual rate of interest shall not exceed _____%.

❏ ADJUSTABLE RATE FINANCING: The initial annual interest rate shall not exceed _____%.

The initial interest rate shall be fixed for _____ months, at which time the interest rate may be increased not more than _____ % per year. The maximum interest rate during the mortgage term shall not exceed _____%. Monthly payments of principal and interest may be adjusted to reflect interest changes.

LOAN COMMITMENT. Buyer agrees to pay all customary financing costs (including closing fees), to apply for financing promptly, and to provide evidence of application promptly upon request by Seller. If Buyer qualifies for the financing described in this Offer or other financing acceptable to Buyer, Buyer agrees to deliver to Seller a copy of the written loan commitment no later than the deadline for loan commitment specified under FINANCING CONTINGENCY. **Buyer's delivery of a copy of any written loan commitment to Seller (even if subject to conditions) shall satisfy the Buyer's financing contingency unless accompanied by a notice of unacceptability.** *CAUTION: BUYER, BUYER'S LENDER, AND AGENTS OF BUYER OR SELLER SHOULD NOT DELIVER A LOAN COMMITMENT TO SELLER WITHOUT BUYER'S PRIOR APPROVAL OR UNLESS ACCOMPANIED BY A NOTICE OF UNACCEPTABILITY.*

SELLER TERMINATION RIGHTS: If Buyer does not make timely delivery of said commitment, Seller may terminate this Offer if Seller delivers a written notice of termination to Buyer prior to Seller's actual receipt of a copy of Buyer's written loan commitment.

FINANCING UNAVAILABILITY: If financing is not available on the terms stated in this Offer (and Buyer has not already delivered an acceptable loan commitment for other financing to Seller), Buyer shall promptly deliver written notice to Seller of same including copies of lender(s') rejection letter(s) or other evidence of unavailability. Unless a specific loan source is named in this Offer, Seller shall then have ten days to give Buyer written notice of Seller's decision to finance this transaction on the same terms set forth in this Offer, and this Offer shall remain in full force and effect, with the time for closing extended accordingly. If Seller's notice is not timely given, this Offer shall be null and void. Buyer authorizes Seller to obtain any credit information reasonably appropriate to determine Buyer's credit worthiness for Seller financing.

ADDITIONAL PROVISIONS/CONTINGENCIES:_____

_____

_____

TITLE EVIDENCE

■ CONVEYANCE OF TITLE: **Upon payment of the purchase price, Seller shall convey the Property by warranty deed (or other conveyance as provided herein)** free and clear of all liens and encumbrances, except: municipal and zoning ordinances and agreements entered under them, recorded easements for the distribution of utility and municipal services, recorded building and use restrictions and covenants, general taxes levied in the year of closing, and _____ (provided none of the foregoing prohibit present use of the Property), which constitutes merchantable title for purposes of this transaction. Seller further agrees to complete and execute the documents necessary to record the conveyance. **Warning: Municipal and zoning ordinances, recorded building and use restrictions, covenants, and easements may prohibit certain improvements or uses and therefore should be reviewed, particularly if Buyer contemplates making improvements to Property or a use other than the current use.**

■ FORM OF TITLE EVIDENCE: Seller shall give evidence of title in the form of an owner's policy of title insurance in the amount of the purchase price on a current ALTA form issued by an insurer licensed to write title insurance in this state. **CAUTION: IF TITLE EVIDENCE WILL BE GIVEN BY ABSTRACT, STRIKE TITLE INSURANCE PROVISIONS AND INSERT ABSTRACT PROVISIONS.**

■ PROVISION OF MERCHANTABLE TITLE: Seller shall pay all costs of providing title evidence. For purposes of closing, title evidence shall be acceptable if the commitment for the required title insurance is delivered to Buyer's attorney or Buyer not less than three business days before closing, showing title to the Property as of a date no more than fifteen days before delivery of such title evidence to be merchantable, subject only to liens that will be paid out of the proceeds of closing and standard title insurance requirements and exceptions, as appropriate. **CAUTION: BUYER SHOULD CONSIDER UPDATING THE EFFECTIVE DATE OF THE TITLE COMMITMENT PRIOR TO CLOSING OR A "GAP ENDORSEMENT," WHICH WOULD INSURE OVER LIENS FILED BETWEEN THE EFFECTIVE DATE OF THE COMMITMENT AND THE DATE THE DEED IS RECORDED.**

■ TITLE ACCEPTABLE FOR CLOSING: If title is not acceptable for closing, Buyer shall notify Seller in writing of objections to title by the time set for closing. In such event, Seller shall have a reasonable time, but not exceeding fifteen days, to remove the objections, and the time for closing shall be extended as necessary for this purpose. In the event that Seller is unable to remove said objections, Buyer shall have five days from receipt of notice thereof to deliver written notice waiving the objections, and the time for closing shall be extended accordingly. If Buyer does not waive the objections, this Offer shall be null and void. Providing title evidence acceptable for closing does not extinguish Seller's obligations to give merchantable title to Buyer.

■ SPECIAL ASSESSMENTS: Special assessments, if any, for work actually commenced or levied prior to date of this Offer shall be paid by Seller no later than closing. All other special assessments shall be paid by Buyer. **Caution: Consider a special agreement if area assessments, property owner's association assessments, or other expenses are contemplated.** "Other expenses" are one-time charges or ongoing-use fees for public improvements (other than those resulting in special assessments) relating to curb, gutter, street, sidewalk, sanitary and storm water and storm sewer (including all sewer mains and hook-up and interceptor charges), parks, street lighting and street trees, and impact fees for other public facilities, as defined under state law.

DELIVERY/RECEIPT. Unless otherwise stated in this Offer, any signed document transmitted by facsimile machine (fax) shall be treated in all manner and respects as an original document, and the signature of any Party upon a document transmitted by fax shall be considered an original signature. Personal delivery to, or actual receipt by, any named Buyer or Seller constitutes personal delivery to, or actual receipt by, Buyer or Seller. Once received, a notice cannot be withdrawn by the Party delivering the notice without the consent of the party receiving the notice. A Party may not unilaterally reinstate a contingency after a notice of a contingency waiver has been received by the other Party. **The delivery/receipt provisions in this Offer may be modified when appropriate (e.g., when mail delivery is not desirable or when a party will not be personally available to receive a notice.)** Buyer and Seller authorize the agents of Buyer and Seller to distribute copies of the Offer to Buyer's lender, appraisers, title insurance companies, and any other settlement service providers for the transaction as defined by the Real Estate Settlement Procedures Act (RESPA).

DEFAULT. Seller and Buyer each have the legal duty to use good faith and due diligence in completing the terms and conditions of this Offer. A material failure to perform any obligation under this Offer is a default that may subject the defaulting party to liability for damages or other legal remedies.

If Buyer defaults, Seller may:
(1) sue for specific performance and request the earnest money as partial payment of the purchase price;
(2) terminate the Offer and have the option to: (a) request the earnest money as liquidated damages or (b) direct Broker to return the earnest money and have the option to sue for actual damages.

If Seller defaults, Buyer may:
(1) sue for specific performance;
(2) terminate the Offer and request the return of the earnest money, sue for actual damages, or both.

In addition, the Parties may seek any other remedies available in law or equity.

The Parties understand that the availability of any judicial remedy will depend upon the circumstances of the situation and the discretion of the courts. If either Party defaults, the Parties may renegotiate the Offer or seek nonjudicial dispute resolution instead of the remedies outlined above. By agreeing to binding arbitration, the Parties may lose the right to litigate in a court of law those disputes covered by the arbitration agreement.

NOTE: IF ACCEPTED, THIS OFFER CAN CREATE A LEGALLY ENFORCEABLE CONTRACT. BOTH PARTIES SHOULD READ THIS DOCUMENT CAREFULLY. BROKERS MAY PROVIDE A GENERAL EXPLANATION OF THE PROVISIONS OF THE OFFER BUT ARE PROHIBITED BY LAW FROM GIVING ADVICE OR OPINIONS CONCERNING YOUR LEGAL RIGHTS UNDER THIS OFFER OR HOW TITLE SHOULD BE TAKEN AT CLOSING. AN ATTORNEY SHOULD BE CONSULTED IF LEGAL ADVICE IS NEEDED.

EARNEST MONEY

■ HELD BY: **Unless otherwise agreed, earnest money** shall be paid to and held in the trust account of the listing broker (Buyer's agent if Property is not listed or Seller's account if no broker is involved) until applied to purchase price or otherwise disbursed as provided in the Offer. **Caution: Should persons other than a broker hold earnest money, an escrow agreement should be drafted by the Parties or an attorney. If someone other than Buyer makes payment of earnest money, consider a special disbursement agreement.**

■ DISBURSEMENT: If negotiations do not result in an accepted offer, the earnest money shall be promptly disbursed (after clearance from payor's depository institution if earnest money is paid by check) to the person(s) who paid the earnest money. At closing, earnest money shall be disbursed according to the closing statement. If this Offer does not close, the earnest money shall be disbursed according to a written disbursement agreement signed by all Parties to this Offer (note: state law provides that an offer to purchase is not a written disbursement agreement pursuant to which the broker may disburse). If said disbursement agreement has not been delivered to broker within sixty days after the date set for closing, broker may disburse the earnest money: (1) as directed by an attorney who has reviewed the transaction and does not represent Buyer or Seller; (2) into a court hearing a lawsuit involving the earnest money and all Parties to this Offer; (3) as directed by court order; or (4) any other disbursement required or allowed by law. Broker may retain legal services to direct disbursement per (1) or to file an interpleader action per (2), and broker may deduct from the earnest money any costs and reasonable attorneys fees, not to exceed $250, prior to disbursement.

■ LEGAL RIGHTS/ACTION: Broker's disbursement of earnest money does not determine the legal rights of the Parties in relation to this Offer. Buyer's or Seller's legal right to earnest money cannot be determined by broker. At least thirty days prior to disbursement per (1) or (4) above, broker shall send Buyer and Seller notice of the disbursement by certified mail. If Buyer or Seller disagree with broker's proposed disbursement, a lawsuit may be filed to obtain a court order regarding disbursement. Small Claims Court has jurisdiction over all earnest money disputes arising out of the sale of residential property with one to four dwelling units and certain other earnest money disputes. Buyer and Seller should consider consulting attorneys regarding their legal rights under this Offer in case of a dispute. Both Parties agree to hold the broker harmless from any liability for good faith disbursement of earnest money in accordance with this Offer or applicable Department of Regulation and Licensing regulations concerning earnest money.

ENTIRE CONTRACT

This Offer, including any amendments to it, contains the entire agreement of the Buyer and Seller regarding the transaction. All prior negotiations and discussions have been merged into this Offer. This agreement binds and inures to the benefit of the Parties to this Offer and their successors in interest.

OPTIONAL PROVISIONS: THE PROVISIONS IN THE NEXT SECTION ARE A PART OF THIS OFFER IF MARKED, SUCH AS WITH AN "X."

THEY ARE NOT PART OF THIS OFFER IF MARKED N/A OR ARE LEFT BLANK.

❏ **SALE OF BUYER'S PROPERTY CONTINGENCY:** This offer is contingent upon the sale and closing of Buyer's property located at_____, no later than _____. Seller may keep Seller's Property on the market for sale and accept secondary offers. **If this contingency is made a part of this Offer, the provision for CONTINUED MARKETING is also a part of this offer unless marked N/A or otherwise deleted.**

❏ **CONTINUED MARKETING:** If Seller accepts a bona fide secondary offer, Seller may give written notice to Buyer of acceptance. If Buyer does not deliver to Seller a written waiver of sale of Buyer's property contingency and

[INSERT OTHER REQUIREMENTS, IF ANY (E.G., PAYMENT OF ADDITIONAL EARNEST MONEY, WAIVER OF ALL CONTINGENCIES, OR PROVIDING EVIDENCE OF SALE OR BRIDGE LOAN, ETC.)] within _____ hours of Buyer's actual receipt of said notice, this Offer shall be null and void.

❏ **SECONDARY OFFER:** This Offer is secondary to a prior accepted offer. This Offer shall become primary upon delivery of written notice to Buyer that this Offer is primary. Unless otherwise provided, Seller is not obligated to give Buyer notice prior to any deadline, nor is any particular secondary buyer given the right to be made primary ahead of other secondary buyers. Buyer may declare this Offer null and void by delivering written notice of withdrawal to Seller prior to delivery of Seller's notice that this Offer is primary. Buyer may not deliver notice of withdrawal earlier than _____ days after acceptance of this Offer. All other Offer deadlines that are run from acceptance shall run from the time this Offer becomes primary.

❏ **PRE/POST-CLOSING OCCUPANCY:** Occupancy of _____ shall be given to Buyer on _____at _____ A.M./P.M. (Seller)(Buyer) [STRIKE ONE] shall pay an occupancy charge of $_____ per day or partial day of pre/post-closing occupancy. Payment shall be due at the beginning of the occupancy period. Any unearned post-closing occupancy fee (shall)(shall not) [STRIKE ONE] be refunded based on actual occupancy. **Caution: Consider a special agreement regarding occupancy, escrow, insurance, utilities, maintenance, keys, etc.**

❏ **INSPECTION CONTINGENCY:** This Offer is contingent upon a licensed home inspector performing a home inspection of the Property, and an inspection, by a qualified independent inspector, of _____ that discloses no defects as defined below. This contingency shall be deemed satisfied unless Buyer, within _____ days of acceptance, delivers to Seller, and to listing broker if Property is listed, a copy of the inspector's written inspection report(s) and a written notice listing the defect(s) identified in the inspection report(s) to which Buyer objects. **Caution: A proposed amendment will not satisfy this notice requirement.** Buyer shall order the inspection and be responsible for all costs of inspection, including any inspections required by lender or as follow-up inspections to the home inspection. **Note: This contingency only authorizes inspections, not testing.**

■ **RIGHT TO CURE:** Seller (shall)(shall not) [STRIKE ONE] have a right to cure the defects. (Seller shall have a right to cure if no choice is indicated.) If Seller has right to cure, Seller may satisfy this contingency by: (1) delivering a written notice within ten days of receipt of Buyer's notice of Seller's election to cure defects; (2) curing the defects in a good and workmanlike manner; and (3) delivering to Buyer a written report detailing the work done no later than three days prior to closing. This Offer shall be null and void if Buyer makes timely delivery of the above notice and report and: (1) Seller does not have a right to cure or (2) Seller has a right to cure but: a) Seller delivers notice that Seller will not cure or b) Seller does not timely deliver the notice of election to cure.

■ **"DEFECT" DEFINED:** For the purposes of this contingency, a defect is defined as a structural, mechanical, or other condition that would have a significant adverse effect on the value of the Property; that would significantly impair the health or safety of future occupants of the Property; or that if not repaired, removed, or replaced would significantly shorten or have a significant adverse effect on the expected normal life of the Property. Defects do not include structural, mechanical, or other conditions the nature and extent of which Buyer had actual knowledge or written notice before signing this Offer.

❏ **ADDENDA:** The attached _____ is/are made part of this Offer.

ADDITIONAL PROVISIONS/CONTINGENCIES:_____

_____

This Offer was drafted on _____ [date] by [Licensee and firm]

_____

_____

(X) Buyer's Signature _____ Print Name Here: _____

Social Security No. or FEIN _____ Date _____

(X) Buyer's Signature _____ Print Name Here: _____

Social Security No. or FEIN _____ Date _____

EARNEST MONEY RECEIPT. Broker acknowledges receipt of earnest money as per EARNEST MONEY section of the above Offer.

_____ Broker (By) _____

SELLER ACCEPTS THIS OFFER. THE WARRANTIES, REPRESENTATIONS, AND COVENANTS MADE IN THIS OFFER SURVIVE CLOSING AND THE CONVEYANCE OF THE PROPERTY. SELLER AGREES TO CONVEY THE PROPERTY ON THE TERMS AND CONDITIONS AS SET FORTH HEREIN AND ACKNOWLEDGES RECEIPT OF A COPY OF THIS OFFER.

(X) Seller's Signature _____ Print Name Here: _____

Social Security No. or FEIN _____ Date _____

(X) Seller's Signature _____ Print Name Here: _____

Social Security No. or FEIN _____ Date _____

This Offer was presented to the Seller by _____ on _____ at_____ A.M./P.M.

THIS OFFER IS REJECTED _____ _____.

                                 Seller Initials   Date

THIS OFFER IS COUNTERED [See attached counter].

                      _____ _____.

                                 Seller Initials   Date

Appendix C
PROPERTY CONDITION DISCLOSURE STATEMENT

SELLER'S DISCLOSURE FORM

Most states now require the seller to disclose any known problems with the home to all would-be buyers. In some states, the disclosure may take the form of a notice drafted by the seller, a real estate agent, or an attorney. Elsewhere, a state-mandated form must be used.

The following is New York's statement, which became mandatory in 2002. It is among the most inclusive, and it's not a bad document to use in your own evaluation of a home. If the seller's disclosure statement doesn't deal with one of the questions on New York's form, go ahead and ask for it.

Name of seller or sellers:

Property address:

The Property Condition Disclosure Act requires the seller of residential real property to cause this disclosure statement or a copy thereof to be delivered to a buyer or buyer's agent prior to the signing by the buyer of a binding contract of sale.

Purpose of Statement:

This is a statement of certain conditions and information concerning the property known to the seller. This disclosure statement is not a warranty of any kind by the seller or by any agent representing the seller in this transaction. It is not a substitute for any inspections or tests, and the buyer is encouraged to obtain his or her own independent professional inspections and environmental tests and also is encouraged to check public records pertaining to the property.

A KNOWINGLY FALSE OR INCOMPLETE STATEMENT BY THE SELLER ON THIS FORM MAY SUBJECT THE SELLER TO CLAIMS BY THE BUYER PRIOR TO OR AFTER THE TRANSFER OF TITLE. IN THE EVENT A SELLER FAILS TO PERFORM THE DUTY PRESCRIBED IN THIS ARTICLE TO DELIVER A DISCLOSURE STATEMENT PRIOR TO THE SIGNING BY THE BUYER OF A BINDING CONTRACT OF SALE, THE BUYER SHALL RECEIVE UPON THE TRANSFER OF TITLE A CREDIT OF FIVE HUNDRED DOLLARS AGAINST THE AGREED UPON PURCHASE PRICE OF THE RESIDENTIAL REAL PROPERTY.

"Residential real property" means real property improved by a one- to four-family dwelling used or occupied, or intended to be used or occupied, wholly or partly, as the home or residence of one or more persons, but shall not refer to (a) unimproved real property upon which such dwellings are to be constructed or (b) condominium units or cooperative apartments or (c) property on a homeowners association that is not owned in fee simple by the seller.

Instructions to the Seller:

(a) Answer all questions based upon your actual knowledge. (b) Attach additional pages with your signature if additional space is required. (c) Complete this form yourself. (d) If some items do not apply to your property, check "NA" (nonapplicable). If you do not know the answer, check "UNKN" (unknown).

Seller's Statement:

The seller makes the following representations to the buyer based upon the seller's actual knowledge at the time of signing this document. The seller authorizes his or her agent, if any, to provide a copy of this statement to a prospective buyer of the residential real property. The following are representations made by the seller and are not the representations of the seller's agent.

General Information

1. How long have you owned the property?

2. How long have you occupied the property?

3. What is the age of the structure or structures? **Note to buyer:** If the structure was built before 1978, you are encouraged to investigate for the presence of lead-based paint.

4. Does anybody other than yourself have a lease, easement, or any other right to use or occupy any part of your property other than those stated in documents available in the public record, such as rights to use a road or path or cut trees or crops?   Yes   No   UNKN   NA

5. Does anybody else claim to own any part of your property?
Yes   No   UNKN   NA   (if yes, explain below)

6. Has anyone denied you access to the property or made a formal legal claim challenging your title to the property?   Yes   No   UNKN   NA   (if yes, explain below)

7. Are there any features of the property shared in common with adjoining landowners or a homeowners association, such as walls, fences, or driveways?
Yes   No   UNKN   NA   (if yes, describe below)

8. Are there any electric or gas utility surcharges for line extensions, special assessments, or homeowners or other association fees that apply to the property?
Yes   No   UNKN   NA   (if yes, describe below)

9. Are there certificates of occupancy related to the property?
Yes   No   UNKN   NA   (if no, describe below)

Environmental

Note to seller: In this section, you will be asked questions regarding petroleum products and hazardous or toxic substances that you know to have been spilled, leaked, or otherwise been released on the property or from the property onto any other property. Petroleum products may include, but are not limited to, gasoline, diesel fuel, home heating fuel, and lubricants. Hazardous or toxic substances are products that could pose short- or long-term danger to personal health or the environment if they are not properly disposed of, applied, or stored. These include, but are not limited to, fertilizers, pesticides and insecticides, paint (including paint thinner, varnish remover, and wood preservatives), treated wood, construction materials (such as asphalt and roofing materials), antifreeze and other automotive products, batteries, cleaning solvents (including septic tank cleaners, household cleaners, and pool chemicals), and products containing mercury and lead.

Note to buyer: If contamination of this property from petroleum products and/or hazardous or toxic substances is a concern to you, you are urged to consider soil and groundwater testing of this property.

10. Is any or all of the property located in a designated floodplain?
Yes   No   UNKN   NA   (if yes, explain below)

11. Is any or all of the property located in a designated wetland?
Yes   No   UNKN   NA   (if yes, explain below)

12. Is the property located in an agricultural district?   Yes   No   UNKN   NA
(if yes, explain below)

13. Was the property ever the site of a landfill?   Yes   No   UNKN   NA
(if yes, explain below)

14. Are there or have there ever been fuel storage tanks above or below the ground on the property? Yes No UNKN NA

> If yes, are they currently in use? Yes No UNKN NA
> Location(s):
>
> Are they leaking or have they ever leaked? Yes No UNKN NA
> (if yes, explain below)

15. Is there asbestos in the structure? Yes No UNKN NA (if yes, state location or locations below)

16. Is lead plumbing present? Yes No UNKN NA (if yes, state location or locations below)

17. Has a radon test been done? Yes No UNKN NA (if yes, attach a copy of the report)

18. Has motor fuel, motor oil, home heating fuel, lubricating oil or any other petroleum product, methane gas, or any hazardous or toxic substance spilled, leaked, or otherwise been released on the property or from the property onto any other property? Yes No UNKN NA (if yes, describe below)

19. Has the property been tested for the presence of motor fuel, motor oil, home heating fuel, lubricating oil, or any other petroleum product, methane gas, or any hazardous or toxic substance? Yes No UNKN NA (if yes, attach report[s])

Structural

20. Is there any rot or water damage to the structure or structures?
Yes No UNKN NA (if yes, explain below)

21. Is there any fire or smoke damage to the structure or structures?
Yes No UNKN NA (if yes, explain below)

22. Is there any termite, insect, rodent, or pest infestation or damage?
Yes No UNKN NA (if yes, explain below)

23. Has the property been tested for termite, insect, rodent, or pest infestation or damage? Yes No UNKN NA (if yes, please attach report[s])

24. What is the type of roof/roof covering (slate, asphalt, other)?
Any known material defects? Yes No UNKN NA (if yes, explain below)

How old is the roof?

Is there a transferable warranty on the roof in effect now?
Yes No UNKN NA (if yes, explain below)

25. Are there any known material defects in any of the following structural systems: footings, beams, girders, lintels, columns, or partitions?
Yes No UNKN NA (if yes, explain below)

Mechanical Systems and Services

26. What is the water source (circle all that apply: well, private, municipal, other)? If municipal, is it metered? Yes No UNKN NA

27. Has the water quality and/or flow rate been tested?
Yes No UNKN NA (if yes, describe below)

28. What is the type of sewage system (circle all that apply: public sewer, private sewer, septic, or cesspool)?
If septic or cesspool, age?

Date last pumped?

Frequency of pumping?

Any known material defects? Yes No UNKN NA (if yes, explain below)

29. Who is your electric service provider?

What is the amperage?

Does it have circuit breakers or fuses?

Private or public poles?

Any known material defects? Yes No UNKN NA (if yes, explain below)

30. Are there any flooding, drainage, or grading problems that resulted in standing water on any portion of the property? Yes No UNKN NA (if yes, state locations and explain below)

31. Does the basement have seepage that results in standing water?
Yes No UNKN NA (if yes, explain below)

Are there any known material defects in any of the following: (If yes, explain below. Use additional sheets if necessary.)

32. Plumbing system?	Yes	No	UNKN	NA
33. Security system?	Yes	No	UNKN	NA
34. Carbon monoxide detector?	Yes	No	UNKN	NA
35. Smoke detector?	Yes	No	UNKN	NA
36. Fire sprinkler system?	Yes	No	UNKN	NA
37. Sump pump?	Yes	No	UNKN	NA
38. Foundation/slab?	Yes	No	UNKN	NA
39. Interior walls/ceilings?	Yes	No	UNKN	NA
40. Exterior walls or siding?	Yes	No	UNKN	NA
41. Floors?	Yes	No	UNKN	NA
42. Chimney/fireplace or stove?	Yes	No	UNKN	NA
43. Patio/deck?	Yes	No	UNKN	NA
44. Driveway?	Yes	No	UNKN	NA
45. Air conditioner?	Yes	No	UNKN	NA
46. Heating system?	Yes	No	UNKN	NA
47. Hot water heater?	Yes	No	UNKN	NA

48. The property is located in the following school district   UNKN

Note: Buyer is encouraged to check public records concerning the property (e.g., tax records and wetland and floodplain maps).

The seller should use this area to further explain any item above. If necessary, attach additional pages and indicate here the number of additional pages attached.

Seller's Certification:

SELLER CERTIFIES THAT THE INFORMATION IN THIS PROPERTY CONDITION DISCLOSURE STATEMENT IS TRUE AND COMPLETE TO THE SELLER'S ACTUAL KNOWLEDGE AS OF THE DATE SIGNED BY THE SELLER. IF A SELLER OF RESIDENTIAL REAL PROPERTY ACQUIRES KNOWLEDGE THAT RENDERS MATERIALLY INACCURATE A PROPERTY CONDITION DISCLOSURE STATEMENT PROVIDED PREVIOUSLY, THE SELLER SHALL DELIVER A REVISED PROPERTY CONDITION DISCLOSURE STATEMENT TO THE BUYER AS SOON AS PRACTICABLE. IN NO EVENT, HOWEVER, SHALL A SELLER BE REQUIRED TO PROVIDE A REVISED PROPERTY CONDITION DISCLOSURE STATEMENT AFTER THE TRANSFER OF TITLE FROM THE SELLER TO THE BUYER OR OCCUPANCY BY THE BUYER, WHICHEVER IS EARLIER.

Seller   date

Seller   date

Buyer's Acknowledgment:

Buyer acknowledges receipt of a copy of this statement, and buyer understands that this information is a statement of certain conditions and information concerning the property known to the seller. It is not a warranty of any kind by the seller or seller's agent and is not a substitute for any home, pest, radon, or other inspections or testing of the property or inspection of the public records.

Buyer   date

Buyer   date

Appendix D

A COMPARISON LIST OF MORTGAGE CANDIDATES

FIXED-RATE MORTGAGE	A	B	C
Lender			
Amount of principal applied for			
Interest rate			
APR			
Is there a lock-in agreement for the interest rate?			
Is there a fee for the lock-in?			
How long is the lock-in period?			
If interest rates drop before closing, can you lock in at the lower rate?			
Term in years			
Down payment required			
Number of points			
Is mortgage insurance required?			
If so, when can it be canceled?			
[A]Mortgage insurance cost per month			
[B]Estimated monthly payment for principal and interest (P&I)			
[C]Estimated monthly escrow for taxes and insurance			
Estimated total monthly payment (A+B+C)			
Application fee			
Attorney fee			
Origination or underwriting fee			
Appraisal fee			
Credit report fee			
Survey cost			
Inspection and test costs			

FIXED-RATE MORTGAGE *(continued)*	A	B	C
Document preparation and recording fees			
Other costs at closing			
Total fees and closing costs			
Can loan be prepaid without penalty?			
If there is a prepayment fee, how much is it?			
How long does the penalty period last?			
Are extra principal payments permitted?			
Title search and title insurance fees for lender			
Can loan be assumed by qualified buyer?			
ADJUSTABLE RATE MORTGAGE	A	B	C
Lender			
Initial interest rate			
Initial APR			
Down payment required			
Number of points			
Initial monthly payment for P&I			
Application fee			
Attorney fee			
Appraisal fee			
Can loan be prepaid without penalty?			
Can loan be assumed by qualified buyer?			
Adjustments			
Date of first adjustment			
Period between adjustments			
Cap for each interest rate adjustment			
Lifetime cap on interest rate			
Index used			
Treasury securities (indicate term)			
LIBOR index			
Other index			

ADJUSTABLE RATE MORTGAGE *(continued)*	A	B	C
Conversion			
Can rate be converted to fixed?			
Date for fixed conversion			
Fee for conversion to fixed			
Amortization			
Is there a cap on monthly payment?			
Can the loan go to negative amortization?			
Is there a cap on negative amortization?			

Appendix E

MORGAGE TYPES AT A GLANCE

Type	Interest Rate	Term	Principal and Interest Payments	Notes
Fixed rate	Fixed.	Typically fifteen, twenty, twenty-five, or thirty years.	Unchanged over the term of the loan.	Typically a few percentage points more expensive than the initial rate of an ARM, but rates do not change over the course of the term.
Adjustable Rate Mortgage (ARM)	Interest rate is based on a mark-up over an in-dependently calculated index or rate, such as the weekly aver-age yield on U.S. Government securities or London Inter-Bank Offered Rate (LIBOR) based on dollar-based securities.	Fixed term, typically based on thirty-year amortization.	Payment subject to adjust-ment according to the terms of the loan agree-ment, typically annually; some ARMs do not begin adjustments until after a period of three, five, or seven years.	Rates are usually lower than fixed-rate mortgages because the borrower shares some of the risk of rising interest rates. Watch carefully for important elements, including the amount the rate can increase per year and the cap or maximum possible rate. A small number of ARMs limit the level of the monthly payment, resulting in negative amortization of the outstanding balance or an extension of the term. Starting rate may be lower than on a fixed-rate loan because borrower shares risk of rising rates with lender. If payments do not increase with interest rates, result may be negative amortization (see GPM below) or an extension of the maturity.

Type	Interest Rate	Term	Principal and Interest Payments	Notes
Graduated payment mortgage (GPM)	Fixed.	Fixed term, typically based on thirty-year amortization.	Payments are artificially lower at the start of the term and then increase according to a schedule in the agreement.	Aimed at first-time homebuyers and others who expect their income to increase in future years. Payments in the early years may not be sufficient to cover interest due, resulting in negative amortization.
Graduated Payment Adjustable	Interest rates based on an independent index, as with an ARM.	Fixed term, typically based on thirty-year amortization.	Payments are artificially lower at the start of the term and then increase according to a schedule in the agreement.	A combination of graduated payments with adjustable interest rates. Adjustments will likely be more severe because of both interest rate changes and graduated payments. Under some agreements, mortgage may go into negative amortization in early years.
Renegotiable Rate Mortgage (RRM)	Typically fixed for three to five years and then renegotiable based on current interest rates.	A short-term loan amortized over a fixed period, typically thirty years.	Payments are fixed during each loan term but subject to change if interest rate changes after renegotiation.	The short-term loan is automatically renewable, but the borrower must decide whether to accept the new rate, refinance, or sell the property. Some RRMs limit the amount of increases in the interest rate with each renegotiation and over the full term of the loan.
Shared Appreciation	Fixed.	Fixed term, typically based on thirty-year amortization.	Fixed.	In return for a loan based on a lower interest rate, the borrower agrees to share with the lender a percentage of the increase in the value of the home when it is sold or at a specified time. This sort of

Type	Interest Rate	Term	Principal and Interest Payments	Notes
Shared Appreciation (continued)				mortgage may be attractive to first-time homebuyers, but it may also rob the owners of the equity they want to use for their next home.
Wraparound Mortgage	Fixed.	Fixed. Can be any term, but some lenders require a short term with a balloon payment.	Fixed.	If an existing mortgage is at a good rate and assumable, the purchaser of a home may want to consider taking over the loan and then *wrapping around* the original mortgage with a second mortgage to pay the seller's price. The entire package can be refinanced later if rates decline. (All FHA and VA mortgages are assumable.)
Balloon payment	Fixed or adjustable.	Fixed. Typically for five to ten years, but can be longer or shorter in term.	Fixed payments. At the end of the term, the debt will not be fully paid; some agreements call only for the payment of interest. Borrower must pay off the outstanding balance with a balloon payment or refinance the loan.	A balloon mortgage usually calls for a much lower monthly payment and a low down payment. In most situations, the balance can be refinanced at the end of the term.

Type	Interest Rate	Term	Principal and Interest Payments	Notes
Reverse Mortgage	Usually fixed, but may be adjustable.	Term is defined in the agreement; usually runs until home is sold or the borrower dies.	Lump sum, monthly, or other scheduled payments from lender to borrower.	A way for homeowners to draw income from the equity in their home. Special programs aimed at older homeowners guarantee against an outstanding balance higher than the value of the home.
Shared Equity	Fixed or adjustable.	Any term.	Depends on loan terms.	An arrangement where a third party—either a family member or an outside investor—copurchases a home with the borrower, sharing the down payment and/or monthly payments. The occupant leases back the property, paying a fair market rent. The cobuyer receives tax benefits in the deal. The shared equity agreement calls for distribution of appreciation in the property at the time of sale or refinancing.
Take Back or Owner-Financed	Usually fixed rate.	Usually short term.	Generally calls for a high down payment and a balloon payment at maturity.	The seller of the property offers a loan to assist the buyer.
Federal Housing Administration (FHA) Insured	Rates are usually below market because of government guarantees.	Fixed.	Payments can be fixed or graduated.	Properties must meet FHA requirements, and lender must be certified by agency.

Type	Interest Rate	Term	Principal and Interest Payments	Notes
Veterans Administration (VA) guaranteed	Rates are usually below market because of VA program.	Fixed, usually thirty years.	Payments can be fixed or graduated.	VA guarantee permits low or no down payment. Participants must meet VA eligibility requirements.
Buy-Down	The interest rate is artificially reduced below market for a specific period.	Fixed.	Payments are fixed for the term of the buy-down and then will rise with interest rate.	Rates can be reduced as an enticement to customers by a lending company or a builder. Or the rates can be reduced as the result of up-front points paid by the buyer.

Appendix F

UNIFORM RESIDENTIAL LOAN APPLICATION

Uniform Residential Loan Application

This application is designed to be completed by the applicant(s) with the lender's assistance. Applicants should complete this form as "Borrower" or "Co-Borrower," as applicable. Co-Borrower information must also be provided (and the appropriate box checked) when ☐ the income or assets of a person other than the "Borrower" (including the Borrower's spouse) will be used as a basis for loan qualification or ☐ the income or assets of the Borrower's spouse will not be used as a basis for loan qualification, but his or her liabilities must be considered because the Borrower resides in a community property state, the security property is located in a community property state, or the Borrower is relying on other property located in a community property state as a basis for repayment of the loan.

I. TYPE OF MORTGAGE AND TERMS OF LOAN

Mortgage Applied for:	☐ V.A. ☐ Conventional ☐ Other: ☐ FHA ☐ FmHA		Agency Case Number	Lender Case Number
Amount $	Interest Rate %	No. of Months	**Amortization Type** ☐ Fixed Rate ☐ GPM	☐ Other (explain): ☐ ARM (type):

II. PROPERTY INFORMATION AND PURPOSE OF LOAN

Subject Property Address (street, city, state, ZIP)	No. of Units
Legal Description of Subject Property (attach description if necessary)	Year Built

Purpose of Loan ☐ Purchase ☐ Construction ☐ Other (explain): ☐ Refinance ☐ Construction-Permanent	Property will be: ☐ Primary Residence ☐ Secondary Residence ☐ Investment

Complete this line if construction or construction-permanent loan.

Year Lot Acquired	Original Cost $	Amount Existing Liens $	(a) Present Value of Lot $	(b) Cost of Improvements $	Total (a+b) $

Complete this line if this is a refinance loan.

Year Acquired	Original Cost $	Amount Existing Liens $	Purpose of Refinance	Describe Improvements ☐ made ☐ to be made Cost $

Title will be held in what Name(s)	Manner in which Title will be held	Estate will be held in: ☐ Fee Simple
Source of Down Payment, Settlement Charges and/or Subordinate Financing (explain)		☐ Leasehold (show expiration date)

III. BORROWER INFORMATION

Borrower	**Co-Borrower**
Borrower's Name (include Jr. or Sr. if applicable)	Co-Borrower's Name (include Jr. or Sr. if applicable)

Social Security Number	Home Phone (incl. area code)	Age	Yrs. School	Social Security Number	Home Phone (incl. area code)	Age	Yrs. School

☐ Married ☐ Unmarried (include single, divorced, widowed) ☐ Separated	Dependents (not listed by Co-Borrower) no. ages	☐ Married ☐ Unmarried (include single, divorced, widowed) ☐ Separated	Dependents (not listed by Co-Borrower) no. ages
Present Address (street, city, state, ZIP) ☐ Own ☐ Rent ____ No. Yrs.		Present Address (street, city, state, ZIP) ☐ Own ☐ Rent ____ No. Yrs.	

If residing at present address for less than two years, complete the following:

Former Address (street, city, state, ZIP) ☐ Own ☐ Rent ____ No. Yrs.	Former Address (street, city, state, ZIP) ☐ Own ☐ Rent ____ No. Yrs.
Former Address (street, city, state, ZIP) ☐ Own ☐ Rent ____ No. Yrs.	Former Address (street, city, state, ZIP) ☐ Own ☐ Rent ____ No. Yrs.

Borrower			IV. EMPLOYMENT INFORMATION	Co-Borrower	
Name and Address of Employer	☐ Self Employed	Yrs. on this job	Name and Address of Employer	☐ Self Employed	Yrs. on this job
		Yrs. employed in this line of work/profession			Yrs. employed in this line of work/profession
Position/Title/Type of Business	Business Phone (incl. area code)		Position/Title/Type of Business	Business Phone (incl. area code)	

If employed in current position for less than two years or if currently employed in more than one position, complete the following:

Name and Address of Employer	☐ Self Employed	Dates (from-to)	Name and Address of Employer	☐ Self Employed	Dates (from-to)
		Monthly Income $			Monthly Income $
Position/Title/Type of Business	Business Phone (incl. area code)		Position/Title/Type of Business	Business Phone (incl. area code)	
Name and Address of Employer	☐ Self Employed	Dates (from-to)	Name and Address of Employer	☐ Self Employed	Dates (from-to)
		Monthly Income $			Monthly Income $
Position/Title/Type of Business	Business Phone (incl. area code)		Position/Title/Type of Business	Business Phone (incl. area code)	

Freddie Mac Form 65   10/92   Page 1 of 4   Borrower _____   Fannie Mae Form 1003   10/92
                                                       Co-Borrower _____

V. MONTHLY INCOME AND COMBINED HOUSING EXPENSE INFORMATION						
Gross Monthly Income	Borrower	Co-Borrower	Total	Combined Monthly Housing Expense	Present	Proposed
Base Empl. Income*	$	$	$	Rent	$	$
Overtime				First Mortgage (P&I)		
Bonuses				Other Financing (P&I)		
Commissions				Hazard Insurance		
Dividends/Interest				Real Estate Taxes		
Net Rental Income				Mortgage Insurance		
OTHER (before completing, see the notice in "describe other income," below)				Homeowner Assn. Dues		
				Other:		
Total	$	$	$	Total	$	$

*Self Employed Borrower(s) may be required to provide additional documentation such as tax returns and financial statements.

Describe Other Income Notice: Alimony, child support, or separate maintenance income need not be revealed if the Borrower (B) or Co-Borrower (C) does not choose to have it considered for repaying this loan.

B/C		Monthly Amount
		$
		$
		$

VI. ASSETS AND LIABILITIES

This statement and any applicable supporting schedules may be completed jointly by both married and unmarried Co-Borrowers if their assets and liabilities are sufficiently joined so that the Statement can be meaningfully and fairly presented on a combined basis; otherwise separate Statements and Schedules are required. If the Co-Borrower section was completed about a spouse, this Statement and supporting schedules must be completed about that spouse also.

Completed [ ] Jointly [ ] Not Jointly

ASSETS	Cash or Market Value	Liabilities and Pledged Assets. List the creditor's name, address, and account number for all outstanding debts, including automobile loans, revolving charge accounts, real estate loans, alimony, child support, stock pledges, etc. Use continuation sheet if necessary. Indicate by (*) those liabilities that will be satisfied upon sale of real estate owned or upon refinancing of the subject property.	Monthly Payt. & Mos. Left to Pay	Unpaid Balance
Description				
Cash deposit toward purchase held by:	$	**LIABILITIES**		
List checking and savings accounts below		Name and Address of Company	$	$
Name and address of Bank, S&L, or Credit Union			Payt./Mos.:	
		Acct. No.		
Acct. no .	$	Name and Address of Company	$	$
Name and address of Bank, S&L, or Credit Union			Payt./Mos:	
		Acct. No.		
Acct. no.	$	Name and Address of Company	$	$
Name and address of Bank, S&L, or Credit Union			Payt./Mos.:	
		Acct. No.		
Acct. no.	$	Name and Address of Company	$	$
Name and address of Bank, S&L, or Credit Union			Payt./Mos.:	
		Acct. No.		
Acct. no.	$	Name and Address of Company	$	$
Stocks & Bonds (company name/ number & description)	$		Payt./Mos.:	
		Acct. No.		
		Name and Address of Company	$	$
			Payt./Mos.:	
Life insurance net cash value				
Face amount:	$	Acct. No.		
Subtotal Liquid Assets	$	Name and Address of Company	$	$
Real estate owned (enter market value from schedule of real estate owned)	$		Payt./Mos.:	
Vested interest in retirement fund	$			
Net worth of businesses owned (attach financial statement)	$	Acct. No.		
Automobiles owned (make and year)	$	Alimony/Child Support/Separate Maintenance Payments Owed to:		
			$	
Other Assets (itemize)	$	Job Related Expense (child care, union dues, etc.)	$	
		Total Monthly Payments	$	
Total Assets a.	$	**Net Worth (a-b)** $	**Total Liabilities b.**	$

VI. ASSETS AND LIABILITIES (cont.)

Schedule of Real Estate Owned (If additional properties are owned, use continuation sheet.)

Property Address (enter S if sold, PS if pending sale, or R if rental being held for income)	Type of Property	Present Market Value	Amount of Mortgages & Liens	Gross Rental Income	Mortgage Payments	Insurance Maintenance Taxes & Misc.	Net Rental Income
		$	$	$	$	$	$
	Totals	$	$	$	$	$	$

List any additional names under which credit has previously been received and indicate appropriate creditor name(s) and account number(s):

Alternate Name	Creditor Name	Account Number

VII. DETAILS OF TRANSACTION

a. Purchase price	$
b. Alterations, improvements, repairs	
c. Land (if acquired separately)	
d. Refinance (include. debts to be paid off)	
e. Estimated prepaid items	
f. Estimated closing costs	
g. PMI, MIP, Funding Fee	
h. Discount (if Borrower will pay)	
i. Total costs (add items a through h)	
j. Subordinate financing	
k. Borrower's closing costs paid by Seller	
l. Other Credits (explain)	
m. Loan amount (exclude PMI, MIP, Funding Fee financed)	
n. PMI, MIP, Funding Fee financed	
o. Loan amount (add m & n)	
p. Cash from/to Borrower (subtract j, k, l, & o from i)	

VIII. DECLARATIONS

If you answer "yes" to any questions a through i, please use continuation sheet for explanation

	Borrower Yes No	Co-Borrower Yes No
a. Are there any outstanding judgments against you?	☐ ☐	☐ ☐
b. Have you been declared bankrupt within the past 7 years?	☐ ☐	☐ ☐
c. Have you had property foreclosed upon or given title or deed in lieu thereof in the last 7 years?	☐ ☐	☐ ☐
d. Are you a party to a lawsuit?	☐ ☐	☐ ☐
e. Have you directly or indirectly been obligated on any loan that resulted in foreclosure, transfer of title in lieu of foreclosure, or judgment? (This would include such loans as home mortgage loans, SBA loans, home improvement loans, educational loans, manufactured [mobile] home loans, any mortgage, financial obligation, bond, or loan guarantee. If "Yes," provide details, including date, name and address of Lender, FHA or VA case number, if any, and reasons for the action.)	☐ ☐	☐ ☐
f. Are you presently delinquent or in default on any Federal debt or any other loan, mortgage, financial obligation bond, or loan guarantee? if "Yes," give details as described in the preceding question.	☐ ☐	☐ ☐
g. Are you obligated to pay alimony, child support, or separate maintenance?	☐ ☐	☐ ☐
h. Is any part of the down payment borrowed?	☐ ☐	☐ ☐
i. Are you a co-maker or endorser on a note?	☐ ☐	☐ ☐
j. Are you a U.S. citizen?	☐ ☐	☐ ☐
k. Are you a permanent resident alien?	☐ ☐	☐ ☐
l. Do you intend to occupy the property as your primary residence? if "Yes," complete question m below.	☐ ☐	☐ ☐
m. Have you had an ownership interest in a property in the last three years?	☐ ☐	☐ ☐
(1) What type of property did you own—principal residence (PR), second home (SH), or investment property (IP)?	_____	_____
(2) How did you hold title to the home—solely by yourself (S), jointly with your spouse (SP), or jointly with another person (O)?	_____	_____

IX. ACKNOWLEDGMENT AND AGREEMENT

The undersigned specifically acknowledge(s) and agree(s) that: (1) the loan requested by this application will be secured by a first mortgage or deed of trust on the property described herein; (2) the property will not be used for any illegal or prohibited purpose or use; (3) all statements made in this application are made for the purpose of obtaining the loan indicated herein; (4) occupation of the property will be as indicated above; (5) verification or reverification of any information contained in the application may be made at any time by the Lender, its agents, successors, and assigns, either directly or through a credit reporting agency, from any source named in this application, and the original copy of this application will be retained by the Lender, even if the loan is not approved; (6) the Lender, its agents, successors, and assigns will rely on the information contained in the application, and I/we have a continuing obligation to amend and/or supplement the information provided in this application of any of the material facts that I/we have represented herein should change prior to closing; (7) in the event my/our payments on the loan indicated in this application become delinquent, the Lender, its agents, successors, and assigns may, in addition to all their other rights and remedies, report my/our name(s) and account information to a credit reporting agency; (8) ownership of the loan may be transferred to successor or assign of the Lender with prior notice to me; (9) the Lender, its agents, successors, and assigns make no representations or warranties, express or implied, to the Borrower(s) regarding the property, the condition of the property, or the value of the property.

Certification: I/We certify that the information provided in this application is true and correct as of the date set forth opposite my/our signature(s) on this application and acknowledge my/our understanding that any intentional or negligent misrepresentation(s) of the information contained in this application may result in civil liability and/or criminal penalties including, but not limited to, fine or imprisonment or both under the provisions of Title 18, United States Code, Section 1001, et seq. and liability for monetary damages to the Lender, its agents, successors and assigns, insurers, and any other person who may suffer any loss due to reliance upon any misrepresentation that I/we have made on this application.

Borrower's Signature	Date	Co-Borrower's Signature	Date
X		X	

X. INFORMATION FOR GOVERNMENT MONITORING PURPOSES

The following information is requested by the Federal Government for certain types of loans related to a dwelling, in order to monitor the Lender's compliance with equal credit opportunity, fair housing, and home mortgage disclosure laws. You are not required to furnish this information but are encouraged to do so. The law provides that a Lender may neither discriminate on the basis of this information nor on whether you choose to furnish it. However, if you choose not to furnish it, under Federal regulations this Lender is required to note race and sex on the basis of visual observation or surname. If you do not wish to furnish the above information, please check the box below. (Lender must review the above material to assure that the disclosure satisfies all requirements to which the Lender is subject under applicable law for the particular type of loan applied for.)

BORROWER ☐ I do not wish to furnish this information

CO-BORROWER ☐ I do not wish to furnish this information

BORROWER	**CO-BORROWER**
Race/National Origin ☐ American Indian or Alaskan Native ☐ Asian or Pacific Islander ☐ Black, not of Hispanic origin ☐ White, not of Hispanic origin ☐ Hispanic ☐ Other (Specify) _____	**Race/National Origin** ☐ American Indian or Alaskan Native ☐ Asian or Pacific Islander ☐ Black, not of Hispanic origin ☐ White, not of Hispanic origin ☐ Hispanic ☐ Other (Specify) _____
Sex ☐ Female ☐ Male	**Sex** ☐ Female ☐ Male

To be completed by Interviewer	Interviewer's Name (print or type)	Name and Address of Interviewer's Employer
This application was taken by: ☐ face-to-face interview ☐ by mail ☐ by telephone	Interviewer's Signature Date	
	Interviewer's Phone Number (incl. area code)	

Continuation Sheet/Residential Loan Application

Use this continuation sheet if you need more space to complete the Residential Loan Application. Mark B for Borrower or C for Co-Borrower.	Borrower:	Agency Case Number:
	Co-Borrower:	Lender Case Number:

VI. ASSETS AND LIABILITIES (cont.)

ASSETS	Cash or Market Value	LIABILITIES	Monthly Payt. & Mos. Left to Pay	Unpaid Balance
Name and address of Bank, S&L, or Credit Union		Name and Address of Company	$ Payt./Mos.:	$
Acct. no .	$	Acct. No.		
Name and address of Bank, S&L, or Credit Union		Name and Address of Company	$ Payt./Mos.:	$
Acct. no.	$	Acct. No.		
Name and address of Bank, S&L, or Credit Union		Name and Address of Company	$ Payt./Mos.:	$
Acct. no.	$	Acct. No.		
Name and address of Bank, S&L, or Credit Union		Name and Address of Company	$ Payt./Mos.:	$
Acct. no.	$	Acct. No.		
Name and address of Bank, S&L, or Credit Union		Name and Address of Company	$ Payt./Mos.:	$
Acct. no.	$	Acct. No.		
Name and address of Bank, S&L, or Credit Union		Name and Address of Company	$ Payt./Mos.:	$
Acct. no.	$	Acct. No.		
Name and address of Bank, S&L, or Credit Union		Name and Address of Company	$ Payt./Mos.:	$
Acct. no.	$	Acct. No.		
Name and address of Bank, S&L, or Credit Union		Name and Address of Company	$ Payt./Mos.:	$
Acct. no.	$	Acct. No.		

Name and address of Bank, S&L, or Credit Union		Name and Address of Company	$ Payt./Mos.:	$
Acct. no.	$	Acct. No.		
Name and address of Bank, S&L, or Credit Union		Name and Address of Company	$ Payt./Mos.:	$
Acct. no.	$	Acct. No.		

I/We fully understand that it is a Federal crime punishable by fine or imprisonment, or both, to knowingly make any false statements concerning any of the above facts as applicable under the provisions of Title 18, United States Code, Section 1001, et seq.

Borrower's Signature :	Date	Co-Borrower's Signature:	Date
X		X	

LAND-BUYING COMPARISON LIST

	#1	#2	#3	#4
Address				
Asking price	$	$	$	$
Real estate taxes for unimproved land	$	$	$	$
Comparable sales in neighborhood	$	$	$	$
Date first listed for sale				
Property square footage or acreage				
Zoning classification				
Zoning for nearby property				
Any restrictions on building on the lot?				
Can the property be subdivided?				
Is there a homeowners association? If so, what are the dues?				
Are any road or utilities improvements planned for the area?				
Is property in a flood zone?				
Has the property ever been used for a dwelling, business, or factory?				
Have hazardous chemicals ever been stored or disposed of on the site?				
Are there any buried fuel tanks on the land? What provisions have been made for cleanup?				
Is the land appropriate for a foundation with basement?				
Setback and sidelot restrictions				

	#1	#2	#3	#4
Any current easements on property?				
Are easements required in order to access property or add utilities?				
Is electricity provided to the property? How far to hookup? Estimated cost to hook up?				
Is natural gas provided to the property? How far to hookup? Estimated cost to hook up?				
Is telephone service provided to the property? How far to hookup? Estimated cost to hook up?				
Is cable television service provided to the property? How far to hookup? Estimated cost to hook up?				
Is municipal water provided to the property? How far to hookup? Estimated cost to hook up?				
Is municipal sewer service provided to the property? How far to hookup?				
Are there any restrictions on number of bathrooms to be hooked up to utilities?				
If the property requires a septic tank, has the land passed a percolation test?				
If the property requires a well, how deep are neighboring wells, and what quality of water has been found?				
Is trash pickup provided by the municipality? If not, is there a private service?				

	#1	#2	#3	#4
Are there any known insect or animal problems on the property?				
Is there an architectural or historical review board that must approve home designs?				
Are there any restrictive covenants in the deed?				
Who owns adjacent properties? Are there any plans on file for construction or subdivision?				
How far to neighborhood schools? Is there bus service from the nearest main road?				
How far to shopping?				
How far to work?				
Notes about the property				

Appendix H

GOOD FAITH ESTIMATE

Lender:	**Sales Price:**
Address:	**Base Loan Amount:**
	Total Loan Amount:
Applicant(s):	**Interest Rate:**
	Type of Loan:
Property Address:	**Preparation Date:**
	Loan Number:

The Information provided below reflects estimates of the charges which you are likely to incur at the settlement of your loan. The fees listed are estimates -- actual charges may be more or less. Your transaction may not involve a fee for every item listed.

The numbers listed beside the estimates generally correspond to the numbered lines contained in the HUD-1 or HUD-1 A settlement statement which you will be receiving at settlement. The HUD-1 or HUD-1A settlement statement will show you the actual cost for items paid at settlement.

800 ITEMS PAYABLE IN CONNECTION WITH LOAN:		**1100 TITLE CHARGES:**	
801 Origination Fee ❷ % + $	$	1101 Closing or Escrow Fee	$
802 Discount Fee ❷ % + $	$	1102 Abstract or Title Search	$
803 Appraisal Fee	$	1103 Title Examination	$
804 Credit Report	$	1105 Document Preparation Fee	$
805 Lender's Inspection Fee	$	1106 Notary Fee	
806 Mortgage Insurance Application Fee	$	1107 Attorney's Fee	
807 Assumption Fee	$	1108 Title Insurance	$
808 Mortgage Broker Fee	$		$
810 Tax Related Service Fee	$		$
811 Application Fee	$		$
812 Commitment Fee	$		$
813 Lender's Rate Lock-in Fee	$		$
814 Processing Fee	$		
815 Underwriting Fee	$	**1200 GOVERNMENT RECORDING AND TRANSFER CHARGES:**	
816 Wire Transfer Fee	$	1201 Recording Fee	$
		1202 City/County Tax/Stamps	$
900 ITEMS REQUIRED BY LENDER TO BE PAID IN ADVANCE:		1203 State Tax/Stamps	$
901 Interest for days ❷ $ /day	$	1204 Intangible Tax	$
902 Mortgage Insurance Premium	$		$
903 Hazard Insurance Premium	$		$
904 County Property Taxes	$		$
905 Flood Insurance	$		$
	$	**1300 ADDITIONAL SETTLEMENT CHARGES:**	
		1301 Survey	$
1000 RESERVES DEPOSITED WITH LENDER:		1302 Pest Inspection	$
1001 Hazard Ins. Mo. ❷ $ Per Mo.	$		$
1002 Mortgage Ins. Mo. ❷ $ Per Mo.	$		$
1004 Tax & Assmt. Mo. ❷ $ Per Mo.	$		$
1006 Flood Insurance	$	**TOTAL ESTIMATED SETTLEMENT CHARGES:**	$
'S'/'B' designates those costs to be paid by Seller/Broker.		"A" designates those costs affecting APR.	
TOTAL ESTIMATED MONTHLY PAYMENT:		**TOTAL ESTIMATED FUNDS NEEDED TO CLOSE:**	
Principal & Interest	$	Down Payment	$
Real Estate Taxes	$	Estimated Closing Costs	$
Hazard Insurance	$	Estimated Prepaid Items / Reserves	$
Flood Insurance	$	Total Paid Item (Subtract)	$
Mortgage Insurance	$	Other	$
Other	$	CASH FROM BORROWER	$
TOTAL MONTHLY PAYMENT	$		

THIS SECTION IS COMPLETED ONLY IF A PARTICULAR PROVIDER OF SERVICE IS REQUIRED. Listed below are providers of service which we required you to use. The charges indicated in the Good Faith Estimate above are based upon the corresponding charge of the below designated providers.

ITEM NO. NAME & ADDRESS OF PROVIDER   TELEPHONE NO.   NATURE OF RELATIONSHIP

These estimates are provided pursuant to the Real Estate Settlement Procedures Act of 1974, as amended (RESPA) Additional Information can be found in the HUD Special Information Booklet, which is to be provided to you by your mortgage broker or lender, if your application is to purchase residential property and the Lender will take a first lien on the property

Applicant	**Date**	**Applicant**
Applicant	**Date**	**Applicant**

☐ This Good Faith Estimate is being provided by a mortgage broker, and no lender has yet been obtained.

INDEX

3/1 adjustable rate mortgage, 56
5/1 adjustable rate mortgage, 57
5/25 balloon mortgage, 58–59
5/25 two-step mortgage, 59
7/1 adjustable rate mortgage, 57
7/23 balloon mortgage, 59
10/1 adjustable rate mortgage, 57

"A" mortgage, 87
abstract fee, 136
adjustable rate mortgage (ARM),
   55–57, 63–67
adjustable versus fixed interest
   rates, 51
adjustment period, ARM, 64
age and condition of home,
   appraising, 19
agent, real estate, 11–12, 37–46
American Moving and Storage
   Association, 176
amortization period, mortgage, 49
amortization, negative, 4
annual percentage rate (APR),
   49–50
application fee, 138
applying for a mortgage, 85–97
appraisal contingency, 29
appraisal fee, 134, 138
appraised value, 25
appraising a home for resale, 154–55
appraising home by yourself, 19–24
appreciation, real estate, 16–17
APR. See annual percentage rate
ARM. See adjustable rate mortgage
asking price, 25
assessed value, 25
assumption fee, 134
attics, appraising, 21
attorney fees at closing, 136, 138
Average Mortgage Rate Index, 66

back ratio, 88–91
balloon mortgage, 58–59
basements, appraising, 21
bathrooms, appraising, 20–21
bedrooms, appraising, 21
biweekly mortgages, 106–8
broker versus agent, 38–39
buy-downs, ARM, 67
buyer's agent, 45–46
buyer's market, 10

carryback second mortgage, 79
Century 21, 38–39
city/county tax or stamps, 137
closets, appraising, 21
closing date, 33–34
closing fees, 133–39
closing on real estate purchase,
   132–42
COFI Cost of Funds Index, 65
Coldwell Banker, 38–39
commercial banks, 76
commissions, real estate agent, 41, 42
commute, checking, 18–19
comparables, appraising, 19
comparison of mortgage candidates,
   204–6
condo insurance, 150
condominiums, 126–28
conforming loans, 77
construction costs for new homes,
   116–17
contingencies in home offer, 27–33
contingencies on land offer, 116
contract term for listing, 40
convertibility, ARM, 66
convertible loans, 67
co-op insurance, 150
cooperatives, 127–28
co-ops, 127–28

cosigner for loan, 95
counteroffer, 27, 34–35
county property taxes, 135
Creative Homeowner, 171
credit life insurance, 100
credit report errors, correcting, 94
credit report fee, 134
credit score, 92–94

debt-to-income ratio, 88–91
deeds, types of, 141
Department of Housing and Urban
    Development, 176
depreciation, real estate, 16–17
discount broker, 41–42
discount fee (points), 133
discrimination against buyers, 34
document preparation fee, 136,
    138–39
doors, appraising, 20
down payment assistance
    programs, 101
down payments, 98–101
duplex developments, 128

earnest money, 28–29
easements on land use, 115
electrical, telephone, and cable
    television wiring, 22
E-Loan, 167–68, 171, 172–75
eplans.com, 122
eplans.com, 168
Equifax, 94
ERA, 38–39
escrow agent, 124–25
escrow fee, 135–36
exclusive agency, 40
exclusive buyer's agreement, 43–44
exclusive right to sell, 40
Experian, 94
exterior and roof, appraising, 24
extra payment mortgages, 106–8

factory-built housing, 120–21
Fair, Isaac credit rating, 92–94

Fannie Mae, 68, 75, 76–77,
    99, 176
Federal Home Loan Mortgage
    Corporation, 54
Federal National Mortgage
    Association (FNMA), 53–54
Federal Trade Commission, 94
Federal Truth in Lending Act, 51
FHA mortgage programs, 68–70
FHA 203K Rehab Program, 70
FHLMC, 54
FICO, 92–94
Fifteen-year fixed rate mortgage,
    54–55
financing contingency, 32
first-time buyer programs, 71–72
Five-year adjustable rate mortgage
    (ARM), 56
fixed versus adjustable interest
    rates, 51
flood insurance, 135, 150–51
floors, appraising, 20
FNMA, 53–54
for sale by owner (FSBO), 11–12, 13,
    35–36, 159–60
Freddie Mac, 68, 75, 77, 99, 176
front ratio, 88–91

Ginnie Mae, 68, 77, 176
Good Faith Estimate, 86, 96–97
Good Faith Estimate, form, 221
government recording and transfer
    charges, 136–37
graduated payment mortgage
    (GPM), 57–58
guaranteed sale by agent, 158–59

hazard insurance premium, 135
heating, cooling, and hot water
    systems, 22–23
home equity conversion mortgage,
    110–12
home equity loan, 108–10
home inspections, 30–32
home insurance, 143–51

home office tax issues, 161
Home Price Comparison Index
  (HPCI), xi
home warranties, 151–52
HomeBuilder.com, 171
home-buying comparison
  list, 178–80
Homestore, 168, 169
HUD-1 Settlement Statement, 96–97

income documentation, 87–88
index, ARM, 65
inspection contingency, 29
insurance claims, 148
insurance, types of home coverage,
  144–48
intangible tax, 137
interest cost, advance payment at
  closing, 134
interest deduction, 3–4
interest rate, mortgage, 49–51
interim cap, ARM, 64–65
Internal Revenue rules on profit
  from sale of home, 160–61
Internet home designs, 121–22,
  168–69
Internet listings, 12–13
Internet mortgage applications,
  167–68
Internet real estate portals, 168
Internet services for home buyers
  and sellers, 166–77
introductory rate, ARM, 64
IRA as source for down
  payment, 100

joint ownership of property, 141–42
jumbo mortgage, 77–78

kickbacks, illegal, 97
kitchen, appraising, 20

land contract, 80
land purchase, 113–17
land-buying comparison list, 218–20

lender's inspection fee, 134
Lending Tree, 167–68, 171
leverage, 2
liability coverage, 146–47
LIBOR index, 66
life insurance as source for down
  payment, 100
lifetime cap, ARM, 65
listing contract, 40–41
loan application fee, 134
loan-to-value (LTV) ratio, 59–60, 80
location, appraising, 19
low-documentation mortgage, 88
low-income buyer programs, 71–72
LTV ratio, 59–60, 80

manufactured homes, 120–21
margin, ARM, 66
market value, 25
MIP, 69
MLS , 6, 13, 43
MMI, 69
mobile homes, 120–21
model homes, 120
modular homes, 120–21
monthly housing ratio, 88–91
mortgage broker, 76
mortgage broker fee, 134
mortgage companies, 75
mortgage defined, 47–48
mortgage for land purchase, 116
mortgage insurance premium
  (MIP), 69
mortgage interest premium, 134–35
mortgage payment table, 50
mortgage portals, Internet, 171–75
mortgage term, 52
mortgage types at a glance, 207–11
Moversguide.com, 176–77
moving, 163–65
moving companies on-line
  resources, 177
moving expenses, 161–62
moving services, on-line, 176–77
Moving.com, 176

Movingcenter.com, 176
MSN HomeAdvisor, 168
Multiple Listing Service (MLS),
    6, 13, 43
mutual mortgage insurance
    (MMI), 69

National Association of Realtors
    (NAR), x
negative amortization, 4
negotiations for purchase, 26–36
neighborhoods, 18–19
new home purchase, 118–25
no-closing-cost loans, 139
no-documentation mortgage, 88
nonconforming loans, 77
nonexclusive agreement for
    listing, 40
notary fee, 136

odors, mold, and stains, 23–24
offer, making an, 25–36
offering price, 25
One-year adjustable rate
    mortgage, 55–56
on-line mortgage applications,
    167–68
open houses, 45
open or nonexclusive agreement for
    listing, 40
origination fee, 133
overpricing home for resale, 155

payment cap, ARM, 65
periodic cap, ARM, 64–65
pest/termite inspection, 137
PITI, 89
PMI, 53–54, 99
points, 3
points, deductibility of, 102
portfolio loan, 77
preapproval for mortgage, 91–92
prepaid points, 102–5
prepayment penalties, 52–53, 66
prequalification for mortgage, 92

prime mortgage, 87
Prime rate index, 66
principal, interest, taxes, and
    insurance (PITI), 89
private mortgage insurance (PMI),
    53–54, 99
production homes, 118–20
Property Condition Disclosure
    Statement, form, 197–203
property insurance, 145–46
protection period for listing, 41
Prudential, 38–39

Quicken, 167–68, 171

racial discrimination in home
    sales, 34
rate lock, mortgage, 86
RE/MAX, 38–39
real estate agent, 11–12, 37–46
real estate investment trusts
    (REIT), 77
Real Estate Settlement Procedures
    Act (RESPA), 96–97
real property loan (mortgage), 48
Realtor.com, 168, 170
recording fees, 137
refinancing a loan, 81–84
Regulation Z, 51
REITs, 77
remodeling home for resale, 157–58
rental trucks for moving, 177
renter's insurance, 149–50
reserves collected at closing, 135
Residential Offer to Purchase, form,
    181–96
restrictions on land use, 115
reverse mortgage, 110–12
Rural Housing Loan Program, 71

sale of previous home
    contingency, 32–33
savings and loans, 76
savings banks, 76
second mortgage, 108–10

security, appraising, 24
self-employed income
documentation, 87–88
seller financing, 76, 78–80, 101
seller's disclosure form, 29
seller's market, 10–11
selling price, 25
selling your home, 153–62
short-term fixed rate mortgage, 59
starting rate, ARM, 64
state mortgage programs, 72–74
state tax or stamps, 137
subordination clause for second
mortgage, 80
Sunsetbooks.com, 171
survey fee, 137

tax basis for resale of home, 3, 161
taxes on sale of home, 160–61
tax-free appreciation, 2, 3
tax-related service fee, 134
termite inspection, 137
Thirty-year fixed rate mortgage, 54
Three-year adjustable rate mortgage
(ARM), 56
time limit for offer, 28
time-shares, 129–31
title examination, 136
title insurance, 136, 139–40
title search, 136

title, forms of real estate, 140–41
top ratio, 88–91
town houses, 128
tract homes, 118–20
Trans Union Corporation, 94
Treasury Bill Index, 65–66
Twenty-year fixed rate mortgage,
54–55

U.S. Postal Service moversguide.com,
176–77
underwriting fee, 138
Uniform Residential Loan
Application, form, 212–17
up-front costs, 49
used homes versus new homes,
16–17
usury, 80
utility bills, appraising, 23

VA mortgage programs, 70–71
vacation homes, 129–31

walls and ceilings, appraising, 19
windows, appraising, 20
wraparound mortgage, 79

zero-cost loans, 103–5
zero-point loans, 102–3

ABOUT THE AUTHOR

Corey Sandler is a former newsman and editor for the Associated Press, Gannett Newspapers, Ziff-Davis Publishing, and IDG. He has written more than 160 books on travel, video games, and computers; his titles have been translated into French, Spanish, German, Italian, Portuguese, Polish, Bulgarian, Hebrew, and Chinese. When he's not traveling, he hides out with his wife and two children on Nantucket Island, 30 miles off the coast of Massachusetts.